TAMBURLAINE THE GREAT
Christopher Marlowe

MANCHESTER
UNIVERSITY PRESS

REVELS STUDENT EDITIONS

Based on the highly respected Revels Plays, which provide a wide range of scholarly critical editions of plays by Shakespeare's contemporaries, the Revels Student Editions offer readable and competitively priced introductions, text and commentary designed to distil the erudition and insights of the Revels Plays, while focusing on matters of clarity and interpretation.

GENERAL EDITOR David Bevington

Ford *'Tis Pity She's a Whore*

Kyd *The Spanish Tragedy*

Marlowe *The Jew of Malta* *Tamburlaine the Great*

Middleton/Rowley *The Changeling*

Middleton/Tourneur *The Revenger's Tragedy*

Webster *The Duchess of Malfi* *The White Devil*

FURTHER TITLES IN PREPARATION

anon. *Arden of Faversham*

Dekker/Rowley/Ford *The Witch of Edmonton*

Fletcher *The Woman's Prize*

Heywood *A Woman Killed with Kindness*

Jonson *The Alchemist* *Bartholomew Fair* *Volpone*

Marston *The Malcontent*

Middleton *A Chaste Maid in Cheapside*

Middleton/Dekker *The Roaring Girl*

Plays on Women: An Anthology

REVELS STUDENT EDITIONS

TAMBURLAINE THE GREAT

Christopher Marlowe

edited by J. S. Cunningham
and Eithne Henson

based on The Revels Plays edition
edited by J. S. Cunningham
published by Manchester University Press, 1981

MANCHESTER
UNIVERSITY PRESS

Manchester and New York

distributed exclusively in the USA
by St. Martin's Press

Introduction, critical apparatus, etc.
© J. S. Cunningham and Eithne Henson 1998

The right of J. S. Cunningham and Eithne Henson to be identified as
the editors of this work has been asserted by them in accordance with
the Copyright, Designs and Patents Act 1988.

Published by Manchester University Press
Oxford Road, Manchester M13 9NR, UK
and Room 400, 175 Fifth Avenue, New York, NY 10010, USA

Distributed exclusively in the USA by St. Martin's Press, Inc., 175 Fifth
Avenue, New York, NY 10010, USA

Distributed exclusively in Canada by UBC Press, University of British
Columbia, 6344 Memorial Road, Vancouver, BC, Canada V6T 1Z2

British Library Cataloguing-in-Publication Data
A catalogue record for this book is available from the British Library

Library of Congress Cataloging-in-Publication Data
Marlowe, Christopher, 1564–1593.
Tamburlaine the Great / Christopher Marlowe; edited by J. S.
Cunningham and Eithne Henson.
p.   cm.—(Revels student editions)
'Based on the Revels plays edition edited by J. S. Cunningham,
published by Manchester University Press, 1981.'
ISBN 0-7190-5436-2 (pbk.)
1. Timur, 1336–1405—Drama. I. Cunningham, J. S. (Jaseph Sandy)
II. Henson, Eithne, 1934– . III. Title. IV. Series.
PR2669.A1   1998b
822'.3—dc21   98-18305

ISBN 0 7190 5436 2   *paperback*

First published 1998
05 04 03 02 01 00 99 98   10 9 8 7 6 5 4 3 2 1

Typeset
by Best-set Typesetter Ltd., Hong Kong
Printed in Great Britain
by Clays Ltd, St. Ives Plc

Preface

In this revision of the Revels *Tamburlaine*, which was published in 1981, the Introduction, text, and footnotes to the text reflect a concentration on the needs of students, teachers, and those concerned with producing the play in the theatre. The punctuation of the text is modernised, and more stage directions are provided; the Introduction seeks to be both informative and evocative, and the footnotes seek to help the contemporary reader clearly and efficiently. The General Editor of the Student Revels, David Bevington, has been very closely and generously involved at every turn, making many helpful suggestions—far more than could be itemised in the notes. John Banks provided vigilant and sensible fine-tuning of the proofs. We also wish to thank Matthew Frost, Stephanie Sloan and Rachel Armstrong, at Manchester University Press, for their prompt and cordial helpfulness during the book's preparation and production.

J.S.C.
E.H.

Tamburlaine

the Great.

Who, from a Scythian Shephearde,
by his rare and woonderfull Conquests,
became a most puissant and migh-
tye Monarque.

And (for his tyranny, and terrour in
Warre) was tearmed,
The Scourge of God.

Deuided into two Tragicall Dis-
courses, as they were sundrie times
shewed vpon Stages in the Citie
of London.

By the right honorable the Lord
Admyrall, his seruantes.

Now first, and newlie published.

LONDON.
Printed by Richard Ihones: at the signe
of the Rose and Crowne neere Hol-
borne Bridge. 1590.

Introduction

PERSPECTIVES ON TIMUR KHAN

In 1996, celebrations were held in Tashkent on the occasion of the 660th anniversary of the birth of Timur Khan. Tashkent is the capital of Uzbekistan (which most people in the West had been only vaguely aware of as a central Asian republic within the former Soviet Union), one of several states in a group deriving a collective identity from Turkic languages like Tatar and Kirghiz. The current projection of Timur as a national hero for Uzbekistan, in the effort to assert cultural identity after the welcomed collapse of the Soviet Union, includes a strong element of ideologically-driven reappraisal. In the words of one report of the celebrations, the purpose was 'the re-packaging of the medieval warlord Tamburlaine as Central Asian Renaissance man' (*Guardian*, 26 October 1996). Turkic superman? Devout and enlightened Islamic prince? Or, the traditional western version, bloodthirsty tyrant? Such alternative judgements of Timur are, of course, generated by rival belief-systems and political convictions and purposes, whether those of his own conflict-ridden period, or those of later times, up to the dramatic cultural and territorial changes of our recent past. One obstacle to the pursuit of a balanced assessment is, in western eyes, also a major element of the material's appeal—that is, the exoticism generated by legend, by geographical and temporal distance, and by romanticised ignorance or half-knowledge. Persepolis! Samarkand!

A major influence on the present-day western perspective is Marlowe's *Tamburlaine*, now some four hundred years from us. Timur Khan was by then thoroughly notorious in the West. Marlowe himself seized upon certain sixteenth-century western narratives which had already highlighted incidents in Timur Khan's career. Marlowe's main English source, George Whetstone's miscellany, *The English Myrror* (1586), is a translation of a French version of a Spanish compendium by Pedro Mexia, which included pages on Tamburlaine (published in 1542). Equally important for the play is the Latin *Vita* of 1553, by the Italian author Perondino ('Petrus

1

Perondinus'), which concentrates on Tamburlaine.

These narrative sources are more heroic romances than dependable history. They emphasise Tamburlaine's extensive military conquests, his close connection with that great city of the Silk Road, Samarkand, his sacking of Damascus, his three-day siege ritual (colour-coded white, red, black) and his climactic defeat of Bayazid, the Ottoman Sultan of Turkey. Exotic, indomitable, portentous, this Tamburlaine is driven essentially by heroic will and insatiable self-aggrandisement. He rises to power, self-made, out of social obscurity, declares himself to be the apocalyptic incarnation of divine wrath, and (more historically) is a brilliant military commander, inspiring complete loyalty during arduous campaigns rivalling those of Alexander the Great.

The sources emphasise, above all, the conflicting qualities and impulses in Tamburlaine himself. This Tamburlaine angrily asserts, when challenged in the name of pity, that he is *not* a man, but 'no other than the ire of God, and the destruction of the world'. He is 'endued with many excellencies and virtues', but the very intensity of his cruelty gives credence, in these sources, to the idea that 'God raised him to chasten the kings and proud people of the earth'. We are constantly pulled in opposite directions. On the one hand, Tamburlaine is 'shrewd, savage, treacherous in mind, and lacking any scruples'; on the other, through such qualities as endurance, boldness, and 'sharpness of wit [intelligence]', he is 'a great man . . . to be praised to the skies for his supreme renown'. He is a 'fierce veteran of wars [who] sought indefatigably, as though it were a wonderful work of virtue, for people he might wage war on'. However, he is also felt to have 'irradiated Scythia with a splendour never beheld in any previous age'. At odds with the conception of Tamburlaine as God's agent of retribution, the sources offer several general reflections on the influence of Fortune. Fortune is 'mistress of human affairs', capriciously degrading Bajazeth (Bayazid) and favouring Tamburlaine. In another view, Tamburlaine is a darling of the stars, who is born 'under a favourable harmony of distinguished constellations and the lucky conjunction of stars of uncommon magnitude'.[1]

The general perspectives on Tamburlaine—wrath of God, darling of Fortune or the stars—are significant in the play less for what they tell us about him than for exemplifying the range and discordance of any human attempts to make sense of life, arbitrary as these often are. What Whetstone describes as Tamburlaine's 'reaching and imaginative mind' is developed, in the two plays, into a continual display of accomplished rhetoric. This rhetoric projects the speaker in the light of, for instance, classical mythology (Jove, Hercules, Achilles), supra-human sponsorship (Fortune, Fate, the 'gods'), and a lofty aesthetic of human thirst for beauty and knowledge. In other words, Marlowe's Tamburlaine idealises heroism and mythologises aspiration.

Much of this is, of course, essentially the discourse of western European classicist culture. But the two plays do not let this discourse pass without challenge. Far from it. Sometimes suffering and atrocity themselves provide the repulsive background to speeches of soaring aspiration and professions of 'honour'. Sometimes Tamburlaine's conduct or rhetoric is denounced, or lamented, not always by figures whose judgement is discredited.

The most significant of these figures is Zenocrate. Few of Marlowe's *dramatis personae* are to be found in his sources, and none of them, even Tamburlaine himself, is fully characterised. We do not find the key figure of Zenocrate at all, nor others who offer forceful denunciations of, or reservations about, Tamburlaine's gross wilfulness and brutality. But their critical and perplexed responses to him have force even within the dramatised world of universal aggressive tyranny. The rival leaders—Tartar, Persian, Turkish, Christian—assume and assert their individual right to world supremacy. Their declamatory egotism feeds off antagonistic belief-systems and chauvinistic bigotry, embellishing these drives with the panoply of high principle. They can be adept at twisting arguments. Expediency, on two prominent occasions, is held to justify bad faith, most notably (and disastrously for them) by the Christian leaders in Part Two. In this anatomising of power-lust and the rhetoric of righteousness, the *Tamburlaine* theatre holds a disturbing mirror up to human history, whether for the fourteenth, the sixteenth, or the twentieth century, not least because in Marlowe's version the central figure so frequently mesmerises, and indeed sometimes gratifies, our attention. Explorer-destroyer? Chivalric monster? Aesthetician of cruelty? Scourge or supplanter of God? As Cosroe, an early victim of Tamburlaine's army declares, in dying:

The strangest men that ever Nature made!
I know not how to take their tyrannies.   (*One* 2.7.40–1)

The first edition of *Tamburlaine the Great*, published in 1590, presents the two plays as considered attempts—which have already been successful on various stages—to establish heroic-tragic theatre in English, at the cost of homespun drama's trivial materials and doggerel verse. The title page, the two verse prologues, and the printer's dedicatory letter emphasise the scope and inventiveness of this theatrical project. The plays are 'two Tragicall Discourses' (narratives). They are to concentrate attention upon a central figure whose meteoric rise to military eminence, and his concomitant display of 'tyranny' and 'terrour', led to his being called 'The Scourge of God'. This figure's career affords an 'honourable and stately . . . history', says the printer, perhaps echoing the Prologue to Part One, which images the scene as 'the stately tent of War'. The plays are, within the tolerances of Elizabethan classification, 'histories', and it is emphasised that the prevailing style—spectacle and speech—will match the scope of the high heroic material. The central figure is characterised by his recourse to portentous hyperbole, 'Threat'ning the world with high astounding terms' (Prologue to Part One, 5).

Timur Khan himself (1336–1405) was indeed committed to ceaseless military conquest. He came to real prominence about 1360, taking over Samarkand in 1366. After years of campaigning, in India, Persia, Moghulistan, and elsewhere, including the climactic sacking of Damascus, Timur's ascendancy reached its peak, to western eyes, when he caused Bayazid to raise the siege of (Christian) Constantinople. This was, in effect, a dramatic intervention in the struggle between the Christian and the Turkish powers. In this crucial battle, at Angora, in 1402, Bayazid was captured, and he died in captivity, perhaps by suicide, in 1403. Timur himself died, old and ill, but still campaigning, in February 1405. Except for the scale of Timur's conquests, and such incidents as the great battle with the Turks, there is little correspondence between historical fact and the western Tamburlaine tradition, which Marlowe depended on, and which he strikingly transformed, above all by making Tamburlaine an eloquent orator. (It is, at the same time, true that a lot of detailed historical work on Turkish and Persian history was published in the west, including England, in the sixteenth century.)

Timur was a devout Muslim, a fact now cherished in Uzbekistan. By contrast, Marlowe's Tamburlaine professes allegiance to many faiths. Unlike Timur, Marlowe's Tamburlaine is monogamous—in, be it said, a somewhat romantic-chivalric mode. Unlike Timur, who came from the ruling caste of khans, Marlowe's Tamburlaine is, crucially, a shepherd. Even his western name, Tamburlaine, demonstrates the gap between fact and fiction. Timur himself was lame in his right leg, and had a damaged right hand and arm, perhaps from wounds received in 1363, and was known contemptuously by his enemies as Timur-i-Lenk (Timur the Lame). The modern western form of his name is used in ignorance of this derivation. Although Perondinus does mention his physical impairments, Marlowe's hero has no disability; indeed, he is projected as an ideal of male physique and bearing.

The discrepancies between fact and historical construct in the transmission of the Timur/Tamburlaine narrative are of great interest in themselves, historiographically. But the issues Marlowe raises are by no means invalidated by the distances between the original events, the source narratives, and the *Tamburlaine* plays in their own day and as we nowadays may respond to them. What issues, for example? The bluster and exclusiveness of rival faiths; vindictive massacre; the sacking and destruction of great cities; genocide; the justification of conquest as a mode of exploring and 'civilising' everywhere *else*; the feared and sanctioned tyranny of patriarchal will, and the definition of maleness as successful aggression.

HEROIC TRAGEDY AS MIRROR

The lives of great men are commonly held up, in Renaissance literature, as instructive large-scale mirrors of heroic life. We will find that effects of mirroring are central to the *Tamburlaine* tragic-heroic theatre. The first Prologue concludes with a reference to this image, and perhaps a pointed hint that 'the Scythian Tamburlaine' will not command full approval:

> View but his picture in this tragic glass
> And then applaud his fortunes as you please.

In the closing scene of Part One, centred on the siege of Damascus, Tamburlaine himself twice turns to the mirror image, using one key phrase to introduce entirely contradictory concepts. First, musing in soliloquy about the elevated human impulse to achieve complete expression of noble themes in poetry, which he sees as a heroic enterprise,

> Wherein as in a mirror we perceive
> The highest reaches of a human wit.   (*One* 5.1.167–8)

(A few moments earlier he has employed poetry, that idealised medium, to send the deputation of virgins from the besieged city to their cruel deaths—in the name of his 'honour'.) Second, later in the scene, he exults publicly in the stage spectacle of the corpses of his opponents as

> . . . objects fit for Tamburlaine,
> Wherein as in a mirror may be seen
> His honour, that consists in shedding blood
> When men presume to manage arms with him.   (*One* 5.1.476–9)

There could hardly be a more emphatic challenge to spectator response than the contrast between these two mirror images, within the broad invitation to see the play itself as a large-scale mirror of momentous events.

Those corpses, 'objects fit for Tamburlaine' in his own estimation, have also been projected, as their death approached, as tragic subjects. Bajazeth and Zabina have been brought to despair and suicide as Tamburlaine's brutalised captives. They have expressed their extreme suffering in anguished words, whose power is not erased by our memory of them as blustering potentates. For Zabina, their degeneration transforms the world itself into hell, and abolishes belief in *any* extra-human source of meaning or justice:

> Then is there left no Mahomet, no God,
> No fiend, no Fortune, nor no hope of end
> To our infamous, monstrous slaveries?   (*One* 5.1.239–41)

Her last words, barely coherent, are the nightmare fragments of the atrocities she has suffered and witnessed. Her corpse and Bajazeth's lie on stage, their brains dashed out on the bars of his cage. In death, they form for Zenocrate a portentous example—a 'tragic glass' (mirror) held up to the futile worship of perishable worldly grandeur, as pursued both by these victims and by Tamburlaine himself. She is moralising the spectacle in the conventional terms familiar from medieval times in sermons and homilies, and in the perennial anthology, *A Mirror for Magistrates*. The corpses also reflect Tamburlaine's cruelty, and Zenocrate's own acknowledged complicity in his behaviour:

> Ah, mighty Jove and holy Mahomet,
> Pardon my love, oh, pardon his contempt
> Of earthly fortune and respect of pity . . .
> And pardon me that was not moved with ruth
> To see them live so long in misery.   (*One* 5.1.364–71)

This is among the moments when Zenocrate herself emerges as a tragic subject.

Drawing an admonitory moral from calamity is, of course, a long-established element in the rhetoric of tragedy. Identifying a particular determinant of catastrophe confers meaning, and may afford consolation as well as admonishment. A climactic fall from eminence may, for example, be explained as the caprice of Fortune, or the design of God, perhaps in retribution for sin or to chastise hubristic pride. Tamburlaine's own fatal sickness occurs shortly after his impious burning of the Koran. But we cannot confidently read his death as a 'mirror' of the anger of the Muslim God. Tamburlaine's attempts to account for his approaching death in terms of divine powers are contradictory and, at times, incoherent. In part, he projects his life as a 'tragic' experience of noble enterprise necessarily never complete, thirst for knowledge never assuaged: 'And shall I die, and this unconquered?' (Two 5.3.151, 159). The play ends with his eldest son's eloquent tribute to him, in terms of 'heaven and earth', but the words prompt an unintended recall of the atrocities committed by Tamburlaine, and the cacophony of attempts throughout the play to account for 'tragical' events by reference to many contrasting myths and creeds. The image in the tragic glass defies a reassuringly definitive interpretation, and consequently, a conclusive 'moral'.

MYTHS AND CREEDS

The text resists our taking a settled view of Tamburlaine himself partly by the diversity of its deployment and interpretation of myth. For one thing, it purges classical mythology of the banal moralising often associated with it. Myth does not, here, merely illustrate orthodox lessons like the punishment of pride. Myth is seen cumulatively in the play as material for human invention. Tamburlaine is likened, by himself and by others, to a range of figures—heavenly Jove, black Jove, Mars, Hercules, Achilles, Phaethon—and the scale of such references, in one view, fits his tremendous ambitions and conquests. He challenges Jove; equally, he imitates Jove, seen as the archetypal rebel. Alternatively, he rejoices in Jove's protection, and in that of Nature, Fortune, the 'fates and oracles of heaven' (One 2.3.7), and his uniquely favourable stars. He proclaims himself Jove's scourge, his 'wrathful messenger' (Two 5.1.92). At his death, he boasts that Jove snatches him to heaven, esteeming him 'much too good for this disdainful earth' (Two 5.3.123). The text does not endorse this boast, but refuses us the reassurance of seeing Tamburlaine's death simply as punishment.

Fortune, Nemesis, Fate, astrological determinants, the will of Jove, Mahomet, a sleepless God of righteous anger, a God of seemingly indiscriminate wrath. The play makes us aware that these are powers that humanity might variously pray to, swear by, imitate, or defy. We might declare one or more of them our propitious guides, or our slaves, or the distant symbols of our thirst for knowledge and felicity. Hell, Elysium, Helicon, Heaven, and Olympus have equal imaginative potency. An authentic poetry of religious faith shares the stage with a blustering impiety and with a zestful assertion of the superiority of earthly joys to heavenly. Faith in providence conflicts with a despairing conviction of doom. What may be Christian immortality to Olympia is immortality of pain to Bajazeth. The Turks call down upon Tamburlaine everlasting torment; but Tamburlaine's burning of the Koran is not indisputably the cause of his death. The play shows how adaptable religious sanctions can be to human purposes—and how readily distorted, though the play does not provide stable criteria for judging rival claims.

THE SCOURGE OF GOD

Marlowe's sources report Tamburlaine's declaration that he is the wrath of God. The plays carry many variants of this, chiefly in Part Two, among them 'the scourge and wrath of God' (*One* 3.3.44), 'The wrathful messenger of mighty Jove, / That with his sword hath quailed all earthly kings' (*Two* 5.1.92–3), and the scourge of 'a God full of revenging wrath, / From whom the thunder and the lightning breaks' (*Two* 5.1.182–3). This last God Tamburlaine declares he will 'obey'. But the characteristic assertion of his role as scourge emphasises not his obedience to a god, but rather his own peremptory will as an extreme destroyer and avenger. Often, Tamburlaine is inflicting punishment as an activity in its own right, rather than punishing or avenging a known fault. He merely invokes when he pleases the idea that he acts on some god's behalf.

The concept of the scourge and the wrath of God has a varied but insistent presence in the Old Testament and the New. It accounts for God's purpose at moments of acute human suffering, and from these Biblical incidents arises a long homiletic tradition, aiming to chasten and console sinners undergoing affliction. Our cruel mortal adversaries are to be thought of as acting out God's will to punish our sinfulness.

Secondary characters complicate our response to the image of Tamburlaine as scourge. Not only do they challenge directly his claim to be God's scourge, they also take part in dramatic events which test the idea that one deity or another superintends human conflict in order to work his or her justice. An exchange between Tamburlaine and the vanquished Turks, early in Act 4 of Part Two, demonstrates the complexity of the idea. Tamburlaine executes his own son in the name of military justice; Calyphas is condemned by his father as a dishonourable 'shame of nature', and his soul is consigned in disgrace to Jove. But the 'Jove' whom Tamburlaine invokes here is not simply a God of honour and justice, but the seeker for absolute power. Tamburlaine emulates him with a vengeance, as he claims to be 'of the mould whereof thyself consists', and thus

> . . . valiant, proud, ambitious,
> Ready to levy power against thy throne,
> That I might move the turning spheres of heaven. (*Two* 4.1.116–18)

The god who is elsewhere invoked to scourge unbelievers is himself celebrated here as an impious rebel. This is a characteristically abrupt change of perspective on divine sanctions for human conduct. Tamburlaine goes on to swear by Mahomet, Jove's 'mighty friend', that he will war on Jove in revenge for sending him such a decadent son as Calyphas. Within a few lines, Tamburlaine is declaring, with outrageous inconsistency, that he is Jove's regent, the manifestation of heavenly power and majesty:

> Villains, these terrors and these tyrannies
> (If tyrannies war's justice ye repute)
> I execute, enjoined me from above,
> To scourge the pride of such as heaven abhors;
> Nor am I made arch-monarch of the world,
> Crowned and invested by the hand of Jove,
> For deeds of bounty and nobility.
> But since I exercise a greater name,
> The scourge of God and terror of the world,
> I must apply myself to fit those terms,
> In war, in blood, in death, in cruelty,
> And plague such peasants as resist in me
> The power of heaven's eternal majesty. (*Two* 4.1.146–58)

He will persist 'a terror to the world' until 'by vision or by speech I hear / Immortal Jove say "Cease, my Tamburlaine"' (*Two* 4.1.199–201). The self-styled scourge both invokes and repudiates divine authority, imitating God even in rebelling against him.

Part Two offers further conflicting conceptions of God and of ethics, fought over by Turks and Christians. These secondary episodes have a bearing on Tamburlaine as scourge, and in particular his experience of being a scourge who is himself scourged. The crucial episode is governed by the adoption by Christians of the duty of scourging 'the infidels' (one thinks of the Crusades, and of Marlowe's *Jew of Malta*).

Turks and Christians, equally enemies of Tamburlaine, meet to conclude a peace in the opening Act of Part Two. Sigismond swears by Christ, Orcanes by Mahomet. Our predispositions are engaged, and implicitly questioned. Sigismond is reluctantly persuaded by his allies that he should treacherously take advantage of a weakness in the Turkish forces. To do so would be, they argue, to avenge previous massacres of Christians, acting in Christ's name to 'scourge their foul blasphemous paganism' (*Two* 2.1.53). This is, of course, to break an oath to your God in order to defeat your God's enemies. Confronted with this betrayal, the Turk Orcanes in his turn calls on the God of the Christians to punish their treachery. Orcanes' 'invocation of God's vengeance carries a true note of limpid religious belief in an immanent Godhead who is above the quarrel of rival faiths. He prays

> That He that sits on high and never sleeps
> Nor in one place is circumscriptible,
> But everywhere fills every continent
> With strange infusion of His sacred vigour,
> May in His endless power and purity
> Behold and venge this traitor's perjury!   (*Two* 2.2.49–54)

This god is aligned, in the dramatic confrontation, with a simple ethical principle, namely, keeping your sworn oath. Sigismond himself does interpret his own prompt defeat as divine punishment. The episode supports, for the moment, the broad principle of integrity. The Christian God has rightly punished the Christians. But Marlowe dramatically leaves a loophole for laconic dissent from the general belief that God has intervened: Gazellus, one of Orcanes' attendants, asserts that the victory is 'but the fortune of the wars, my lord, / Whose power is often proved a miracle' (*Two* 2.3.31–2).

As this complex scene expands further, clarity turns into belligerent confusion, principle into the hubbub of obsession and random assertion. When, shortly afterwards, Tamburlaine suffers bereavement, his polluting egotism emphasises the scourging of the scourge:

Proud fury and intolerable fit
That dares torment the body of my love
And scourge the scourge of the immortal God!   (*Two* 2.4.78–80)

In Tamburlaine's climactic burning of the Koran, 'Mahomet' is defied in the name of the generalised God of revenge whose scourge Tamburlaine rantingly claims to be. Within minutes, Tamburlaine is desperately looking to wage war against the gods themselves. And he interprets his own death in conflicting ways. Now it is seen as his elevation to a higher throne; now as the triumph over him of an 'eyeless monster'. It is *not* shown clearly as the final scourging of the scourge. After all, one of the play's strongest intimations is that the role of human beings in history may be no more—and for some, terribly, no less than they assert it to be, including the assertion that they act on behalf of a god. Where Tamburlaine's 'Will and Shall' are imposed in God's name, we experience a frightening sense of the collapse of divine mystery into human arbitrariness—but without the confidence that 'God' is *there* at all, other than in the words which different people use of him.

Frequently, Tamburlaine's assertion of his wrath has the character of the Christian Apocalypse, the Last Judgement. It is as if Tamburlaine were to bring his principal victims to face the two questions drawn from Kent and Edgar by the sight of Lear with the dead Cordelia in his arms: 'Is this the promised end? / Or image of that horror?' (5.3.238–9) The wrath of God visited on human beings in *this* life prefigures His final wrath, which will precede the coming of grace. In Revelation, it is wielded by the personified Word of God, who treads the winepress of God's wrath, and out of whose mouth 'goeth a sharp sword, that with it he should smite the nations' (19.13). For a bloodthirsty tyrant to *announce* himself as the bearer of this final terror strains all tolerance of the idea that God uses human scourges for his own high purposes. No redemptive consequence of his tyranny is offered by Tamburlaine. Indeed, the god associated with him as scourge is often, quite simply, the god of war.

Marlowe, then, has subjected the received idea of the scourge of God to intense dramatic pressure, increasing the audience's need to embrace orthodox convictions, but denying us clear grounds of true belief, and clear ethical criteria. The need for secure faith increases in ratio to the scale of human suffering which we contemplate, and this in its turn subjects religious belief to great strain. This is a turbulent dramatisation of the chaos of claims and counter-claims by which human beings attempt to justify action. The concept of the 'scourge of god' is perhaps the most potent of the play's challenges as we look in its mirror of conflict and suffering, explanation and rationalisation.

FIRE, ACTUAL AND APOCALYPTIC

Earthly conquest and heavenly retribution are insistently character-ised by fire in the play. 'Let there be a fire presently' (*Two* 5.1.177): Tamburlaine is about to burn the Koran. Throughout the two plays, fire runs from literal to metaphorical, from action to speech. Burnt scriptures dare God from heaven—or 'Mahomet' from hell. Wildfire erupts in Zabina's madness. Basilisks, the serpent-cannons, flash. A burning town kindles portentous fiery dragons. Fiery impressions joust in air. The Furies bear the fires of hell. Auster and Aquilon, the south and north winds, strike lightning from cloudy chariot clashes. A fatal illness extinguishes the sun, 'golden ball of heaven's eternal fire' (*Two* 2.4.2). The death of a fiery spirit exhausts the living fire of heaven. Phaethon drives the chariot of his father, the sun-god, through heaven. Such correspondences thrive on the vividness and scope of Renaissance meteorology as it moves from the sublunary (ruled by the moon) to the celestial, impregnated throughout with classical legend and myth.

To enjoy 'the fire of this martial flesh' (*Two* 4.1.106) is to burn others, and be burned. Flesh is 'martial' both by nature (which is itself seen as 'strife'), and in the specially intense life of 'the jealousy [zeal] of wars' (104). In the name of this 'natural' energy, ironically, Tamburlaine sees fit to kill his own son. Seen one way, the warrior as a fiery prodigy burns away the drossy 'earth' which muddies human vision and clogs aspiration. Seen another way, in the light of human kindness, the warrior outrages nature, becoming a 'monster' whose only distinction is an appalling elemental imbalance. As the baffled Meander says:

> Some powers divine, or else infernal, mixed
> Their angry seeds at his conception;
> For he was never sprung of human race.   (*One* 2.6.9–11)

The constellations, meteors, fiery visions, which prefigure and reflect careers of conquest, are abnormal, yet they are phenomena of nature. They threaten the stable order and announce apocalypse, yet they behave according to observed patterns by which we know the nature of fire, which naturally ascends (aspires) up to what Renaissance cosmology believed to be the highest of the universe's concentric spheres, that of fire. In fire, the spiritual and the physical meet, the normal and the perverted, creation and destruction, intense energy and its goal of ultimate knowledge and power. These contrasts and correspondences mark the poetry from page to page. Heroic zeal thirsts for imagined heavens; equally, it wields the fires of hell, savouring the obscene delights of the torturer. The disastrous career of Phaethon, who almost scorched the whole earth driving his sun-god father's chariot out of control, may be invoked to justify a career that will 'think of naught but blood and war' (*One* 1.2.55), and this relates to the sense of Tamburlaine as a madman— 'The poisoned brains of this proud Scythian' (*Two* 3.1.68). Alternatively, Tamburlaine can draw from the Phaethon story the lesson that what was wrong was merely the failure of Zeus's son to drive *well* (a good example of unconventional moralising of myth).

In Tamburlaine himself, fire predominates dramatically over the other elements of his make-up. Paradoxically, however, he claims for beauty the power to redress such imbalance through its own fire: Zenocrate's eyes, he recalls after her death, 'shot fire from their ivory bowers / And tempered every soul with lively heat' (*Two* 2.4.9–10). Clearly, this is a tempering process that is foreign to Tamburlaine's nature. In dying, his own body is consumed with a fever which is expressive of his entire insatiable career. But his dying is also seen as a breaking free of the fiery spirit from the body which tried to contain it. His furious killing of his own son had been aptly cursed by his enemies:

> May never spirit, vein, or artier feed
> The cursèd substance of that cruel heart,
> But, wanting moisture and remorseful blood,
> Dry up with anger and consume with heat! (*Two* 4.1.178–81)

But we also hear Tamburlaine's death celebrated as fire's apotheosis—that is, its highest destiny. In relation to the pervasive imagery of fire, the portentous central figure resists, as in other ways, our necessary attempts to judge.

POWER AND KNOWLEDGE

Fire, we have seen, is both positive and negative, destruction and aspiration. Conquest, itself impelled by fiery ambition, is also seen both positively and negatively in the play. 'Give me a map' (*Two* 5.3.124). Tamburlaine makes this request as he faces the onset of death, at the end of Part Two. It enables him to review his long career of conquest, and brings home to him how much remains for his sons to accomplish. He had meant to cut a canal linking the Mediterranean with the Red Sea, so that 'men might quickly sail to India' (136). Looking west from Africa, we see unimaginable riches. Looking east from the Antarctic, there is as much territory again, 'never . . . described, / Wherein are rocks of pearl that shine as bright / As all the lamps that beautify the sky' (*Two* 5.3.156–8). Tamburlaine's motives include discovering the unknown, acquiring untold riches, and facilitating trade. But the insistent refrain of this long testamentary speech emphasises, above all, imperial power: 'And shall I die, and this unconquerèd?' (159).

This range of motives characterised the political and mercantile enterprise of the western powers, and their conflict, in Marlowe's own time. Economic and political power was embodied in the making and owning of maps, with the promise of untold riches in newly-discovered lands. In dramatising what we would call 'the theatre of war', Marlowe is greatly indebted to one of the most important cartographers of his time, Abraham Ortelius, who published at Antwerp in 1570 his tellingly-entitled world atlas, the *Theatrum Orbis Terrarum*. As Tamburlaine's followers narrate their conquests, Marlowe's finger moves across Ortelius's page, picking out place-names and planning marches. The prestige of this atlas, like that of Mercator, was immense. To Tamburlaine, a career of conquest not only exerts power—it *confers* it, and particularly in its mapping and naming of the world as discovery progresses:

> I will confute those blind geographers
> That make a triple region in the world,
> Excluding regions which I mean to trace,
> And with this pen reduce them to a map,
> Calling the provinces, cities, and towns
> After my name and thine, Zenocrate.   (*One* 4.4.79–84)

Much of the world is yet to find, and the conventions governing cartography are themselves a focus of power. As the choice of the zero meridian of longtitude is in dispute, a burning commercial and political issue in Marlowe's day, the powerful might dream of making an arbitrary choice: 'Here at Damascus will I make the point / That shall begin the perpendicular' (85–6). The sword, in this view, is the map-maker's true pen, redrawing boundaries and breaking from the strait-jacket of old-style maps, correcting ignorance, bestowing names. Tamburlaine, eager to rule Egypt, rejects Zenocrate's plea that he should spare Damascus, and make a league with her father: 'And wouldst thou have me buy thy father's love / With such a loss?' (87–8). Power and knowledge, inquisitiveness and exploitation, finding and naming, are locked together in Tamburlaine's career.

A sonorous roll-call of proper names can register powerfully, not just as random exoticism, but as an act of appropriation, naming the world, both known and as yet unknown:

From Scythia to the oriental plage
Of India, where raging Lantchidol
Beats on the regions with his boist'rous blows,
That never seaman yet discoverèd . . .   (*Two* 1.1.68–71)

The play draws extensively on a mystique of knowledge and naming, applied to celestial, infernal, and terrestrial worlds. The 'axletree of heaven' runs through the centre of the earth. Aspiration upwards through the spheres is a correlative of the drive to discover unknown lands, both declared to be 'natural' activities. Astrology sees the planets as jewels; cartography maps the routes to mines of silver. Conquest itself is, in one view, a means of *knowing* what has, in anticipation, already been vividly imagined.

The play does not assert that what is found disappoints expectation; but clearly, the quest for the perfect realisation of an infinite possibility is at once admirable and self-contradictory. And thirst for experience can, in this play, be represented as at once profoundly gratified and insatiable: attainment both satisfies and endlessly stimulates hunger. The play excites disdain for limits but brings them, in conclusion, poignantly to bear. And it has insistently shown how the idealised human energies of finding and naming are deformed by the brutal realities of conquest and subjugation. The imperial chariot is drawn by brutalised kings, themselves despots in their day. A city is rased to the ground simply because it is where Zenocrate dies. 'The sweet fruition of an earthly crown' (*One* 2.7.29) was acclaimed as an immaculate reward for conquest. This affirmation relates to humanistic idealisation of the pursuit of knowledge, both earthly and heavenly:

> Our souls, whose faculties can comprehend
> The wondrous architecture of the world
> And measure every wand'ring planet's course,
> Still climbing after knowledge infinite
> And always moving as the restless spheres . . .   (*One* 2.7.21–5)

But the 'earthly crown' handed on to Tamburlaine's sons is as hazardous as the chariot of Apollo was in Phaethon's hands. Attempted world domination nourishes rebellion (by its own logic) at its own cost. The expansive geography of conquest shrinks to the anxieties of government:

> The nature of these proud rebelling jades
> Will take occasion by the slenderest hair
> And draw thee piecemeal like Hippolytus
> Through rocks more steep and sharp than Caspian clifts.
>   (*Two* 5.3.239–42)

GENDER

Conquest, rule, and dynastic succession are, of course, men's business in the play. Its expected readers are also defined, in the first published edition, in terms of class and gender, as 'gentlemen and courteous readers whosoever', who may turn to it as recreation after their 'serious affairs and studies' (To the Gentlemen Readers, 1, 5–6). However, throughout the play we are continually brought face to face with questions about what makes a man, and distinguishes him from a woman, and what makes 'nobility', as distinct from being a 'peasant', 'villain', 'slave', or Scythian shepherd. At the outset, we meet, in Mycetes, the king who is not a king, the man who is not a man: he is not fit for rule because he lacks the power of rhetoric—he cannot produce 'a great and thund'ring speech' (*One* 1.1.3)—and has to ask his brother to deputise. Cosroe's speech, in response, introduces one of the play's great sources of rhetorical description, Renaissance astrology, here deployed to attack his brother's weakness. He was born, his brother scornfully insists, under Cynthia (the moon) and the evil planet Saturn, and lacks the qualities of kingliness and wit that the sun and Mercury would have bestowed. The moon, always female, is inconstant, 'wat'ry', and has no generative power, borrowing her light from her brother the sun. Even

Mycetes is not too dim to understand the insult, and plays childishly with the idea that he could put Cosroe to death, and then with the idea of mercy: 'Yet live, yea, live, Mycetes wills it so' (*One* 1.1.27). Throughout the play, we see the exercise of 'will', and the power of granting life and death, as a definition of masculine greatness, above all exemplified by Tamburlaine. Mycetes, playing at king, sending a thousand horse against Tamburlaine, asks for approval—'Is it not a kingly resolution?'—and is mocked by his brother's sarcastic 'It cannot choose, because it comes from you' (55–6).

Mycetes's charge to Theridamas is inept: he is to 'come smiling home' from defeating Tamburlaine 'As did Sir Paris with the Grecian dame', alluding not to the successful *end* of war, but its cause. Grotesquely, though Mycetes is a coward, he glories in the idea of his 'milk-white steeds' coming back 'All loaden with the heads of killèd men', and 'Besmeared with blood', because 'that makes a dainty show' (65–6, 77–80). Later, he is brought face to face with the reality of war, and movingly laments its invention (a powerful classical *topos*), as he slinks off to hide his crown. However ambivalent the play may be about the legitimacy of butchery as the touchstone of successful masculinity, effeminate men are a source of very successful comedy, whether in 'camp' speech, or in exchanges with 'witty' (intelligent) opponents—here, Cosroe and Tamburlaine himself. Although, like Calyphas in Part Two, Mycetes comes to see the evil of war, neither of these men can carry full moral weight.

There is a jarring contrast between Tamburlaine's courtly praise of Zenocrate and his martial exhortations to his sons, two of whom are fitting successors. After his invitation to thrust their hands into his bloody wound (a disquieting travesty of Jesus's invitation to Thomas), they are ready to follow him in self-mutilation. Our first introduction to them, however, sitting by their mother, shows Tamburlaine disturbed by their apparent effeminacy, with its suggestion of Oedipal attachment: 'their looks are amorous' (*Two* 1.3.21), he complains, their hair is soft and blond instead of black and bristly. This chimes with the colour-coding of gender, where black symbolises the most ferocious male barbarity (including the massacre of women and children) while women are signalled by 'bright', white, and silver. Here, the boys' youthful softness, Tamburlaine fears,

Bewrays they are too dainty for the wars.
Their fingers made to quaver on a lute,

> Their arms to hang about a lady's neck,
> Their legs to dance and caper in the air.   (*Two* 1.3.28–31)

Zenocrate defends their prowess at courtly equestrian war-play—tilting at a glove—which belongs with the code of chivalry. Mycetes had pettishly evoked this code against Tamburlaine: 'Thou break'st the law of arms unless thou kneel / And cry me "Mercy, noble King"' (*One* 2.4.21–2). But Tamburlaine's wars are played by different rules: his 'honour' does mean that he sportingly sends a thousand men to even up the odds against Cosroe, but it also means that he is obliged to massacre a town's inhabitants simply because he has said he will. Two of his sons pass his test of martial masculinity, but Calyphas proposes to 'accompany my gracious mother' (*Two* 1.3.66), pointing out that his father and brothers are more than enough to conquer the world. This leads to a still bloodier tirade from Tamburlaine. Zenocrate's unwonted protest that he will dismay his sons 'before they come to prove / The wounding troubles angry war affords' (86–7) leads to protestations, even more gory, from the sons.

After Zenocrate's death, Calyphas again points out, following his father's lecture on the art of war, that 'this is dangerous to be done. / We may be slain or wounded ere we learn' (*Two* 3.2.93–4). The comedy lies in the inappropriateness of tone, the clash of values: of course the emperor has no clothes on, but this must not be allowed to intrude on the mighty rhetoric of slaughter. When the time does come for battle, Calyphas uses Tamburlaine's own rhetoric of invincible personal power to justify staying in his tent:

> My father were enough to scare the foe.
> You do dishonour to his majesty
> To think our helps will do him any good.   (*Two* 4.1.19–21)

Changing his ground to moral scruple, he argues that he knows 'what it is to kill a man; / It works remorse of conscience in me' (27–8), but this argument does not persuade his brothers. He is a coward, but his fantasies fall within the male code: the stake for his card-game is the right to kiss 'the fairest of the Turks' concubines' ahead of his companion, and he jokes about amorous battle with 'a naked lady in a net of gold'. As the alarm of real battle sounds, he continues the 'camp' joking: 'What a coil they keep! I believe there will be some hurt done anon amongst them' (74–5). Ironically, this is his last speech, before his father kills him.

This deed of Tamburlaine's is universally deprecated: by his captive enemies, who define it as 'barbarous damnèd tyranny', and even by his three closest allies and his sons, who beg him for mercy. He defends the deed by appeal to 'the argument of arms' and 'the jealousy [zeal] of wars', his own extreme version of the code of warfare. The Sultan had earlier disqualified him from the ranks of chivalry: after Tamburlaine's massacre of the inhabitants of Damascus, 'Without respect of sex, degree, or age' (*One* 4.1.62), the Sultan describes him as a 'Merciless villain, peasant ignorant / Of lawful arms or martial discipline' (64–5). Tamburlaine is not a gentleman, and he does not understand that slaughter has its own rules.

How, then, do warriors deal with *real* women, as opposed to effeminate men? At her first appearance, Zenocrate looks like the heroine of romance, helpless, asking for pity for 'a silly maid' in a 'distressed plight', and Tamburlaine marshals magnificent Renaissance hyperbole to woo her. She is 'lovelier than the love of Jove' (Juno), and therefore a fit mate for one who constantly relates himself to Jove. She is 'Brighter than is the silver Rhodope', a silver-bearing mountain, and 'Fairer than whitest snow on Scythian hills' (*One* 1.2.87–9). Conventionally, such praise relates women to classical goddesses, to precious metal or jewels, and to landscape and heavenly bodies. Here, as in Theridamas's later praise of Olympia, the stress is on moon-like qualities of coldness, brightness, fairness, adding up to dazzling beauty, but also implying chastity.

Besides praise, Tamburlaine also offers material inducements: the play is full of heaped riches, often exotic in origin, silks, jewels, golden chains, such as adorn, for instance, Holbein's Ambassadors or the many portraits of Queen Elizabeth. Here, Zenocrate is promised robes of 'Median silk, / Enchased with precious jewels of mine own' (95–6). Throughout the play, Tamburlaine is composing her, as here, in *tableaux*. Such emblematic presentations formed a significant part of political life at the Tudor court. Expensively costumed and staged masques, processions, triumphal arches, and shows like Elizabeth's Acession Day Tilts presented the sovereign and her courtiers in flattering roles—as figures from myth or chivalric romance—often intended as an exercise in public relations for the presenter, and a means to royal favour. In Tamburlaine's imagined masque, Zenocrate is to be the goddess Diana, drawn by 'milk-white harts upon an ivory sled'. She is to travel

> ... amidst the frozen pools
> And scale the icy mountains' lofty tops,
> Which with thy beauty will be soon resolved.   (99–101)

(It is notable that such global warming is rarely able to melt Tamburlaine's cruel determination.)

There is, in heroic romance, always an uneasy relation between Venus and Mars, between the emasculating blandishments of love— the music, sex, and dancing that Tamburlaine feared his sons would favour—and true martial toughness. Here, amusingly, Techelles challenges Tamburlaine: 'What now? In love?', eliciting the revealing reply: 'Techelles, women must be flatterèd. / But this is she with whom I am in love' (106–8). Devoted male friendship is a crucial component of the martial code, and Tamburlaine's relationship with his three lieutenants is, he claims, like that of 'Pylades and Orestes', classical models of such friendship. He rejoices in his generals more 'Than doth the King of Persia in his crown', and their bonding does indeed survive throughout his career. Zenocrate values still more highly the lives of the virgins of her native city: they were 'dearer . . . / Than her own life' (*One* 5.1.338–9) or anything but her love for Tamburlaine. For Tamburlaine is as happy in his wooing as in his friends. Initially, Zenocrate has no choice: she 'must be pleased perforce. Wretched Zenocrate!' (*One* 1.2.258), but we must suppose that the courtship later succeeds. In spite of Agydas's comic picture of Tamburlaine, who, when she looks for 'amorous discourse / Will rattle forth his facts of war and blood' (*One* 3.2.44–5) (a joke that costs his life), Zenocrate 'digests' her 'rape' (kidnapping) and returns his love (6, 8).

The siege of Damascus impels women to demonstrate their initiative and eloquence, but also makes clear their incapacity to breach the bastions of male pride. Their pleas for Damascus are cogent and moving, but they fall on male ears deafened with 'honour'. When the speaker for the virgins bitterly reproaches the Governor for ignoring the 'tears of wretchedness and blood' of the wives and children of the city, he too pleads 'love of honour' to excuse himself to the 'lovely virgins' (*One* 5.1.25, 34–5). Their chastity, beauty, and tears are described as bargaining counters to soften Tamburlaine, but their eloquent pleas to him in the name of old age, family relationships, and on behalf of virgins, children, and innocent citizens receive the expected reply: 'Virgins, in vain ye labour to prevent / That which mine honour swears shall be performed' (106–7). The phallic impaling of the virgins on soldiers' spears becomes for him another relished *tableau*, this time an illustration from a *danse macabre*.

Zenocrate's actual powerlessness, in spite of all the praise, is demonstrated when she pleads: 'Yet would you have some pity for my sake, / Because it is my country's, and my father's', to which Tamburlaine's answer is 'Not for the world, Zenocrate, if I have sworn' (*One* 4.2.123–5). When she explains why she is sad—'to see my father's town besieged, / The country wasted where myself was born' (*One* 4.4.69–70)—Tamburlaine, as we have seen, merely proposes to reduce the world to a map, drawn by his sword, and, presumably to console her, will call 'the provinces, cities, and towns / After my name and thine, Zenocrate' (83–4).

Tamburlaine's response to Zenocrate's tears is to remark, exquisitely, how lovely they make her look! His long soliloquy, analysing the effect of beauty on himself, reaches a peak of solipsism and insensitivity in the question 'What is beauty, saith my sufferings, then?' (*One* 5.1.160). His paean of praise for the 'immortal flowers of poesy' as representing 'The highest reaches of a human wit' (although even poesy, he feels, cannot fully express beauty), is checked by a 'masculine' thought:

But how unseemly is it for my sex,
My discipline of arms and chivalry,
My nature, and the terror of my name,
To harbour thoughts effeminate and faint!   (174–7)

But he concludes that a warrior 'rapt with love / Of fame, of valour, and of victory, / Must needs have beauty beat on his conceits' (180–2), and, prompted further by Theridamas, agrees to spare the Sultan.

Zenocrate's later sorrow for the fall of Damascus comes close to reproaching Tamburlaine, as does her reaction to the sight of the dead Bajazeth and Zabina, but her eloquence is seldom able to modify his actions. Once she is herself dead, in Part Two, his cruelty is untempered. His richly Petrarchan lament for her poignantly conveys deeply-felt grief. But 'Black is the beauty of the brightest day' (*Two* 2.4.1), reduces the world to the colour of martial cruelty, and he burns the town where she dies, merely as a symbol of mourning. Her portrait is enlisted into his belligerent world, as she is metamorphosed from an icon of peace and mercy into Bellona, goddess of war, who 'Threw naked swords and sulphur balls of fire / Upon the heads of all our enemies' (*Two* 3.2.40–2). Here, as elsewhere, women suffer his cruelty: the Turkish concubines are forced to bury Calyphas, lest the soldiers should be sullied by his effeminacy, and are then doled out for mass rape: 'And let them equally serve all your turns' (*Two* 4.3.73). Their appeal to 'pity us . . . and save our honours' (83) is inevitably ignored; women's 'honour' is at issue only when they are men's own property.

Olympia mirrors Zenocrate. She is stoically chaste, eloquent, and quick-witted, but, unlike Zenocrate, she is not swayed by courtship. Techelles fails to allure her, given her experience of war, with his inept masque-like picture of a martial Tamburlaine, who

> . . . makes the mighty god of arms his slave;
> On whom Death and the Fatal Sisters wait
> With naked swords and scarlet liveries;
> Before whom, mounted on a lion's back,
> Rhamnusia bears a helmet full of blood
> And strews the way with brains of slaughtered men. (*Two* 3.4.53–8)

Her response is to beg to be allowed to burn herself to death. Techelles has praised her for killing her son and burning the boy and her husband: ''Twas bravely done, and like a soldier's wife' (38), but she has still higher value as a sexual commodity: 'Madam, sooner shall fire consume us both / Than scorch a face so beautiful as this' (72–3). When Theridamas himself describes her, his rhetorical praise of her beauty repeats Tamburlaine's conceit of light: her beauty lights his tent; she is the moon, who makes his joys ebb and flow. He woos her with another *tableau*: she shall wear a golden robe, and sit 'like to Venus in her chair of state' (*Two* 4.2.42) among marble turrets, a static emblem of the consort, with Theridamas, by implication, as a Mars who

> . . . will cast off arms and sit with thee,
> Spending my life in sweet discourse of love.   (44–5)

When she refuses him, he threatens rape: 'I must and will be pleased, and you shall yield' (53). However, when she has tricked him with the ointment, the symbolic rape of the stabbing is one that she has planned, and Theridamas's lament mirrors Tamburlaine's, except that Olympia's beauty is to light up Hades, rather than heaven.

THE TWO PARTS

Plays in two or more parts, like *Tamburlaine* and Shakespeare's *Henry IV* and *Henry VI*, raise interesting questions about structure. How do the two parts of *Tamburlaine* relate to each other? Part One was completed, it seems clear, as a self-sufficient play, first staged in 1587–88. The sequel is a creative and critical response by Marlowe himself—written soon afterwards—to the way he had already developed the Tamburlaine story.

Part One ends with a ceremonious speech from Tamburlaine himself. Zenocrate, so recently eloquent on the dangers of earthly pomp, is now herself crowned. Tamburlaine will bury 'with honour' the broken 'Turk and his great emperess', echoing the refrain of Zenocrate's lament over these brutalised victims. Zenocrate has called for 'a league of honour' with Egypt, and this has been achieved. In the aftermath of gloating destruction, and the clash of opposing views of Tamburlaine, the closing note of Part One is of ritual celebration.

If Marlowe had not written Part Two, the first play might have seemed to raise questions about tyrannical self-assertion which it evaded following through; it might have stood as a powerful enigma, ending inconclusively as a challenging invitation to admire a frighteningly single-minded heroic monster. In the event, Part One is the major 'source' of Part Two, not simply because Marlowe had already used up most of the 'historical' material he had been drawing on. Part Two pursues themes and relationships (especially that of Tamburlaine and Zenocrate) in a deliberate response to the first play.

There are many connections and contrasts between the two Parts. Part One, for instance, had repeatedly drawn attention to dissolution, that of the world and that of the individual life, when 'our bodies turn to elements' (*One* 1.2.235). Bajazeth and Alcidamus were powerful emblems of death visited on a tyrant and on a heroic lover. Climactically, Tamburlaine's own encounter with Death is dramatised at the end of Part Two in relation to other deaths, occurring in both Parts of the play, and with particular reference to the theme of the scourge of God, which, as we have seen, had already been announced in Part One.

Mirroring being an insistent element in *Tamburlaine*, it is appropriate that episodes and characters from one Part are mirrored pointedly in the other. Tamburlaine's early attack on Cosroe, break-

ing their league, was not so much a betrayal as a piece of opportun-
ism. In sharp contrast, Part Two explores the Christian Sigismond's
'Machiavellian' treachery towards Orcanes the Turk. Mycetes (in
Part One) finds a counterpart in Almeda, eventually crowned as a
mock-king, and he is also echoed in Calyphas, effete like Mycetes
(but like him a sharp critic of warfare). Callapine's tempting of
Almeda from his responsibility to Tamburlaine contrasts with
Tamburlaine's own winning of Theridamas from Mycetes in Part
One. The torture of Bajazeth finds a counterpart in the bridling of
the captive Turkish kings. Each of the Parts features a siege. However, the siege of Babylon in the sequel includes the callous treatment of the Governor of the city, a cynical oath-breaking by
Tamburlaine not matched by anything in Part One. The courtship
of Zenocrate in Part One is reflected in Theridamas's pursuit of
Olympia. Within Part Two, Olympia's noble killing of her son
stands in striking contrast to Tamburlaine's murder of his son
Calyphas.

Tamburlaine's first words in Part Two, heralded by 'drums and
trumpets', eloquently celebrate

> . . . Zenocrate, the world's fair eye
> Whose beams illuminate the lamps of heaven,
> Whose cheerful looks do clear the cloudy air
> And clothe it in a crystal livery.   (*Two* 1.3.1–4)

She and her sons form a *tableau* for this eulogy, but she herself
protests against the martial element in this theatrical moment, and
the polarities of Part One, between the martial and the merciful,
between 'wrath' and 'ruth', are re-stated. Within a few lines,
Tamburlaine is recalling Bajazeth's imprisonment (in Part One), in
an exhortation to his sons to 'shine in complete virtue' (that is,
courage), but expressed in the scowling rhetoric of blood-thirst:

> And sprinkled with the brains of slaughtered men,
> My royal chair of state shall be advanced;
> And he that means to place himself therein
> Must armèd wade up to the chin in blood.   (*Two* 1.3.81–4)

This announces the mood in which ritual blood-letting, the murder
of Calyphas, and the feeding of raw flesh to the 'pampered jades'—
the bridled kings—can occur, recalling the gloating banquet of Part
One. And, as we have seen, our aversion to such atrocities is most
persuasively voiced in the play by women.

STAGING AND ACTING

Tamburlaine's initial act of self-realisation is expressed by a symbolic change of costume—rags into armour, shepherd into chivalric leader. This is to acknowledge, and at a stroke to fulfil, one dramatic imperative which also applies to heroic leadership. The actor *becomes* the role; Tamburlaine becomes what his armour proclaims him to be. This symbolic act of transformation relates to the insistence in the play on heroism as courage and address. Heroism, like theatre, centres on self-production. The heroic code wills us to 'wear ourselves and never rest' (*One* 2.7.26), to 'put on our meet encount'ring minds' (like actors' costumes) (*One* 2.6.19). To 'bear / A mind courageous and invincible' (*Two* 1.3.72–3) associates with legendary physical prowess—strength to 'bear the axis of the world' (*Two* 5.3.59), like Atlas. This is a distended boast, but also a daring conviction. 'Virtue' in the plays is commonly used to mean ideal manly power and fortitude: 'complete virtue' shines in 'complete armour'. In this vision, Tamburlaine's character and his staged image mirror each other almost too exactly. The dark side of this, repeatedly, is narcissism and brutal self-will.

The play draws continuously upon a conception of event and appearance as making essence manifest. In this theatre, 'showing' is power, and power lies in eloquence of gesture and in the symbols of passion and of authority. Zenocrate's picture and her statue are set up as icons in the place where she dies, to draw the stars in admiration out of their orbit. A dying lover makes a 'virtue' of the physical sight of his love. The 'virtues' of a crown lie in its burnished appearance. Tributary kings render up their crowns, crowns are served at banquets. The stare of imperious displeasure moves an adversary to suicide, or terrorises an entire army. A black army of Moors is the fear of death incarnate. Colours take on sonority; sound has a brazen shine.

The *Tamburlaine* text in performance requires carefully-staged rituals of entry and departure; coronations, a banquet, the formal surrender and return of tributary crowns; a funeral march to music, 'the town burning'; a dying speech paced in sensitive harmony with music played to a sounding close; a stylised *tableau*, ending with the solemn drawing of an arras. Costumes must be sumptuously elaborate. Dress, accoutrements, flags, are colour-coded (white, red, black) through successive days of siege. The text implies a stirring repertory of sound-effects: 'hear the clang / Of Scythian trumpets, hear the basilisks'(*One* 4.1.1–2), and 'The crack, the echo, and the soldiers' cry' (*Two* 3.3.60). Battle noises offstage are timed to occur in the intervals of speech onstage. And the play's formal speeches must appear spontaneous, without sacrificing their firm rhythmical and syntactical structure. Rhetorical address, by no means all declamatory, is here a disciplined medium for the voice. Tamburlaine himself must show innocent elation, mischievous verve, grief, brooding introspection, magnanimity, quiet acceptance of mortality, futile rage, and gloating vindictiveness. These very distinct feelings have to register clearly without the support of a clear line of 'character development'.

Those who aspire to the high style and the stately effect, however, are frequently exposed in *Tamburlaine* as laughable. Some of the play's comedy is associated with the theatrical grandeur of ceremonial, through the 'low' public pageants it often imitates. When Tamburlaine distributes the Turkish queens to his troops, he reminds us of the gloating which Shakespeare's Cleopatra came to fear from the Roman crowd (whose 'quick comedians / Extemporally will stage us' (*Antony and Cleopatra*, 5.2.212–13)):

> *Theridamas.* It seems they meant to conquer us, my lord,
>   And make us jesting pageants for their trulls.
> *Tamburlaine.* And now themselves shall make our pageant,
>   And common soldiers jest with all their trulls.
>
>   (*Two* 4.3.88–91)

In Tamburlaine's treatment of such victims as Bajazeth and Orcanes, he casts himself in the role of the director of a pageant, inviting a coarse response from the crowd-audience. Such moments blatantly break the high style, but they are true to one thoroughly-developed aspect of the Tamburlaine figure. His brutality and his zest repeatedly find expression in gleeful or sardonic mockery.

Joseph Hall, in 1597, thought the acting style of Edward Alleyn, the notorious inaugural Tamburlaine, indiscriminately pretentious: 'The stalking steps of his great personage, / Gracèd with huf-cap termes and thundring threats'. In the same context Hall writes pungently about farcical intrusion in tragic theatre:

>   mids the silent rout
> Comes leaping in a selfe-misformèd lout,
> And laughes, and grins, and frames his Mimik face,
> And justles straight into the Princes place.[2]

The printer of the first edition of *Tamburlaine* claims to have edited out 'some fond and frivolous jestures' which will offend the wise, though their 'graced deformities' have pleased the groundlings. We can only speculate about these materials, allegedly removed in the name of high seriousness. Nevertheless, there are many passages of comic writing in the text as it stands, which have been emphasised in several modern productions.

In any case, it is inescapable that in so extravagant a play the balances of seriousness and levity, admiration and mockery, are capable of sudden alteration, especially in performance. A display of ebullient cruelty—'Holla, ye pampered jades of Asia' (*Two* 4.3.1)— might excite an astonished nervous laughter from the audience. A passage of flat, gloating banter might freeze mirth at its source. The actors in the early production may have taken their cue from an audience needing more relief than Marlowe allowed from 'stately' emphasis in both language and spectacle. But it is clear that Marlowe's text itself constantly asks painful questions: do we laugh at the caged Bajazeth, at (and with) the sardonic and effete Calyphas, at the 'pampered jades' and the violated queens? To find that we do, or that we hesitate to do so, is to register the strains of responding to a brutal 'scourge of God'.

Tamburlaine waited some three hundred years for its revival in the professional theatre, after dropping out of the repertoire at some time in the mid-seventeenth century. Tyrone Guthrie produced an abridged and conflated version of both Parts at London's Old Vic and at Stratford in 1951: Donald Wolfit played Tamburlaine, and Jill Balcon Zenocrate. This version was staged again, at Stratford, Ontario, and in New York, with Anthony Quayle in the central role.

In 1976, the National Theatre production of *Tamburlaine* convincingly established the integrity of the play, presenting at each performance a virtually complete text of both Parts, with an interval between them. Peter Hall directed the play in a production style essentially true to the many indications the text carries of Marlowe's conception of it. Pageantry, effects of *tableau*, formal groupings, firm and measured utterance, echoed and assisted the poetry at every point. Most significantly, the stage-set and the visual style evoked emblematic and symbolic meanings boldly, not as a pious revival but as living theatre: white and black, mercy and doom, pliancy and resolution, fire and dross, life and death, male and female. A circular lighting grid picked out a matching area on the stage below it, on which a map of the world was projected before the play began, shading off into *terra incognita*. A red stain flooded the stage circle at moments of horrific conquest. A trap at the centre of this stage circle served a range of purposes, concentrating our attention on the ways in which extremes of experience impinge on each other. The trap served as a raised plinth for Zenocrate in grief, a pit for cremations and the burning of the Koran, a tomb for Tamburlaine and Zenocrate as the chariot backed offstage at the end of Part Two. The white-red-black colour-coding of Tamburlaine's three-day sieges was thoroughly observed; and it was supplemented by the adoption of a symbolic or evocative colour-scheme for each dramatic group— Turks, Egyptians, Christians. The text rings with 'triples', both literal and metaphorical, and the production responded with formal stage-groupings: three sons, three physicians, three followers of Tamburlaine, all grouped at the death of Zenocrate, and equally bold and simple groupings at other times. Maximum symbolic impact was achieved at such peak moments as the siege of Babylon: the governor hanging in cruciform posture formed a background to Tamburlaine pulled in his coach by vanquished kings wearing crowns of thorns.

These bold contrasts and expansive evocations provided a vivid context within which the play's human implications were explored. Here, the single most surprising discovery was the diversity of engagement among the characters and between the characters and their audience. Crucial, of course, is the response to Tamburlaine himself. Albert Finney drew his followers, and often the audience, into a delighted and mirthful partisanship with his rise to power. That rise was itself conceived of as an opportunistic and daring self-production by Tamburlaine, based partly on perceptive and irreverent mimicry of the bogus grandeur he observes in others, such as Bajazeth. The more the audience is drawn into sympathetic alignment with Tamburlaine, the more embarrassing is their realisation that this is, in effect, complicity with a spirit of gloating atrocity and hubristic pride. Zenocrate, played by Susan Fleetwood, emerged as a fully-conceived figure whose relation to Tamburlaine is complex and painful. Her entry during the battle for Damascus was closely parallel to the entries of Tamburlaine's victims themselves at the successive moments of hideous conquest. The production allowed no compromise with such painful implications as these. It confirmed how continually in Marlowe's play the grotesque impinges on the beautiful, the true heroic coarsens into ranting automatism, and mirth is chastened by our being brought to acknowledge the dark side of the joke.[3]

A very different interpretation of the play was the Royal Shakespeare Company production at The Swan Theatre, which opened on 13 August 1992, directed by Terry Hands, with Antony Sher as Tamburlaine and Claire Benedict as Zenocrate. This production emphasised the grotesque with energy and relish, using many surreal properties and effects. It gave us a Tamburlaine who was inventively sadistic and athletic, aboundingly scornful of the established emperors he confronted. The production lacked the chivalric and processional elements of the National Theatre version, but heightened the elements of exoticism, barbarity, and horror, all oppressively close at hand in the intimate Swan, with its apron stage.

THE TEXT

It is generally accepted that the first published text of the play, the octavo edition of 1590, enjoys clear authority. It may well have been printed from Marlowe's own manuscript, or from that of a scribe. The text lacks the kind of detailed instruction that a theatre copy would have generated. For instance, it carries too few precise and detailed stage directions, fails to signal all entries and exits, and omits some necessary scene divisions. Conversely, the text indicates with a Latin flourish its status as a 'classical' work, in two distinct five-act Parts. There remains, however, the problem of the passages of 'low' comedy, which the printer, in his dedicatory letter, claims to have edited out. Some such passages remain, in this 1590 text (and all texts thereafter), and the gaps where cuts were made are not clearly evident. It is possible that the printer was making cuts on Marlowe's own direct instructions.

The later octavos, of 1593 (the year of Marlowe's death) and 1597, have no independent authority. They introduce minor errors, but also provide some helpful minor corrections. There is also a quarto, in two volumes, of 1605–6, which has no special authority.

The punctuation of the first published texts is to some extent 'rhetorical' in character, indicating emphatic delivery, sometimes at the cost of syntactical sense. Punctuation of the present edition aims to observe modern conventions. Although it is light, compared to the original, it keeps one of the main rhetorical strengths of the play—not simply the popularly-acclaimed 'mighty line', but the firm and lucid sentence and paragraph structure, sustained through so many speeches.

The other main, and essential, intervention of a modern editor, is in providing consistent scene-divisions, and, above all, informative directions for stage action. (All such editorial additions are in square brackets.) A lot *happens* on stage in *Tamburlaine*—a fact easily obscured, for the mere reader of the play, in the absence of many significant stage-directions.

FURTHER READING

In 1964, Clifford Leech influentially reviewed developments in Marlowe criticism and scholarship as a preface to his anthology, *Marlowe: A Collection of Critical Essays* (Englewood Cliffs, N. J.). 'The wide differences' he observed among recent interpretations of Marlowe had effectively displaced the old-fashioned, almost unanimous view of his works. *Tamburlaine* was no longer seen as a monotonous, feebly-dramatised series of episodes whose central figure was mostly a mouthpiece for a 'dazzled' and precocious author. The 'intellectual quality' of Marlowe's address to the writing of the play was now being emphasised; the complexity of the texts was gaining recognition; much more was coming to be known about Elizabethan theatre and society.

Among the most influential works within Leech's survey were: Eugene Waith's *The Herculean Hero* (London, 1962), David Bevington's *From Mankind to Marlowe* (Cambridge, Mass., 1962), and—at a surprising distance in time—T. S. Eliot's essay on Marlowe of 1919 (*Selected Essays*, London, 1932). Waith had broken away from such discussions of *Tamburlaine* as had centered on mere authorial approval or disapproval of the central figure. He sees the play as re-defining a specific kind of heroic character which is in itself a compound of opposed impulses and attitudes:

> In the depiction of the Herculean hero there is no relaxation of the tensions between his egotism and altruism, his cruelties and benefactions, his human limitations and his divine potentialities. (86)

Bevington's work was, at the same time, bringing us closer to an understanding of the formative development of drama and theatre leading up to Marlowe. Eliot had sought to define in the plays a 'powerful and mature tone' of farce, a dramatic idiom 'not unlike caricature' (*Selected Essays*, 1932, 123, 125). Leech's prefatory essay took this line of definition further: the comic element, in conveying 'the ludicrous gap between aspiration and any possible fulfilment', was an integral part of *Tamburlaine* as a tragedy (*Marlowe*, 1964, 5). See also Leech's essay, 'Marlowe's Humor' (in R. Hosley, ed., *Essays on Shakespeare and Elizabethan Theater in Honor of Hardin Craig*, London, 1963, 69–81).

The years since 1964 have, of course, extended our knowledge of Marlowe's life, his resources, the theatre, and the culture of his time. There have been deeply influential productions of *Tamburlaine*, especially that in the National Theatre in 1976—which itself drew on advances in scholarly knowledge. It would now be true to say that something of a critical consensus has emerged, to the effect that the two parts of *Tamburlaine* are a fully-controlled dramatic achievement, drawing on rich theatrical resources in ways that challenge the audience to reckon with contradictions and ironies, and disturbing implications, in this narrative of tyrannical self-assertion. Judith Weil, for instance, in *Christopher Marlowe: Merlin's Prophet* (Cambridge, 1977), emphasised the 'dialectical vigour' of the two *Tamburlaine* plays, and their dramatic ironies, texts imposing on their audience 'the burdens of inference and interpretation': 'Tamburlaine cannot fully outrun our perception that his power falls far short of his hopes and that it does enormous damage to other men' (117, 106, 107–8).

Some such view of the *Tamburlaine* plays gains support from many quarters. For instance, there are two informative discussions of the challenges we are subjected to in the theatre: David Hard Zucker's *Stage and Image in the Plays of Christopher Marlowe* (Salzburg, 1972), and George L. Geckle's *Tamburlaine and Edward II: Text and Performance* (London, 1988). Simon Shepherd's *Marlowe and the Politics of Elizabethan Theatre* (Brighton, 1986) offers a stimulating discussion of, among other things, gender in Marlowe's theatre. Emily C. Bartels's essay, 'The Double Vision of the East: Imperialist Self-Construction in Marlowe's *Tamburlaine*, Part One', advances discussion of the play's ideological cross-currents with reference to sixteenth century mercantile and colonial competition, from a Bakhtinian and feminist perspective, that also derives strength from the work of Edward Said (*Renaissance Drama*, New Series XXIII, Evanston, 1992; reprinted in Bartels, *Spectacles of Strangeness*, Philadelphia, 1993).

It would be wrong, while pointing briefly towards some contemporary criticism on *Tamburlaine*, to neglect to mention two pioneer

works of scholarship from as long ago as the 1920s. Both are by Ethel
Seaton. One, 'Marlowe's Map', investigated in detail the influential
presence behind *Tamburlaine* of the great atlas of Abraham Ortelius,
and what might be called the ideology of map-making in the sixteenth century (*Essays and Studies*, X, 1924). The second, 'Fresh
Sources for Marlowe', broke new ground, very influentially for
subsequent critics and editors (*R.E.S.*, V, 1929). This piece of
scholarship has been most recently reflected in the comprehensive
anthology, *Christopher Marlowe, the Plays and their Sources*, ed. Vivien
Thomas and William Tydeman, London and New York, 1994.

Some four hundred years on from the first production of
Marlowe's *Tamburlaine*, a wealth of editorial, theatrical, and critical
attention is being given to the play. The relevant periodicals, such as
Renaissance Drama, are, of course, invaluable guides to this many-
sided engagement with the play, which is now typically seen as
eminently stageable in its full length, and particularly challenging to
us in our time.

NOTES

1 For a selection from Marlowe's main sources, see *Tamburlaine the Great*, ed. J. S.
  Cunningham, Manchester and Baltimore, 1981, 318–29.
2 *Virgidemiarum*, 1.3.16–17, 33–6. *Collected Poems*, ed. A. Davenport, London, 1949,
  14–15.
3 For a fuller account of this production, see J. S. Cunningham and Roger Warren,
  '*Tamburlaine the Great* Re-discovered', *Shakespeare Survey* 31 (1978), 155–62.

Abbreviations

Bevington	David Bevington and Eric Rasmussen (ed.), Marlowe, *Tamburlaine* in *Christopher Marlowe: 'Doctor Faustus' and Other Plays* (Oxford, 1995); also suggestions communicated by David Bevington.
Ellis-Fermor	*Tamburlaine the Great*, ed. Una Ellis-Fermor (London, 1930); second edition, revised, 1951.
Heninger	S. K. Heninger, Jr, *A Handbook of Renaissance Meteorology* (Durham, N. C., 1960).
Kocher	Paul H. Kocher, *Christopher Marlowe. A Study of his Thought, Learning, and Character* (New York, 1946).
OED	*Oxford English Dictionary*
Parr	Johnstone Parr, *Tamburlaine's Malady* (Alabama, 1953).
Pendry-Maxwell	Marlowe, *Complete Plays and Poems*, ed. E. D. Pendry and J. C. Maxwell (London, 1976).
Seaton	Ethel Seaton, 'Marlowe's Map', *Essays and Studies by Members of the English Association*, X (1924), 13–35.
Whetstone	George Whetstone, *The English Myrror* (London, 1586). Facsimile, 1973, *The English Experience*, No. 632 (Amsterdam and New York).
Woolf	*Tamburlaine the Great*, ed. Tatiana M. Woolf (London, 1964).

Quotations from Marlowe, *Doctor Faustus*, are from the Bevington and Rasmussen edition cited above. Shakespeare quotations are from *The Complete Works*, ed. Stanley Wells and Gary Taylor, Compact Edition (Oxford, 1988).

TAMBURLAINE
THE GREAT

Part One

[DRAMATIS PERSONAE

The Prologue.
MYCETES, *King of Persia.*
COSROE, *his brother.*

MEANDER ⎫
THERIDAMAS ⎪   5
MENAPHON ⎬ *Persian lords.*
ORTYGIUS ⎪
CENEUS ⎭

TAMBURLAINE, *a Scythian shepherd.*
ZENOCRATE, *daughter of the Sultan of Egypt.*   10
ANIPPE, *her maid.*
TECHELLES, *follower of Tamburlaine.*
USUMCASANE, *follower of Tamburlaine.*

MAGNETES ⎫
AGYDAS ⎭ *Median lords attending Zenocrate.*   15

BAJAZETH, *Emperor of the Turks.*
ZABINA, *Empress of the Turks.*
EBEA, *her maid.*

KING OF FEZ ⎫
KING OF MOROCCO ⎬ *tributary kings to Bajazeth.*   20
KING OF ARGIER ⎭

SULTAN OF EGYPT.
CAPOLIN, an *Egyptian.*
ALCIDAMUS, *King of Arabia.*

---

2. *MYCETES*] not in history a king of Persia. Marlowe may be adapting the name 'Mesithes' found by chance in a work he knew on Persian history.

3. *COSROE*] name of a Persian king of later date.

8. *CENEUS*] a standard emendation displacing the early texts' *Conerus*; these early texts read '*Cene*' as the speech-heading at 1.1.140.

10. *ZENOCRATE*] Evidently Marlowe invented the name and the character.

12. *TECHELLES*] name of a warrior of a later date.

13. *USUMCASANE*] a Persian king of later date, mentioned ('Usancasan') by Whetstone, one of Marlowe's main sources.

14. *MAGNETES*] a standard editorial expansion of the early texts' speech-heading *Mag.* (see *One* 1.2.0.2n.).

21. *ARGIER*] Algiers.

24. *ALCIDAMUS*] Given this name by Marlowe, the King of Arabia occurs in his major sources, as does the Sultan of Egypt.

GOVERNOR OF DAMASCUS.   25
FOUR VIRGINS OF DAMASCUS.
A Spy, Messengers (including PHILEMUS), Lords, Soldiers,
    Bassoes, two Moors, Citizens, Attendants.]

---

28. *Bassoes*] pashas (high officials of the former Ottoman Empire).

To the Gentlemen Readers and others that take pleasure
in reading Histories.

Gentlemen and courteous readers whosoever: I have here
published in print for your sakes the two tragical discourses of
the Scythian shepherd Tamburlaine, that became so great a
conqueror and so mighty a monarch. My hope is that they will
be now no less acceptable unto you to read after your serious   5
affairs and studies than they have been, lately, delightful for
many of you to see, when the same were showed in London
upon stages. I have purposely omitted and left out some fond
and frivolous jestures, digressing and, in my poor opinion, far
unmeet for the matter, which I thought might seem more   10
tedious unto the wise than any way else to be regarded—
though, haply, they have been of some vain conceited fondlings greatly gaped at, what times they were showed upon the
stage in their graced deformities. Nevertheless, now to be
mixtured in print with such matter of worth, it would prove a   15
great disgrace to so honourable and stately a history. Great
folly were it in me to commend unto your wisdoms either the
eloquence of the author that writ them or the worthiness of
the matter itself; I therefore leave unto your learned censures
both the one and the other, and myself the poor printer of   20
them unto your most courteous and favourable protection;
which if you vouchsafe to accept, you shall evermore bind me
to employ what travail and service I can to the advancing and
pleasuring of your excellent degree.

Yours, most humble at commandment,   25
R. J.
Printer.

---

2. *discourses*] narratives, tales.

9. *jestures*] clearly associated with 'jest' rather than merely a variant spell-
ing of our 'gestures'.

10. *unmeet*] unfit.

12–13. *fondlings*] fools.

13. *what times*] when.

14. *graced*] favoured, applauded (by the vulgar).

19. *censures*] judgments.

22. *which*] i.e. the printer's dedicatory gesture.

23. *travail*] labour.

24. *degree*] rank, station.

26–7. *R. J. Printer*] Richard Jones is named in the Stationers' Register
entry for the play, but the play was probably printed for him by Thomas
Orwin. Jones was the publisher.

The Prologue

From jigging veins of rhyming mother-wits,
And such conceits as clownage keeps in pay,
We'll lead you to the stately tent of War,
Where you shall hear the Scythian Tamburlaine
Threat'ning the world with high astounding terms   5
And scourging kingdoms with his conquering sword.
View but his picture in this tragic glass
And then applaud his fortunes as you please.

---

1. *jigging*] may serve here generally for doggerel metre; more precisely, it
could allude to the farcical 'jigs' used as interludes or end-pieces, in which
the 'extemporall wit' of comic actors like Tarlton or Kempe could be employed. Marlowe's disparaging words anticipate many later attacks, but his
own work includes, or has had interpolated, scenes of farce and horseplay.

mother-wits] those relying on their mere unschooled impulses.

2. *conceits*] fanciful actions, tricks.

6. *scourging*] an early hint of the 'scourge of God' theme (see Introduction, pp. 8–12).

7. *tragic glass*] The sense of Tamburlaine as a mirror, whether for rulers or
tyrants or common men, is continually present in the play. The metaphor is
ubiquitous in texts moralising the spectacle of human life (e.g. *A Mirror for
Magistrates*) and/or discussing the nature of theatre (e.g. 'to hold as 'twere the
mirror up to nature', *Hamlet*, 3.2.21–2).

Act 1

SCENE I

[*Enter*] MYCETES, COSROE, MEANDER, THERIDAMAS,
ORTYGIUS, CENEUS, [MENAPHON,] *with others.*

Mycetes. Brother Cosroe, I find myself aggrieved
Yet insufficient to express the same,
For it requires a great and thund'ring speech.
Good brother, tell the cause unto my lords;
I know you have a better wit than I.   5
Cosroe. Unhappy Persia, that in former age
Hast been the seat of mighty conquerors
That in their prowess and their policies
Have triumphed over Afric, and the bounds
Of Europe where the sun dares scarce appear   10
For freezing meteors and congealèd cold—
Now to be ruled and governed by a man
At whose birth-day Cynthia with Saturn joined,

1.1.] Scene divisions are in Latin throughout both Parts in the early texts.
Location: at the Persian court.

2. *insufficient*] not competent, unfit. Mycetes' coy recognition of his own
inadequacy is apter than he knows.

5. *wit*] wisdom, good judgment. The word clings ironically to Mycetes,
both in this sense and in others, linking his lack of sense with his effete relish
of frilly effects ('a pretty toy to be a poet'). Cf. his regrettable (unwitting?)
wordplay at 22, and Tamburlaine's taunting 'Are you the witty King of
Persia?' at *One* 2.4.23.

7. *mighty conquerors*] Cosroe invokes the memory of Cyrus the Great,
whose Persian empire stretched from India to Egypt, and Darius his
successor.

9.] Cambyses 'triumphed over Afric', i.e. conquered Egypt.

11. *freezing . . . cold*] sleet and snow. At this time, 'meteor' could include
'clouds, dew, winds, lightning, comets, [and] rainbows' (Heninger, 3–4).

13. *birth-day*] i.e. the actual day of his birth, not the anniversary
occasions.

13–15.] 'According to Cosroe, Mycetes was born under Saturn (hence,

And Jove, the Sun, and Mercury denied
To shed their influence in his fickle brain!   15
Now Turks and Tartars shake their swords at thee,
Meaning to mangle all thy provinces.
Mycetes. Brother, I see your meaning well enough,
And through your planets I perceive you think
I am not wise enough to be a king;   20
But I refer me to my noblemen
That know my wit, and can be witnesses:
I might command you to be slain for this!
Meander, might I not?
Meander. Not for so small a fault, my sovereign lord.   25
Mycetes. I mean it not, but yet I know I might.
Yet live, yea, live, Mycetes wills it so.
Meander, thou my faithful counsellor,
Declare the cause of my conceivèd grief
Which is, God knows, about that Tamburlaine,   30
That like a fox in midst of harvest time
Doth prey upon my flocks of passengers,
And, as I hear, doth mean to pull my plumes.
Therefore 'tis good and meet for to be wise.
Meander. Oft have I heard Your Majesty complain   35
Of Tamburlaine, that sturdy Scythian thief,
That robs your merchants of Persepolis
Trading by land unto the Western Isles,

---

sluggish, cold and gloomy) and the Moon or Cynthia (hence, fickle and
irresolute), with no qualities of Jove or Jupiter (majestic, jovial), the Sun
(royal, sanguine), or Mercury (eloquent, ingenious)' (Bevington).

14. *denied*] refused.

16. *thee*] i.e. Persia.

19. *your planets*] your citing of astrology.

22. *wit . . . witnesses*] The inept wordplay contributes to the characterisa-
tion of Mycetes and helps prepare us for Tamburlaine's own imperious
command over words.

29. *conceivèd*] mentally produced.

32. *passengers*] travellers.

33. *pull my plumes*] pull out the feathers in my royal crest; humiliate me.

34. *meet . . . wise*] sensible to be intelligently prepared.

36. *sturdy*] fierce, rebellious.

Scythian] Tartar; Tartary often means the whole of Central and North-
Eastern Asia.

38. *Western Isles*] possibly Britain, or the West Indies.

And in your confines with his lawless train
Daily commits incivil outrages, 40
Hoping, misled by dreaming prophecies,
To reign in Asia, and with barbarous arms
To make himself the monarch of the East.
But ere he march in Asia, or display
His vagrant ensign in the Persian fields, 45
Your Grace hath taken order by Theridamas,
Charged with a thousand horse, to apprehend
And bring him captive to Your Highness' throne.
Mycetes. Full true thou speak'st, and like thyself, my lord,
Whom I may term a Damon for thy love. 50
Therefore 'tis best, if so it like you all,
To send my thousand horse incontinent
To apprehend that paltry Scythian.
How like you this, my honourable lords?
Is it not a kingly resolution? 55
Cosroe. It cannot choose, because it comes from you.
Mycetes. Then hear thy charge, valiant Theridamas,
The chiefest captain of Mycetes' host,
The hope of Persia, and the very legs
Whereon our state doth lean, as on a staff 60
That holds us up and foils our neighbour foes:
Thou shalt be leader of this thousand horse,
Whose foaming gall with rage and high disdain

---

39. *confines*] border regions.
40. *incivil*] barbarous.
43. *monarch of the East*] The phrase returns with Cosroe's usurpation of Mycetes' titles (161), and becomes a focus for Tamburlaine's ambition (*One* 1.2.184).
45. *vagrant ensign*] i.e. roving army.
46. *taken order by*] ordered.
47. *Charged with*] in command of.
49. *like thyself*] true to your nature.
50. *Damon*] Damon offered himself as a hostage for his friend Pythias. This classical model of friendship suits Tamburlaine's loyalty and generosity better than it does the decadent Persians.
51. *if so it like*] if it pleases.
52. *incontinent*] immediately.
56. *choose*] help being kingly. (Ironic.)
58. *host*] army.
63. *gall*] spite.

Have sworn the death of wicked Tamburlaine.
Go frowning forth, but come thou smiling home,   65
As did Sir Paris with the Grecian dame.
Return with speed, Time passeth swift away,
Our life is frail, and we may die today.
Theridamas. Before the moon renew her borrowed light
　　Doubt not, my lord and gracious sovereign,   70
　　But Tamburlaine and that Tartarian rout
　　Shall either perish by our warlike hands
　　Or plead for mercy at Your Highness' feet.
Mycetes. Go, stout Theridamas; thy words are swords,
　　And with thy looks thou conquerest all thy foes.   75
　　I long to see thee back return from thence,
　　That I may view these milk-white steeds of mine
　　All loaden with the heads of killèd men,
　　And from their knees even to their hoofs below
　　Besmeared with blood, that makes a dainty show.   80
Theridamas. Then now, my lord, I humbly take my leave.
　　　　　　　　　　　　　　　　　　　　　Exit.

Mycetes. Theridamas, farewell ten thousand times.
　　Ah, Menaphon, why stay'st thou thus behind
　　When other men press forward for renown?
　　Go, Menaphon, go into Scythia,   85
　　And foot by foot follow Theridamas.
Cosroe. Nay, pray you, let him stay. A greater task
　　Fits Menaphon than warring with a thief:
　　Create him prorex of Assyria,
　　That he may win the Babylonians' hearts,   90
　　Which will revolt from Persian government
　　Unless they have a wiser king than you.

---

66. *Sir Paris*] Paris abducted Helen, triggering the Trojan war. Noble
characters are often given anachronistic titles in chivalric romances.
　67–8.] typically banal.
　71. *rout*] mob.
　74. *stout*] brave.
　87. *task*] usually accepted by editors as the word omitted in early texts.
　89. *prorex*] viceroy.
　Assyria] The early texts read 'Africa' or 'all Affrica'. The emendation to
'Assyria' gains support from *Two* 5.1.63 ff., where the period of Assyrian rule
over Babylon is spoken of in the dramatic present tense.
　90–1.] Babylon was part of the Persian empire.

Mycetes. 'Unless they have a wiser king than you!'
  These are his words, Meander, set them down.
Cosroe. And add this to them, that all Asia   95
  Lament to see the folly of their king.
Mycetes. Well, here I swear by this my royal seat—
Cosroe. You may do well to kiss it, then.
Mycetes. —Embossed with silk as best beseems my state,
  To be revenged for these contemptuous words.   100
  Oh, where is duty and allegiance now?
  Fled to the Caspian or the Ocean main?
  What, shall I call thee brother? No, a foe,
  Monster of Nature, shame unto thy stock,
  That dar'st presume thy sovereign for to mock.   105
  Meander, come, I am abused, Meander.
                              Exit [with MEANDER *and others].*

            Manent COSROE *and* MENAPHON.

Menaphon. How now, my lord, what, mated and amazed
  To hear the King thus threaten like himself?
Cosroe. Ah, Menaphon, I pass not for his threats.
  The plot is laid by Persian noblemen   110
  And captains of the Median garrisons
  To crown me emperor of Asia.
  But this it is that doth excruciate
  The very substance of my vexèd soul:
  To see our neighbours that were wont to quake   115
  And tremble at the Persian monarch's name
  Now sits and laughs our regiment to scorn;
  And that which might resolve me into tears,

---

97. *seat*] throne. (But Cosroe, in 98, sarcastically takes it in the sense of 'backside'.)

99. *state*] rank, also the theatrical throne on its dais (assisting the wordplay).

102. *Ocean main*] ocean.

106.2. *Manent*] They remain.

107. *mated*] abashed, daunted.

109. *pass*] care.

113. *excruciate*] torment.

114. *substance*] essence.

117. *sits . . . laughs*] Elizabethan plural.

regiment] rule, royal authority.

118. *resolve me into*] reduce me to, dissolve me into.

    Men from the farthest equinoctial line
    Have swarmed in troops into the Eastern India,   120
    Lading their ships with gold and precious stones,
    And made their spoils from all our provinces.
Menaphon. This should entreat Your Highness to rejoice,
    Since Fortune gives you opportunity
    To gain the title of a conqueror   125
    By curing of this maimèd empery.
    Afric and Europe bordering on your land
    And continent to your dominions,
    How easily may you with a mighty host
    Pass into Graecia, as did Cyrus once,   130
    And cause them to withdraw their forces home
    Lest you subdue the pride of Christendom!
                            [*A trumpet sounds.*]
Cosroe. But Menaphon, what means this trumpet's sound?
Menaphon. Behold, my lord, Ortygius and the rest,
    Bringing the crown to make you emperor.   135

Enter ORTYGIUS *and* CENEUS, *bearing a crown, with others.*

Ortygius. Magnificent and mighty prince Cosroe,
    We in the name of other Persian states
    And commons of this mighty monarchy
    Present thee with th'imperial diadem.
Ceneus. The warlike soldiers and the gentlemen   140
    That heretofore have filled Persepolis
    With Afric captains taken in the field—
    Whose ransom made them march in coats of gold,
    With costly jewels hanging at their ears
    And shining stones upon their lofty crests—   145

---

119. *equinoctial line*] the equator.
121. *Lading*] loading.
122. *made their spoils from*] looted.
123. *entreat*] persuade.
124.] With this sense of Fortune giving political opportunity which must be seized, compare *Two* 2.1.11–13. Fortune is more often seen as chance ('the fortune of the wars'), or as Tamburlaine's sponsor, or even his slave.
126. *empery*] rule; dominion; empire.
128. *continent to*] connected to.
130.] In fact, it was Darius, not Cyrus, who subdued Greek Asia Minor.
137. *states*] persons of high estate.
143. *made them*] made them so rich as to.

Now living idle in the wallèd towns,
Wanting both pay and martial discipline,
Begin in troops to threaten civil war
And openly exclaim against the King.
Therefore, to stay all sudden mutinies,   150
We will invest Your Highness emperor;
Whereat the soldiers will conceive more joy
Than did the Macedonians at the spoil
Of great Darius and his wealthy host.

Cosroe. Well, since I see the state of Persia droop   155
And languish in my brother's government,
I willingly receive th'imperial crown
And vow to wear it for my country's good,
In spite of them shall malice my estate.

Ortygius. And in assurance of desired success   160
We here do crown thee monarch of the East,
Emperor of Asia and of Persia,
Great lord of Media and Armenia,
Duke of Assyria and Albania,
Mesopotamia and of Parthia,   165
East India and the late-discovered isles,
Chief lord of all the wide vast Euxine Sea
And of the ever-raging Caspian Lake.
Long live Cosroë, mighty emperor!

Cosroe. And Jove may never let me longer live   170
Than I may seek to gratify your love
And cause the soldiers that thus honour me

---

147. *Wanting*] in need of.

150. *stay*] prevent.

151. *invest*] crown.

152. *conceive*] experience.

153–4.] Alexander the Great defeated Darius III (not the Darius of 7 and 130) in 333 and 331 B.C.

155. *state*] imperial rule.

159. *them shall malice*] those who may seek to injure my authority, or regard it with malice.

163. *Media*] on the Caspian Sea, near Persia.

166. *the late-discovered isles*] perhaps islands near Indonesia, discovered by Drake.

167. *Euxine Sea*] Black Sea.

170. *Jove may*] may Jove.

171. *gratify*] repay.

To triumph over many provinces!
By whose desires of discipline in arms
I doubt not shortly but to reign sole king,   175
And with the army of Theridamas,
Whither we presently will fly, my lords,
To rest secure against my brother's force.
Ortygius. We knew, my lord, before we brought the crown,
Intending your investion so near   180
The residence of your despisèd brother,
The lords would not be too exasperate
To injure or suppress your worthy title.
Or if they would, there are in readiness
Ten thousand horse to carry you from hence   185
In spite of all suspected enemies.
Cosroe. I know it well, my lord, and thank you all.
Ortygius. Sound up the trumpets, then. God save the King!
                                   [*Trumpets sound.*] *Exeunt.*

SCENE 2

[*Enter*] TAMBURLAINE *leading* ZENOCRATE; TECHELLES,
USUMCASANE, *other* Lords [*among them* MAGNETES *and*
AGYDAS] *and* Soldiers *loaden with treasure.*

Tamburlaine. Come, lady, let not this appal your thoughts;
The jewels and the treasure we have ta'en
Shall be reserved, and you in better state
Than if you were arrived in Syria,
Even in the circle of your father's arms,   5
The mighty Sultan of Egyptia.

---

177. *fly*] hasten.
178. *rest*] remain.
180. *investion*] investiture.
182. *too exasperate*] so exasperated as: i.e. we were not afraid of opposition
to your crowning, even though planned to occur in your brother's palace.
184. *Or if they would*] or if they did actually rebel.

1.2. Location: in Scythia, ancient region of south-eastern Europe and
Asia, north of the Black Sea.
0.3. loaden] laden.
3. *reserved*] kept intact.
better state] greater splendour.

Zenocrate. Ah, shepherd, pity my distressèd plight
    (If, as thou seem'st, thou art so mean a man)
    And seek not to enrich thy followers
    By lawless rapine from a silly maid   10
    Who, travelling with these Median lords
    To Memphis, from my uncle's country of Media,
    Where all my youth I have been governèd,
    Have passed the army of the mighty Turk,
    Bearing his privy signet and his hand   15
    To safe conduct us thorough Africa.
Magnetes. And, since we have arrived in Scythia,
    Besides rich presents from the puissant Cham
    We have His Highness' letters to command
    Aid and assistance if we stand in need.   20
Tamburlaine. But now you see these letters and commands
    Are countermanded by a greater man,
    And through my provinces you must expect
    Letters of conduct from my mightiness
    If you intend to keep your treasure safe.   25
    But since I love to live at liberty,
    As easily may you get the Sultan's crown
    As any prizes out of my precinct;
    For they are friends that help to wean my state
    Till men and kingdoms help to strengthen it,   30
    And must maintain my life exempt from servitude.
    But tell me, madam, is Your Grace betrothed?
Zenocrate. I am, my lord—for so you do import.

---

8. *mean*] lowly.
10. *rapine*] theft.
silly] helpless.
12. *Memphis*] ancient centre of Lower Egypt, on the Nile.
13. *governèd*] brought up.
15. *privy . . . hand*] a document signed and sealed.
16. *safe conduct us*] require our unimpeded passage.
thorough Africa] i.e. through the Middle East to Africa.
18. *Cham*] emperor of Tartary.
22. *countermanded*] revoked by a contrary command.
25. *your treasure*] your wealth; but with a suggestion also of virgin purity.
28. *precinct*] sphere of control.
29. *wean my state*] assist the growth of my power.
33. *import*] imply (i.e. that he is a lord).

Tamburlaine. I am a lord, for so my deeds shall prove,
    And yet a shepherd by my parentage.   35
    But lady, this fair face and heavenly hue
    Must grace his bed that conquers Asia
    And means to be a terror to the world,
    Measuring the limits of his empery
    By east and west as Phoebus doth his course.   40
    Lie here, ye weeds that I disdain to wear!
    This complete armour and this curtle-axe
    Are adjuncts more beseeming Tamburlaine.
    And madam, whatsoever you esteem
    Of this success, and loss unvaluèd,   45
    Both may invest you empress of the East;
    And these that seem but silly country swains
    May have the leading of so great an host
    As with their weight shall make the mountains quake,
    Even as when windy exhalations,   50
    Fighting for passage, tilt within the earth.
Techelles. As princely lions when they rouse themselves,
    Stretching their paws and threat'ning herds of beasts,
    So in his armour looketh Tamburlaine.
    Methinks I see kings kneeling at his feet,   55
    And he with frowning brows and fiery looks
    Spurning their crowns from off their captive heads.
Usumcasane. And making thee and me, Techelles, kings,
    That even to death will follow Tamburlaine.

---

37. *his bed that*] i.e. the bed of him who.

39. *empery*] dominion.

40. *Phoebus*] the sun. Tamburlaine's empire, he asserts, will be boundless.

41. *weeds*] garments (here, those of a shepherd).

42. *curtle-axe*] cutlass.

43. *adjuncts more beseeming*] equipment more suitable to.

44–5. *whatsoever . . . unvaluèd*] whatever you think about what has happened, and of your unassessable loss.

45. *success*] outcome.

47. *these*] i.e. Usumcasane and Techelles.

silly] lowly, simple.

49–51.] Earthquakes were thought to be caused by pressure from compressed underground vapours.

51. *tilt*] joust.

57. *Spurning*] literally, kicking.

Tamburlaine. Nobly resolved, sweet friends and followers.   60
  These lords, perhaps, do scorn our estimates,
  And think we prattle with distempered spirits;
  But since they measure our deserts so mean
  That in conceit bear empires on our spears,
  Affecting thoughts coequal with the clouds,   65
  They shall be kept our forcèd followers
  Till with their eyes they view us emperors.
Zenocrate. The gods, defenders of the innocent,
  Will never prosper your intended drifts
  That thus oppress poor friendless passengers.   70
  Therefore at least admit us liberty,
  Even as thou hopest to be eternised
  By living Asia's mighty emperor.
Agydas. I hope our lady's treasure and our own
  May serve for ransom to our liberties.   75
  Return our mules and empty camels back,
  That we may travel into Syria,
  Where her betrothèd lord, Alcidamus,
  Expects th'arrival of Her Highness' person.
Magnetes. And wheresoever we repose ourselves   80
  We will report but well of Tamburlaine.
Tamburlaine. Disdains Zenocrate to live with me?
  Or you, my lords, to be my followers?
  Think you I weigh this treasure more than you?
  Not all the gold in India's wealthy arms   85
  Shall buy the meanest soldier in my train!
  Zenocrate, lovelier than the love of Jove,

---

61. *These lords*] i.e. Zenocrate's attendants.
estimates] attributed, or asserted, value.
62. *with distempered spirits*] in intemperate or deranged states of mind.
63. *measure . . . mean*] assess our deserts as worthless.
64. *That in conceit*] who in our imagination.
65. *Affecting*] aspiring to.
coequal with] as lofty as.
69. *prosper*] cause to prosper.
drifts] purposes.
72. *eternised*] made immortal.
73. *living*] living in the future.
79. *Expects*] awaits.
87. *the love of Jove*] Juno.

Brighter than is the silver Rhodope,
Fairer than whitest snow on Scythian hills,
Thy person is more worth to Tamburlaine   90
Than the possession of the Persian crown,
Which gracious stars have promised at my birth.
A hundred Tartars shall attend on thee,
Mounted on steeds swifter than Pegasus;
Thy garments shall be made of Median silk,   95
Enchased with precious jewels of mine own,
More rich and valurous than Zenocrate's;
With milk-white harts upon an ivory sled
Thou shalt be drawn amidst the frozen pools
And scale the icy mountains' lofty tops,   100
Which with thy beauty will be soon resolved.
My martial prizes, with five hundred men,
Won on the fifty-headed Volga's waves,
Shall all we offer to Zenocrate,
And then my self to fair Zenocrate.   105
Techelles. [*Aside to Tamburlaine*] What now? In love?
Tamburlaine [*Aside*] Techelles, women must be flatterèd.
    But this is she with whom I am in love.

                    Enter a Soldier.

Soldier. News, news!
Tamburlaine. How now, what's the matter?   110
Soldier. A thousand Persian horsemen are at hand,
    Sent from the King to overcome us all.

---

88. *Rhodope*] mountains famous for silver mines, and supposedly named
after a queen of Thrace who claimed to be more beautiful than Juno.

92. *gracious stars*] the 'happy stars' of *One* 5.1.359, and the 'gracious
aspect' of *Two* 3.5.80; emphasised in Marlowe's sources.

94. *Pegasus*] winged horse of classical mythology, later the favourite steed
of the Muses.

96. *Enchased*] adorned. Marlowe uses the word elsewhere of jewelled
crowns, thrones, and canopies, and (by a characteristic extension) of the
night sky.

97. *valurous*] valuable.

101. *resolved*] melted.

103. *fifty-headed Volga*] Ortelius's maps emphasise the Volga's numerous
major tributaries.

104. *Shall all we*] all of these we shall.

Tamburlaine. How now, my lords of Egypt and Zenocrate!
　　Now must your jewels be restored again,
　　And I that triumphed so be overcome?　　　　　　　115
　　How say you, lordings, is not this your hope?
Agydas. We hope yourself will willingly restore them.
Tamburlaine. Such hope, such fortune, have the thousand
　　　　horse.
　　Soft ye, my lords and sweet Zenocrate:
　　You must be forcèd from me ere you go.　　　　　　　120
　　A thousand horsemen! We five hundred foot!
　　An odds too great for us to stand against.
　　But are they rich? And is their armour good?
Soldier. Their plumèd helms are wrought with beaten gold,
　　Their swords enamelled, and about their necks　　　125
　　Hangs massy chains of gold down to the waist—
　　In every part exceeding brave and rich.
Tamburlaine. Then shall we fight courageously with them,
　　Or look you I should play the orator?
Techelles. No: cowards and faint-hearted runaways　　130
　　Look for orations when the foe is near.
　　Our swords shall play the orators for us.
Usumcasane. Come, let us meet them at the mountain top,
　　And with a sudden and an hot alarm
　　Drive all their horses headlong down the hill.　　　135
Techelles. Come, let us march.
Tamburlaine. Stay, Techelles, ask a parley first.

　　　　　The Soldiers [*of Tamburlaine*] *enter.*

　　Open the mails, yet guard the treasure sure.
　　Lay out our golden wedges to the view,
　　That their reflections may amaze the Persians.　　　140
　　　　　　　　　　[*Soldiers lay out gold ingots.*]

---

　　118. *Such hope, such fortune*] The King's forces have just as much hope of
good fortune—i.e. none at all.
　　119. *Soft ye*] gently, steady.
　　127. *brave*] showy, fine.
　　129.] Or do you expect me to defeat them by eloquence?
　　138. *mails*] bags containing Tamburlaine's booty.
　　139. *wedges*] ingots.
　　140. *amaze*] dazzle, stun.

And look we friendly on them when they come;
But if they offer word or violence
We'll fight five hundred men-at-arms to one
Before we part with our possession.
And 'gainst the general we will lift our swords   145
And either lance his greedy thirsting throat
Or take him prisoner, and his chain shall serve
For manacles, till he be ransomed home.
Techelles. I hear them come; shall we encounter them?
Tamburlaine. Keep all your standings, and not stir a foot;   150
    Myself will bide the danger of the brunt.

Enter THERIDAMAS *with others.*

Theridamas. Where is this Scythian Tamburlaine?
Tamburlaine. Whom seek'st thou, Persian? I am
    Tamburlaine.
Theridamas. [*Aside*] Tamburlaine? A Scythian shepherd, so
    embellishèd
    With nature's pride and richest furniture?   155
    His looks do menace heaven and dare the gods;
    His fiery eyes are fixed upon the earth,
    As if he now devised some stratagem,
    Or meant to pierce Avernus' darksome vaults
    And pull the triple-headed dog from hell.   160
Tamburlaine. [*Aside to Techelles*] Noble and mild this Persian
    seems to be,
    If outward habit judge the inward man.

---

146. *lance*] slit open.
147. *chain*] i.e. of office.
148. *home*] to the full.
150. *standings*] stations.
151. *brunt*] attack, onset.
155. *furniture*] trappings, equipment.
157–8.] Tamburlaine's angry brooding looks resemble descriptions of classical heroes like Odysseus and Ajax. The iconic relation of looks and feelings to words is often emphasised in the play.
159. *Avernus*] the lake near Naples, closely associated with Aeneas's descent into the underworld, and used to mean Hades.
160. *And*] emended from the early texts' 'To'.
triple-headed dog] Cerberus, the guardian of the underworld. Hercules descends into Hades to fetch him in Ovid's *Metamorphoses*, 7.409 ff.
162. *habit*] bearing, demeanour, garb.

Techelles. [*Aside to Tamburlaine*] His deep affections make him
    passionate.
Tamburlaine. [*Aside to Techelles*] With what a majesty he rears
    his looks!
    [*To Theridamas*] In thee, thou valiant man of Persia,   165
    I see the folly of thy emperor.
    Art thou but captain of a thousand horse,
    That by characters graven in thy brows,
    And by thy martial face and stout aspect,
    Deserv'st to have the leading of an host?   170
    Forsake thy king and do but join with me,
    And we will triumph over all the world.
    I hold the Fates bound fast in iron chains,
    And with my hand turn Fortune's wheel about,
    And sooner shall the sun fall from his sphere   175
    Than Tamburlaine be slain or overcome.
    Draw forth thy sword, thou mighty man-at-arms,
    Intending but to raze my charmèd skin,
    And Jove himself will stretch his hand from heaven
    To ward the blow and shield me safe from harm.   180
                [*He indicates the gold ingots.*]
    See how he rains down heaps of gold in showers
    As if he meant to give my soldiers pay;
    And as a sure and grounded argument
    That I shall be the monarch of the East,
    He sends this Sultan's daughter rich and brave   185

    163.] His deep feelings (declared in his face) betoken a passionate nature.
    168. *characters*] distinctive marks.
    168–70.] Cf. the celebration of Tamburlaine at *One* 2.1.3–4, and the
disclosure of personality through *aspect*—expression, face. For astrological
'aspect', see *Two* 3.5.80.
    169. *stout aspect*] brave look.
    173.] *the Fates*] the three goddesses who in Greek mythology control
human destiny: Clotho, Atropos, and Lachesis; as in *Two*, Prologue 5. Cf.
the 'Fatal Sisters' of *Two* 2.4.98–100.
    174.] Tamburlaine is said to have made Fortune stop her wheel, at *One*
5.1.374–5. Fortune may be actively partisan with Tamburlaine: cf. *One*
2.2.73, *Two* 1.1.60, etc.
    175.] Marlowe's astronomy is Ptolemaic: the sun orbits the earth.
    his] its.
    185. *brave*] fine, splendid.

To be my queen and portly emperess.
If thou wilt stay with me, renownèd man,
And lead thy thousand horse with my conduct,
Besides thy share of this Egyptian prize
Those thousand horse shall sweat with martial spoil   190
Of conquered kingdoms and of cities sacked;
Both we will walk upon the lofty clifts,
And Christian merchants that with Russian stems
Plough up huge furrows in the Caspian Sea
Shall vail to us as lords of all the lake.   195
Both we will reign as consuls of the earth,
And mighty kings shall be our senators.
Jove sometimes maskèd in a shepherd's weed,
And by those steps that he hath scaled the heavens
May we become immortal like the gods.   200
Join with me now in this my mean estate
(I call it mean, because, being yet obscure,
The nations far removed admire me not),
And when my name and honour shall be spread
As far as Boreas claps his brazen wings   205
Or fair Boötes sends his cheerful light,
Then shalt thou be competitor with me
And sit with Tamburlaine in all his majesty.
Theridamas. Not Hermes, prolocutor to the gods,

---

186. *portly*] stately.
188. *with my conduct*] under my leadership. Second syllable of 'conduct' stressed.
192. *clifts*] cliffs.
193.] and Christian merchant ships that with their Russian timber prows.
195. *vail*] salute by lowering sail.
198. *Jove*] Jove killed his father, Saturn, and elsewhere in the play is a model of revolt against authority; here the mirror for aspiration from a lowly position.
    maskèd] disguised himself (for instance, in courting Mnemosyne).
    weed] clothes. The sight of shepherds in love can stop divine wrath at *One* 5.1.183–7. Cf. *One* 4.2.108, *One* 4.4.17, and *Two* 3.2.12.
199. *that*] by which.
203. *admire*] marvel at.
205–6.] the furthest northern distances: *Boreas* is the north wind, *Boötes* a northern constellation containing the bright star Arcturus.
207. *competitor*] partner.
209. *Hermes*] messenger of the gods.
    prolocutor] advocate.

Could use persuasions more pathetical.   210
Tamburlaine. Nor are Apollo's oracles more true
    Than thou shalt find my vaunts substantial.
Techelles. We are his friends, and if the Persian king
    Should offer present dukedoms to our state,
    We think it loss to make exchange for that   215
    We are assured of by our friend's success.
Usumcasane. And kingdoms at the least we all expect,
    Besides the honour in assured conquests
    Where kings shall crouch unto our conquering swords
    And hosts of soldiers stand amazed at us,   220
    When with their fearful tongues they shall confess
    'These are the men that all the world admires'.
Theridamas. What strong enchantments 'tice my yielding
        soul?
    Are these resolvèd, noble, *Scythians*?
    But shall I prove a traitor to my king?   225
Tamburlaine. No, but the trusty friend of Tamburlaine.
Theridamas. Won with thy words and conquered with thy
        looks,
    I yield myself, my men and horse to thee,
    To be partaker of thy good or ill
    As long as life maintains Theridamas.   230
Tamburlaine. Theridamas, my friend, take here my hand,
    Which is as much as if I swore by heaven
    And called the gods to witness of my vow.
    Thus shall my heart be still combined with thine
    Until our bodies turn to elements   235

---

210. *pathetical*] moving.
212. *vaunts*] brags.
substantial] firmly based.
214. *present*] immediate.
to our state] to exalt our standing.
215. *that*] that which.
221. *fearful*] awed, full of fear.
confess] acknowledge.
223. *'tice*] entice.
224.] Theridamas is surprised that 'barbaric' Scythians should appear
brave and noble.
227.] See *One* I.I.74–5.
235–6.] until our bodies disintegrate into their constituent elements at
death.

And both our souls aspire celestial thrones.
Techelles and Casane, welcome him.
Techelles. Welcome, renownèd Persian, to us all.
Usumcasane. Long may Theridamas remain with us!
Tamburlaine. These are my friends, in whom I more rejoice   240
    Than doth the King of Persia in his crown;
    And by the love of Pylades and Orestes,
    Whose statues we adore in Scythia,
    Thyself and them shall never part from me
    Before I crown you kings in Asia.   245
    Make much of them, gentle Theridamas,
    And they will never leave thee till the death.
Theridamas. Nor thee nor them, thrice-noble Tamburlaine,
    Shall want my heart to be with gladness pierced
    To do you honour and security.   250
Tamburlaine. A thousand thanks, worthy Theridamas.
    And now, fair madam, and my noble lords,
    If you will willingly remain with me
    You shall have honours as your merits be—
    Or else you shall be forced with slavery.   255
Agydas. We yield unto thee, happy Tamburlaine.
Tamburlaine. For you then, madam, I am out of doubt.
Zenocrate. I must be pleased perforce. Wretched Zenocrate!
                           Exeunt.

[*Finis Actus primi.*]

242.] Pylades and Orestes, archetypes of loyal friendship, ready to die for each other at Taurus (in 'Scythia'). Contrast Mycetes' effete appeal to a similar model at *One* I.I.50.

244. *them*] they. Orthodox Elizabethan grammar.

249. *want*] lack (my whole-hearted protection and honour).

256. *happy*] fortunate—an insistent word for Tamburlaine.

257. *out of doubt*] assured (of your readiness to remain).

258.2.] The end of Act I. (Conclusions to all Acts are declared in Latin in the early texts.)

Act 2

[*Enter*] COSROE, MENAPHON, ORTYGIUS, CENEUS,
with other Soldiers.

Cosroe. Thus far are we towards Theridamas
    And valiant Tamburlaine, the man of fame,
    The man that in the forehead of his fortune
    Bears figures of renown and miracle.
    But tell me, that hast seen him, Menaphon,   5
    What stature wields he, and what personage?
Menaphon. Of stature tall, and straightly fashionèd,
    Like his desire, lift upwards and divine;
    So large of limbs, his joints so strongly knit,
    Such breadth of shoulders as might mainly bear   10
    Old Atlas' burden; 'twixt his manly pitch
    A pearl more worth than all the world is placed,
    Wherein by curious sovereignty of art
    Are fixed his piercing instruments of sight,
    Whose fiery circles bear encompassèd   15
    A heaven of heavenly bodies in their spheres
    That guides his steps and actions to the throne

2.1. Location: in Scythia.

3–4.] recalling the 'characters graven in thy [Theridamas's] brows' at *One*
1.2.168. The image contributes to the projection of Tamburlaine himself as
a figure of Apocalypse. Cf. Revelation 7.3: 'We have sealed the servants of
our God in their foreheads'.

5. *that hast*] you that have.

8. *lift*] lifted, aspiring.

10. *mainly*] by main force.

11. *Atlas*] a Titan compelled by Zeus to support the sky on his shoulders.
pitch] breadth of shoulders.

12. *pearl*] i.e. his head.

13. *curious*] ingenious. The art is that of divine creation.

15–17.] Tamburlaine's fiery eyes are planetary spheres which propitiously
guide his career of aspiration.

Where honour sits invested royally;
Pale of complexion—wrought in him with passion,
Thirsting with sovereignty, with love of arms;   20
His lofty brows in folds do figure death,
And in their smoothness amity and life;
About them hangs a knot of amber hair
Wrappèd in curls, as fierce Achilles' was,
On which the breath of heaven delights to play,   25
Making it dance with wanton majesty;
His arms and fingers long and sinewy,
Betokening valour and excess of strength;
In every part proportioned like the man
Should make the world subdued to Tamburlaine.   30
Cosroe. Well hast thou portrayed in thy terms of life
The face and personage of a wondrous man.
Nature doth strive with Fortune and his stars
To make him famous in accomplished worth,
And well his merits show him to be made   35
His fortune's master and the king of men
That could persuade at such a sudden pinch,
With reasons of his valour and his life,
A thousand sworn and overmatching foes.
Then, when our powers in points of swords are joined   40
And closed in compass of the killing bullet,
Though strait the passage and the port be made

18.] 'Honour' is attributed to Tamburlaine in relation to a variety of
codes, some of them in conflict with conventional expectations.

20. *Thirsting with sovereignty*] closely echoed at *One* 2.6.31. This theme
holds right through the play to Tamburlaine's dying fever.

21. *in folds do figure*] when frowning, prefigure.

23. *amber hair*] So Achilles is described in Homer and elsewhere.

30. *Should*] who should.

31. *terms of life*] lifelike or lively terms.

33–4.] Nature's gifts, good fortune, and astrological influence compete in
assisting Tamburlaine.

37. *pinch*] crisis.

38.] i.e. by the example of his valorous life.

39.] i.e. a thousand enemies who are sworn to oppose him, and who are
numerically overpowering.

40–1.] i.e. then, when our armies are joined in sword-fights and in
bullet-range.

42–3.] i.e. however well Mycetes is shielded by his troops.

42. *strait . . . port*] narrow, the road and gateway.

That leads to palace of my brother's life,
Proud is his fortune if we pierce it not.
And when the princely Persian diadem   45
Shall overweigh his weary witless head
And fall like mellowed fruit, with shakes of death,
In fair Persia noble Tamburlaine
Shall be my regent and remain as king.
Ortygius. In happy hour we have set the crown   50
    Upon your kingly head, that seeks our honour
    In joining with the man ordained by heaven
    To further every action to the best.
Ceneus. He that with shepherds and a little spoil
    Durst, in disdain of wrong and tyranny,   55
    Defend his freedom 'gainst a monarchy—
    What will he do supported by a king,
    Leading a troop of gentlemen and lords,
    And stuffed with treasure for his highest thoughts?
Cosroe. And such shall wait on worthy Tamburlaine.   60
    Our army will be forty thousand strong
    When Tamburlaine and brave Theridamas
    Have met us by the river Araris,
    And all conjoined to meet the witless king
    That now is marching near to Parthia,   65
    And with unwilling soldiers faintly armed,
    To seek revenge on me and Tamburlaine.
    To whom, sweet Menaphon, direct me straight.
Menaphon. I will, my lord.   *Exeunt.*

SCENE 2

[*Enter*] MYCETES, MEANDER, *with other* Lords *and* Soldiers.

Mycetes. Come, my Meander, let us to this gear;
    I tell you true, my heart is swoll'n with wrath

---

43. *palace of my brother's life*] i.e. Mycetes' heart.
44.] He will have to be incredibly fortunate for us not to break through his defences.
51. *that seeks*] you who seek.
59.] and given riches commensurate with his loftiest wishes.
63. *Araris*] Ortelius's map marks the Araxes in Armenia as the Araris.

2.2. Location: in Scythia.
1. *gear*] business.

On this same thievish villain Tamburlaine,
And of that false Cosroe, my traitorous brother.
Would it not grieve a king to be so abused   5
And have a thousand horsemen ta'en away?
And, which is worst, to have his diadem
Sought for by such scald knaves as love him not?
I think it would; well then, by heavens I swear,
Aurora shall not peep out of her doors   10
But I will have Cosroë by the head
And kill proud Tamburlaine with point of sword.
Tell you the rest, Meander; I have said.

Meander. Then, having passed Armenian deserts now
And pitched our tents under the Georgian hills,   15
Whose tops are covered with Tartarian thieves
That lie in ambush waiting for a prey,
What should we do but bid them battle straight,
And rid the world of those detested troops?
Lest, if we let them linger here a while,   20
They gather strength by power of fresh supplies.
This country swarms with vile outrageous men
That live by rapine and by lawless spoil,
Fit soldiers for the wicked Tamburlaine.
And he that could with gifts and promises   25
Inveigle him that led a thousand horse,
And make him false his faith unto his king,
Will quickly win such as are like himself.
Therefore cheer up your minds, prepare to fight.
He that can take or slaughter Tamburlaine   30

5.] The line is a weak counterpart of Tamburlaine's 'Is it not passing brave to be a king', *One* 2.5.53.

8. *scald*] low, contemptible.

10. *Aurora*] Roman goddess of the dawn.

11. *Cosroë*] three syllables here, but (as with other proper names in the play) it may be more or less elided to suit the metre.

13. *said*] finished speaking.

14–5.] Mycetes, 'marching near to Parthia' (south-east of the Caspian), has crossed Armenia and reached the foothills of the Caucasus. Parthia and Armenia are now both ruled by Cosroe.

22. *outrageous*] fierce, violent.

26. *him*] i.e. Theridamas.

27. *false*] break, violate.

Shall rule the province of Albania.
Who brings that traitor's head, Theridamas',
Shall have a government in Media,
Beside the spoil of him and all his train.
But if Cosroë (as our spials say,   35
And as we know) remains with Tamburlaine,
His Highness' pleasure is that he should live
And be reclaimed with princely lenity.

                    [*Enter a* Spy.]

Spy. An hundred horsemen of my company,
    Scouting abroad upon these champian plains,   40
    Have viewed the army of the Scythians,
    Which make report it far exceeds the King's.
Meander. Suppose they be in number infinite,
    Yet being void of martial discipline,
    All running headlong after greedy spoils   45
    And more regarding gain than victory,
    Like to the cruel brothers of the earth
    Sprung of the teeth of dragons venomous,
    Their careless swords shall lance their fellows' throats
    And make us triumph in their overthrow.   50
Mycetes. Was there such brethren, sweet Meander, say,
    That sprung of teeth of dragons venomous?
Meander. So poets say, my lord.
Mycetes. And 'tis a pretty toy to be a poet.
    Well, well, Meander, thou art deeply read,   55

---

31. *Albania*] on the Caspian Sea, near Armenia, not in the Balkans.
32. *Who*] he who.
    Theridamas'] genitive, in apposition to 'traitor's'.
34.] as well as the confiscated property of Theridamas and his followers.
35. *spials*] spies.
38. *lenity*] mercy.
40. *champian*] level and open.
42. *Which*] i.e. the horsemen.
45. *after greedy spoils*] greedy for plunder. Meander's trick intended to
distract Tamburlaine's army is a futile counterpart of Tamburlaine's own
display of gold to assist his winning over of Theridamas.
47–8.] Armed men sprang up from the dragons' teeth sown by Cadmus,
and attacked each other.
54. *toy*] trifle, plaything.

And having thee I have a jewel sure.
Go on, my lord, and give your charge, I say.
Thy wit will make us conquerors today.
Meander. Then, noble soldiers, to entrap these thieves
    That live confounded in disordered troops,   60
    If wealth or riches may prevail with them,
    We have our camels laden all with gold
    Which you that be but common soldiers
    Shall fling in every corner of the field,
    And while the baseborn Tartars take it up,   65
    You, fighting more for honour than for gold,
    Shall massacre those greedy-minded slaves.
    And when their scattered army is subdued
    And you march on their slaughtered carcasses,
    Share equally the gold that bought their lives   70
    And live like gentlemen in Persia.
    Strike up the drum, and march courageously!
    Fortune herself doth sit upon our crests.
Mycetes. He tells you true, my masters, so he does.
    Drums, why sound ye not when Meander speaks?   75
                                Exeunt.

SCENE 3

[*Enter*] COSROE, TAMBURLAINE, THERIDAMAS, TECHELLES,
    USUMCASANE, ORTYGIUS, *with others.*

Cosroe. Now, worthy Tamburlaine, have I reposed
    In thy approvèd fortunes all my hope.
    What think'st thou, man, shall come of our attempts?
    For even as from assurèd oracle,

---

    57. *charge*] orders.
    58. *wit*] intelligence, inventiveness.
    59–67.] a stratagem much praised in the military manuals of Marlowe's
day.
    75.1. Exeunt] One editor adds *Flourish of drums*, but perhaps Mycetes
fails to rouse martial noise.

    2.3. Location: in Scythia.
    2. *approvèd*] proved or established by experience.

I take thy doom for satisfaction.   5
Tamburlaine. And so mistake you not a whit, my lord,
    For fates and oracles of heaven have sworn
    To royalise the deeds of Tamburlaine
    And make them blest that share in his attempts.
    And doubt you not but, if you favour me   10
    And let my fortunes and my valour sway
    To some direction in your martial deeds,
    The world will strive with hosts of men-at-arms
    To swarm unto the ensign I support.
    The host of Xerxes, which by fame is said   15
    To drink the mighty Parthian Araris,
    Was but a handful to that we will have.
    Our quivering lances shaking in the air
    And bullets like Jove's dreadful thunderbolts
    Enrolled in flames and fiery smouldering mists   20
    Shall threat the gods more than Cyclopian wars;
    And with our sun-bright armour as we march
    We'll chase the stars from heaven and dim their eyes
    That stand and muse at our admirèd arms.
Theridamas. [*To Cosroe*] You see, my lord, what working
        words he hath!   25
    But when you see his actions top his speech,
    Your speech will stay, or so extol his worth
    As I shall be commended and excused
    For turning my poor charge to his direction.

---

5. *doom*] judgment or opinion, though these synonyms lack the appropriate portentousness, which ironically anticipates Cosroe's fall.

8. *royalise*] render famous, celebrate.

9. *them*] those persons.

11–12. *sway . . . direction in*] exert some authority over.

16. *Parthian Araris*] The legendary drinking dry of the river Araxes by
Xerxes' army is narrated by Herodotus.

17. *that*] the number.

18–21.] The Cyclopes, imprisoned by their brother Cronus, were freed by
Zeus and made in return the thunder and lightning of his wrath. They are
here merged with the Titans who made war on Zeus.

27–9.] either you will be dumbstruck, or you will praise him so highly that
I shall be excused for putting my force under his command.

29. *charge*] army.

And these his two renownèd friends, my lord,   30
Would make one thrust and strive to be retained
In such a great degree of amity.
Techelles. With duty and with amity we yield
Our utmost service to the fair Cosroe.
Cosroe. Which I esteem as portion of my crown.   35
Usumcasane and Techelles both,
When she that rules in Rhamnus' golden gates
And makes a passage for all prosperous arms
Shall make me solely emperor of Asia,
Then shall your meeds and valours be advanced   40
To rooms of honour and nobility.
Tamburlaine. Then haste, Cosroë, to be king alone,
That I with these my friends and all my men
May triumph in our long-expected fate.
The King your brother is now hard at hand;   45
Meet with the fool and rid your royal shoulders
Of such a burden as outweighs the sands
And all the craggy rocks of Caspia.

[*Enter a* Messenger.]

Messenger. My lord, we have discovered the enemy
Ready to charge you with a mighty army.   50
Cosroe. Come, Tamburlaine, now whet thy wingèd sword
And lift thy lofty arm into the clouds,
That it may reach the King of Persia's crown

30–2.] And these renowned friends, Techelles and Usumcasane, arc such as would make one wish to press forward and strive to remain united with in comradeship.

33. *yield*] offer in sign of service.

35. *portion of my crown*] an integral part of my kingly estate.

37. *she*] Nemesis, whose temple stood at Rhamnus in Attica. There is dramatic irony in Cosroe's proudly invoking the assistance of the goddess of retribution for *hubris* (overweening pride).

38. *makes . . . for*] assists the progress of.

40. *meeds*] merit, excellence.

41. *rooms*] positions, offices.

42. *king alone*] sole king (but with a proleptic irony, here and in the next two lines, in that Cosroe will soon be displaced by the new emperor, Tamburlaine).

48. *Caspia*] the Caspian Sea.

And set it safe on my victorious head.

Tamburlaine. [*Brandishing his sword*] See where it is, the
    keenest curtle-axe   55
    That e'er made passage thorough Persian arms.
    These are the wings shall make it fly as swift
    As doth the lightning or the breath of heaven,
    And kill as sure as it swiftly flies.

Cosroe. Thy words assure me of kind success.   60
    Go, valiant soldier, go before and charge
    The fainting army of that foolish king.

Tamburlaine. Usumcasane and Techelles, come:
    We are enough to scare the enemy,
    And more than needs to make an emperor.   [*Exeunt.*]   65

SCENE 4

To the battle [enter Soldiers, *and exeunt], and* MYCETES *comes
out alone with his crown in his hand, offering to hide it.*

Mycetes. Accurst be he that first invented war!
    They knew not, ah, they knew not, simple men,
    How those were hit by pelting cannon shot
    Stand staggering like a quivering aspen leaf
    Fearing the force of Boreas' boist'rous blasts.   5
    In what a lamentable case were I
    If nature had not given me wisdom's lore!

---

57. *wings*] literally, the cross-piece of his cutlass.
shall] that shall.
59–60. *sure . . . assure*] pronounced with two and three syllables
respectively.
60. *kind*] fitting.
64. *scare*] An alternative reading would be 'scar'.
65.] another proleptic irony.

2.4. Location: in Scythia.
0.2. offering to] trying to.
1–5.] An elegy by Tibullus (1.10) castigates the same cursed inventor—
'tell me, who invented the terrifying sword?'—and develops the theme of the
madness of war by contrast with primeval happiness.
3. *were*] i.e. who were.
5. *Boreas*] the north wind.

For kings are clouts that every man shoots at,
Our crown the pin that thousands seek to cleave.
Therefore in policy I think it good   10
To hide it close: a goodly stratagem,
And far from any man that is a fool.
So shall not I be known, or if I be,
They cannot take away my crown from me.
Here will I hide it in this simple hole.   15

[He tries to hide the crown.]

Enter TAMBURLAINE.

Tamburlaine. What fearful coward straggling from the camp
    When kings themselves are present in the field?
Mycetes. Thou liest.
Tamburlaine. Base villain, dar'st thou give the lie?
Mycetes. Away, I am the King, go, touch me not   20
    Thou break'st the law of arms unless thou kneel
    And cry me 'Mercy, noble King!'
Tamburlaine. Are you the witty King of Persia?
Mycetes. Ay, marry, am I; have you any suit to me?
Tamburlaine. I would entreat you to speak but three wise
    words.   25
Mycetes. So I can when I see my time.
Tamburlaine. *[Finding the crown]* Is this your crown?
Mycetes. Ay, didst thou ever see a fairer?
Tamburlaine. You will not sell it, will ye?

[He takes the crown.]

Mycetes. Such another word, and I will have thee executed.   30
    Come, give it me.
Tamburlaine. No, I took it prisoner.
Mycetes. You lie, I gave it you.
Tamburlaine. Then 'tis mine.
Mycetes. No, I mean, I let you keep it.   35

---

8. *clouts*] targets in archery. Great skill is needed to split the *pin* (9) at the centre.

19. *give the lie*] blatantly accuse of lying (an insult to Tamburlaine's honour).

23. *witty*] wise, intelligent. Mycetes has prized this quality persistently, and has been distinguished for lacking it.

24. *marry*] i.e. by the Virgin Mary (an oath).

Tamburlaine. Well, I mean you shall have it again.
                              [*He returns the crown.*]
     Here, take it for a while. I lend it thee,
     Till I may see thee hemmed with armèd men.
     Then shalt thou see me pull it from thy head.
     Thou art no match for mighty Tamburlaine.   [*Exit.*]   40
Mycetes. O gods, is this Tamburlaine the thief?
     I marvel much he stole it not away.
                    Sound trumpets to the battle, and he runs in.

SCENE 5

[*Enter*] COSROE, TAMBURLAINE, THERIDAMAS, MENAPHON,
MEANDER, ORTYGIUS, TECHELLES, USUMCASANE, *with others.*

Tamburlaine. [*Presenting Cosroe with Mycetes' crown*] Hold
     thee, Cosroe, wear two imperial crowns.
     Think thee invested now as royally,
     Even by the mighty hand of Tamburlaine,
     As if as many kings as could encompass thee
     With greatest pomp had crowned thee emperor.   5
Cosroe. So do I, thrice-renownèd man-at-arms,
     And none shall keep the crown but Tamburlaine.
     Thee do I make my regent of Persia,
     And general lieutenant of my armies.
     Meander, you that were our brother's guide   10
     And chiefest counsellor in all his acts,
     Since he is yielded to the stroke of war,
     On your submission we with thanks excuse
     And give you equal place in our affairs.
Meander. [*Kneeling*] Most happy emperor, in humblest terms   15

42.1. Sound . . . to] give the signal to.

2.5. Location: in Scythia. In the interval between the previous scene and
this one, Tamburlaine has presumably seized Mycetes' crown, which he now
presents to Cosroe.
  1. *Hold thee, Cosroe*] here, Cosroe.
  two . . . crowns] Cosroe was crowned 'Emperor of Asia' at *One* 1.1.162.
  7. *keep*] protect.
  12. *yielded . . . war*] i.e. slain in battle.
  15. *happy*] fortunate.

I vow my service to Your Majesty,
With utmost virtue of my faith and duty.
Cosroe. Thanks, good Meander. [*Meander rises.*] Then,
    Cosroë, reign,
And govern Persia in her former pomp.
Now send embassage to thy neighbour kings   20
And let them know the Persian king is changed
From one that knew not what a king should do
To one that can command what 'longs thereto.
And now we will to fair Persepolis
With twenty thousand expert soldiers.   25
The lords and captains of my brother's camp
With little slaughter take Meander's course
And gladly yield them to my gracious rule.
Ortygius and Menaphon, my trusty friends,
Now will I gratify your former good   30
And grace your calling with a greater sway.
Ortygius. And as we ever aimed at your behoof
And sought your state all honour it deserved,
So will we with our powers and our lives
Endeavour to preserve and prosper it.   35
Cosroe. I will not thank thee, sweet Ortygius;
Better replies shall prove my purposes.
And now, Lord Tamburlaine, my brother's camp
I leave to thee and to Theridamas,
To follow me to fair Persepolis.   40
Then will we march to all those Indian mines
My witless brother to the Christians lost,

---

17. *virtue*] strength, active commitment.
20. *embassage*] ambassadorial message.
23. *'longs*] belongs, is fitting.
28. *yield them*] bow down.
30. *gratify . . . good*] requite . . . service.
31. *calling*] allegiance.
sway] scope of command.
32. *behoof*] advancement.
33. *sought your state*] sought for your royal status.
it] that it.
36. *thank*] i.e. merely thank.
40. *To follow me*] i.e. to follow me later.
41. *Indian mines*] fabulously rich source of precious minerals and jewels.

And ransom them with fame and usury.
And till thou overtake me, Tamburlaine,
Staying to order all the scattered troops,   45
Farewell, lord regent, and his happy friends!
I long to sit upon my brother's throne.
Menaphon. Your Majesty shall shortly have your wish,
And ride in triumph through Persepolis.
          Exeunt [COSROE, MENAPHON, MEANDER, ORTYGIUS].

          Manent TAMBURLAINE, THERIDAMAS, TECHELLES,
                    USUMCASANE.

Tamburlaine. 'And ride in triumph through Persepolis!'   50
Is it not brave to be a king, Techelles?
Usumcasane and Theridamas,
Is it not passing brave to be a king,
And ride in triumph through Persepolis?
Techelles. O my lord, 'tis sweet and full of pomp.   55
Usumcasane. To be a king is half to be a god.
Theridamas. A god is not so glorious as a king.
I think the pleasure they enjoy in heaven
Cannot compare with kingly joys in earth:
To wear a crown enchased with pearl and gold,   60
Whose virtues carry with it life and death;
To ask, and have; command, and be obeyed;
When looks breed love, with looks to gain the prize—
Such power attractive shines in princes' eyes.
Tamburlaine. Why, say, Theridamas, wilt thou be a king?   65
Theridamas. Nay, though I praise it, I can live without it.
Tamburlaine. What says my other friends, will you be kings?
Techelles. Ay, if I could, with all my heart, my lord.
Tamburlaine. Why, that's well said, Techelles, so would I.
And so would you, my masters, would you not?   70

---

43. *with . . . usury*] gaining renown and profit.
53. *passing brave*] surpassingly glorious.
60. *enchased*] set.
61. *virtues*] special powers.
63. *prize*] i.e. of the courtiers' love.
65–74.] a highly dramatic colloquial exchange, playing pentameters
against prose, as a collective conviction builds up.
70. *my masters*] i.e. good sirs.

Usumcasane. What then, my lord?

Tamburlaine. Why then, Casane, shall we wish for aught
    The world affords in greatest novelty,
    And rest attemptless, faint and destitute?
    Methinks we should not. I am strongly moved   75
    That if I should desire the Persian crown
    I could attain it with a wondrous ease.
    And would not all our soldiers soon consent
    If we should aim at such a dignity?

Theridamas. I know they would, with our persuasions.   80

Tamburlaine. Why then, Theridamas, I'll first essay
    To get the Persian kingdom to myself;
    Then thou for Parthia, they for Scythia and Media.
    And if I prosper, all shall be as sure
    As if the Turk, the Pope, Afric, and Greece   85
    Came creeping to us with their crowns apace.

Techelles. Then shall we send to this triumphing king
    And bid him battle for his novel crown?

Usumcasane. Nay, quickly then, before his room be hot.

Tamburlaine. 'Twill prove a pretty jest, in faith, my friends.   90

Theridamas. A jest, to charge on twenty thousand men?
    I judge the purchase more important far.

Tamburlaine. Judge by thyself, Theridamas, not me,
    For presently Techelles here shall haste
    To bid him battle ere he pass too far   95

---

73. *in greatest novelty*] however pricelessly new.

74. *attemptless*] inactive.

75. *moved*] convinced.

83. *they*] i.e. Techelles and Usumcasane.

85.] 'Tamburlaine names the four potentates whose submission would virtually make him emperor of the world: the Turkish emperor representing Anatolia, some of the western Black Sea coast, the Levant, and several African provinces; the Pope being the spiritual head of Christendom; the Soldan of Egypt standing for the chief empire of the African continent; the Emperor of Greece the surviving eastern Roman or Byzantine Empire with its seat at Constantinople' (Ellis-Fermor).

86. *creeping*] i.e. on their knees.

apace] in a rush.

88. *novel*] newly-acquired.

89. *before . . . hot*] before he has established his authority by wielding it eagerly.

92. *purchase*] enterprise.

And lose more labour than the gain will 'quite.
Then shalt thou see the Scythian Tamburlaine
Make but a jest to win the Persian crown.
Techelles, take a thousand horse with thee
And bid him turn him back to war with us   100
That only made him king to make us sport.
We will not steal upon him cowardly,
But give him warning and more warriors.
Haste thee, Techelles, we will follow thee.
                                    [*Exit* TECHELLES.]
What saith Theridamas?
Theridamas.   Go on, for me.   *Exeunt.*   105

SCENE 6

[*Enter*] COSROE, MEANDER, ORTYGIUS, MENAPHON,
                    with other Soldiers.

Cosroe. What means this devilish shepherd, to aspire
          With such a giantly presumption,
          To cast up hills against the face of heaven,
          And dare the force of angry Jupiter?
          But as he thrust them underneath the hills   5
          And pressed out fire from their burning jaws,
          So will I send this monstrous slave to hell
          Where flames shall ever feed upon his soul.
Meander. Some powers divine, or else infernal, mixed

---

96. *lose*] i.e. before we lose.
'*quite*] requite, repay.
98. *a jest to win*] a mere frolic of winning.
99. *horse*] horsemen.
102–3.] Recalling these lines establishes the contrast with the betrayal of
Orcanes by Sigismond in Part Two: cf. *Two* 2.2.24–6.
103. *and more warriors*] i.e. and allow him to reinforce his army.
105. *for me*] as far as I am concerned.

2.6. Location: in Scythia.
2–6.] 'One of the Titans, Enceladus, was trapped by Zeus under Mount
Etna, from which he continued to belch out fire and smoke. He is sometimes
identified with Typhon or Typhoeus, who was a giant' (Woolf).
9–10.] Tamburlaine himself recasts this diagnosis of perversion, seeing
elemental strife—angry seeds—as natural, at *One* 2.7.18–20.

Their angry seeds at his conception;   10
For he was never sprung of human race,
Since with the spirit of his fearful pride
He dares so doubtlessly resolve of rule
And by profession be ambitious.
Ortygius. What god or fiend or spirit of the earth,   15
    Or monster turnèd to a manly shape,
    Or of what mould or mettle he be made,
    What star or state soever govern him,
    Let us put on our meet encount'ring minds,
    And, in detesting such a devilish thief   20
    In love of honour and defence of right,
    Be armed against the hate of such a foe,
    Whether from earth, or hell, or heaven he grow.
Cosroe. Nobly resolved, my good Ortygius;
    And since we all have sucked one wholesome air,   25
    And with the same proportion of elements
    Resolve, I hope we are resembled,
    Vowing our loves to equal death and life.
    Let's cheer our soldiers to encounter him,
    That grievous image of ingratitude,   30
    That fiery thirster after sovereignty,
    And burn him in the fury of that flame
    That none can quench but blood and empery.
    Resolve, my lords and loving soldiers, now,
    To save your king and country from decay.   35

---

12. *fearful*] fearsome.

13. *doubtlessly*] without misgiving.

resolve of] determine firmly to achieve.

14. *by profession*] by vocation, professedly.

17. *mould or mettle*] substance or temperament.

19. *meet encount'ring*] needfully steeled (to battle).

25. *sucked*] inhaled (associating, of course, with the nourishment of breast-feeding).

25–8.] 'As we, being men, have all lived by breathing the same vital air, and shall all dissolve at death into the same proportions of the elements of which we are made, I hope we will also resemble each other in vowing, out of mutual love, to meet death or life resolutely together' (Ellis-Fermor).

33. *blood and empery*] bloodshed and conquest.

35. *decay*] overthrow, fall.

Then strike up drum! [*Sound drum.*] And all the stars
  that make
The loathsome circle of my dated life,
Direct my weapon to his barbarous heart
That thus opposeth him against the gods
And scorns the powers that govern Persia!   [*Exeunt.*]   40

[SCENE 7]

Enter [Soldiers] *to the battle, and after the battle enter*
COSROE *wounded,* THERIDAMAS, TAMBURLAINE,
TECHELLES, USUMCASANE, *with others.*

Cosroe. Barbarous and bloody Tamburlaine,
    Thus to deprive me of my crown and life!
    Treacherous and false Theridamas,
    Even at the morning of my happy state,
    Scarce being seated in my royal throne,   5
    To work my downfall and untimely end!
    An uncouth pain torments my grievèd soul,
    And Death arrests the organ of my voice,
    Who, entering at the breach thy sword hath made,
    Sacks every vein and artier of my heart.   10
    Bloody and insatiate Tamburlaine!
Tamburlaine. The thirst of reign and sweetness of a crown,
    That caused the eldest son of heavenly Ops

36–7. *make . . . life*] determine the detestable conclusion of my fore-
doomed lifespan.
  39. *him*] himself.

  2.7. Location: in Scythia.
  0.1. Enter . . . enter] Modern editors have, if they wish, to supply '*Exeunt*'
at the end of 2.6, and the scene division above this direction. In practice
Cosroe probably remains, and is encountered in battle which moves offstage,
after which he re-enters with his victorious adversaries.
  7. *uncouth*] appalling, strange.
  9. *Who*] i.e. Death.
  10. *artier*] Arteries were believed to contain an ethereal fluid, the 'vital
spirits'.
  13–15.] Rhea, or Ops, mother of Zeus, saved him from being swallowed
by his father Cronos; and Zeus became supreme among the gods by over-
throwing his father.

To thrust his doting father from his chair
And place himself in th'empyreal heaven,   15
Moved me to manage arms against thy state.
What better precedent than mighty Jove?
Nature, that framed us of four elements
Warring within our breasts for regiment,
Doth teach us all to have aspiring minds.   20
Our souls, whose faculties can comprehend
The wondrous architecture of the world
And measure every wand'ring planet's course,
Still climbing after knowledge infinite
And always moving as the restless spheres,   25
Wills us to wear ourselves and never rest
Until we reach the ripest fruit of all,
That perfect bliss and sole felicity,
The sweet fruition of an earthly crown.
Theridamas. And that made me to join with Tamburlaine,   30
For he is gross and like the massy earth
That moves not upwards, nor by princely deeds
Doth mean to soar above the highest sort.
Techelles. And that made us, the friends of Tamburlaine,
To lift our swords against the Persian king.   35
Usumcasane. For as, when Jove did thrust old Saturn down,
Neptune and Dis gained each of them a crown,
So do we hope to reign in Asia
If Tamburlaine be placed in Persia.
Cosroe. The strangest men that ever Nature made!   40
I know not how to take their tyrannies.
My bloodless body waxeth chill and cold,
And with my blood my life slides through my wound.
My soul begins to take her flight to hell,

---

15. *th'empyreal heaven*] the immovable heaven beyond the moving celestial spheres. *Empyreal* associates aptly with *imperial*, describing human rule.
    16. *manage*] wield.
    19. *regiment*] supremacy.
    25. *restless spheres*] Cf. the 'turning spheres' of *One* 4.2.39.
    26. *Wills*] standard Elizabethan plural.
    31–2. *he ... That*] anyone ... who.
    36–7.] Neptune and Dis ruled with Jove (Zeus) after the overthrow of Saturn (Cronos). Neptune ruled the sea and Dis the underworld.
    40.] For Nature as making prodigies or monsters, cf. *One* 1.1.104.

And summons all my senses to depart.									45
The heat and moisture, which did feed each other,
For want of nourishment to feed them both
Is dry and cold, and now doth ghastly death
With greedy talons gripe my bleeding heart
And like a harpy tires on my life.									50
Theridamas and Tamburlaine, I die,
And fearful vengeance light upon you both!

               [*He dies.*]
    He [Tamburlaine] takes the crown and puts it on.

Tamburlaine. Not all the curses which the Furies breathe
 Shall make me leave so rich a prize as this.
 Theridamas, Techelles, and the rest,							55
 Who think you now is King of Persia?
All. Tamburlaine! Tamburlaine!
Tamburlaine. Though Mars himself, the angry god of arms,
 And all the earthly potentates conspire
 To dispossess me of this diadem,								60
 Yet will I wear it in despite of them
 As great commander of this eastern world,
 If you but say that Tamburlaine shall reign.
All. Long live Tamburlaine, and reign in Asia!
Tamburlaine. So, now it is more surer on my head					65
 Than if the gods had held a parliament
 And all pronounced me King of Persia. [*Exeunt.*]

     Finis Actus secundi.

 46–8.] 'Blood, the element which combines the properties of moisture and heat, being removed, the balance of the "temperament" or constitution is destroyed and only the properties of cold and dryness, those of the melancholy humour in the constitution of man, and of the earth in the material universe, remain' (Ellis-Fermor).
 48. *Is*] Elizabethan usage.
 49. *talons gripe*] claws grip and tear.
 50. *harpy*] clawed and winged female monster of legend.
tires] preys.
 53. *Furies*] snake-haired goddesses of vengeance.

Act 3

SCENE I

[*Enter*] BAJAZETH, *the Kings of* FEZ, MOROCCO, *and*
ARGIER, [Basso,] *with others, in great pomp.*

Bajazeth. Great kings of Barbary, and my portly bassoes,
We hear the Tartars and the eastern thieves,
Under the conduct of one Tamburlaine,
Presume a bickering with your emperor
And thinks to rouse us from our dreadful siege   5
Of the famous Grecian Constantinople.
You know our army is invincible;
As many circumcisèd Turks we have
And warlike bands of Christians renied
As hath the ocean or the Terrene sea   10
Small drops of water when the moon begins
To join in one her semicircled horns.
Yet would we not be braved with foreign power,
Nor raise our siege before the Grecians yield
Or breathless lie before the city walls.   15

3.1. Location: at the Turkish siege of Constantinople (modern Istanbul).
0.1–2. *FEZ, MOROCCO*, and *ARGIER*] 'These kingdoms are all marked by
Ortelius along the north coast of Africa; together they make up, as Marlowe
notes, the district known generally as Barbary' (Ellis-Fermor).
1. *portly*] stately.
bassoes] bashaws, pashas.
4. *bickering*] skirmish, or quarrel.
your emperor] i.e. I myself, Emperor of the Turks.
5. *dreadful*] fear-inspiring.
9. *renied*] apostate (who have denied Christianity).
10. *the Terrene sea*] the Mediterranean.
11–12.] i.e. when tides are high at full moon.
13. *braved with . . . power*] menaced by . . . army.
14. *raise*] end or suspend.
15. *breathless lie*] lie dead.

Fez. Renownèd emperor and mighty general,
      What if you sent the bassoes of your guard
      To charge him to remain in Asia,
      Or else to threaten death and deadly arms
      As from the mouth of mighty Bajazeth?   20
Bajazeth. Hie thee, my basso, fast to Persia.
      Tell him thy lord the Turkish emperor,
      Dread lord of Afric, Europe, and Asia,
      Great king and conqueror of Graecia,
      The ocean Terrene, and the coal-black sea,   25
      The high and highest monarch of the world,
      Wills and commands (for say not I 'entreat')
      Not once to set his foot in Africa
      Or spread his colours in Graecia,
      Lest he incur the fury of my wrath.   30
      Tell him I am content to take a truce
      Because I hear he bears a valiant mind.
      But if, presuming on his silly power,
      He be so mad to manage arms with me,
      Then stay thou with him; say I bid thee so;   35
      And if before the sun have measured heaven
      With triple circuit thou regreet us not,
      We mean to take his morning's next arise
      For messenger he will not be reclaimed,
      And mean to fetch thee in despite of him.   40
Basso. Most great and puissant monarch of the earth,

---

18. *charge him*] order Tamburlaine.
21. *Persia*] i.e. Tamburlaine, the new ruler of Persia.
24, 29.] 'Graecia' can, like other proper names, gain a lightly-stressed
syllable when scansion requires.
25. *coal-black sea*] Black Sea.
29. *spread his colours*] advance his banners.
32. *bears a valiant mind*] For this significant description of martial character, cf. *Two* 1.3.72–3, *Two* 3.2.143.
33. *silly power*] feeble, rustic army (though *OED* also gives 'sorry, scanty',
first entry 1593).
34. *mad to*] mad as to.
manage arms] trade blows.
37. *regreet*] greet again.
38–9.] we will interpret the rising of the next morning's sun as token that
Tamburlaine refuses to be reclaimed to, or restrained by, the duty he owes
(Bevington).

Your basso will accomplish your behest
And show your pleasure to the Persian,
As fits the legate of the stately Turk.   *Exit* Basso.
Argier. They say he is the King of Persia;   45
But if he dare attempt to stir your siege
'Twere requisite he should be ten times more,
For all flesh quakes at your magnificence.
Bajazeth. True, Argier, and tremble at my looks.
Morocco. The spring is hindered by your smothering host,   50
For neither rain can fall upon the earth
Nor sun reflex his virtuous beams thereon,
The ground is mantled with such multitudes.
Bajazeth. All this is true as holy Mahomet,
And all the trees are blasted with our breaths.   55
Fez. What thinks Your Greatness best to be achieved
In pursuit of the city's overthrow?
Bajazeth. I will the captive pioners of Argier
Cut off the water that by leaden pipes
Runs to the city from the mountain Carnon;   60
Two thousand horse shall forage up and down,
That no relief or succour come by land;
And all the sea my galleys countermand.
Then shall our footmen lie within the trench,
And with their cannons mouthed like Orcus' gulf   65
Batter the walls, and we will enter in;
And thus the Grecians shall be conquerèd.   *Exeunt.*

---

46. *stir*] molest, disturb.

49. *tremble*] Bajazeth moves the verb into the plural: 'all men tremble'.

52. *reflex*] cast.

53. *mantled*] overspread.

54. *Mahomet*] Mohammed. First syllable stressed, as commonly in the two Parts.

55. *blasted*] withered.

58. *will*] command that.

pioners] sappers, tunnel-diggers.

60. *Carnon*] Marlowe may have confused Constantinople's famous aqueduct with the sea inlet, the Golden Horn, since the name 'Carnon' is near the Turkish for 'horn'.

63. *countermand*] keep under control.

64. *footmen*] infantry.

65. *Orcus' gulf*] hell.

SCENE 2

[*Enter*] AGYDAS, ZENOCRATE, ANIPPE, *with others.*

Agydas. Madam Zenocrate, may I presume
　　　To know the cause of these unquiet fits
　　　That work such trouble to your wonted rest?
　　　'Tis more than pity such a heavenly face
　　　Should by heart's sorrow wax so wan and pale,   5
　　　When your offensive rape by Tamburlaine
　　　(Which of your whole displeasures should be most)
　　　Hath seemed to be digested long ago.
Zenocrate. Although it be digested long ago,
　　　As his exceeding favours have deserved,   10
　　　And might content the Queen of heaven as well
　　　As it hath changed my first conceived disdain,
　　　Yet since a farther passion feeds my thoughts
　　　With ceaseless and disconsolate conceits
　　　Which dyes my looks so lifeless as they are,   15
　　　And might, if my extremes had full events,
　　　Make me the ghastly counterfeit of death.
Agydas. Eternal heaven sooner be dissolved,
　　　And all that pierceth Phoebe's silver eye,
　　　Before such hap fall to Zenocrate!   20
Zenocrate. Ah, life and soul, still hover in his breast
　　　And leave my body senseless as the earth,
　　　Or else unite you to his life and soul,
　　　That I may live and die with Tamburlaine!

　　3.2. Location: in Scythia.
　　6. *rape*] seizure.
　　7. *displeasures*] troubles.
　　8. *digested*] got over.
　　11. *the Queen of heaven*] Juno.
　　13. *since*] i.e. since then.
　　a farther passion] a deeper feeling—i.e. love for Tamburlaine, experienced as a matter of life and death.
　　14. *conceits*] fancies.
　　16–17.] and might, if what I imagine at worst came to pass (or, if my extreme feelings took their full hold), make me the very picture of death. The sense is developed in her next speech.
　　19.] and all that the moon looks down upon.
　　21–4.] Zenocrate addresses her own life and soul, the 'you' of 23.
　　23. *his*] Tamburlaine's.

Enter [aside] TAMBURLAINE *with* TECHELLES *and others.*

Agydas. With Tamburlaine? Ah, fair Zenocrate,   25
    Let not a man so vile and barbarous,
    That holds you from your father in despite
    And keeps you from the honours of a queen—
    Being supposed his worthless concubine—
    Be honoured with your love, but for necessity.   30
    So now the mighty Sultan hears of you,
    Your Highness needs not doubt but in short time
    He will, with Tamburlaine's destruction,
    Redeem you from this deadly servitude.
Zenocrate. Agydas, leave to wound me with these words,   35
    And speak of Tamburlaine as he deserves.
    The entertainment we have had of him
    Is far from villainy or servitude,
    And might in noble minds be counted princely.
Agydas. How can you fancy one that looks so fierce,   40
    Only disposed to martial stratagems?
    Who when he shall embrace you in his arms
    Will tell how many thousand men he slew;
    And when you look for amorous discourse
    Will rattle forth his facts of war and blood,   45
    Too harsh a subject for your dainty ears.
Zenocrate. As looks the sun through Nilus' flowing stream,
    Or when the morning holds him in her arms,
    So looks my lordly love, fair Tamburlaine;
    His talk much sweeter than the Muses' song   50
    They sung for honour 'gainst Pierides,

---

27. *despite*] contemptuous defiance.
30. *but for necessity*] except for what you are obliged to pretend.
31. *So*] if.
35. *leave to*] cease to.
37. *entertainment*] gracious treatment.
38. *villainy*] indignity, insult.
39. *counted*] accounted.
45. *facts*] exploits.
47. *Nilus'*] the Nile's.
48. *the morning*] Aurora, who embraces Phoebus, the sun.
50–1.] The daughters of Pierus were defeated in a singing contest by the Muses, and were turned into magpies for their effrontery.

    Or when Minerva did with Neptune strive;
    And higher would I rear my estimate
    Than Juno, sister to the highest god,
    If I were matched with mighty Tamburlaine.   55
Agydas. Yet be not so inconstant in your love,
    But let the young Arabian live in hope
    After your rescue to enjoy his choice.
    You see, though first the King of Persia,
    Being a shepherd, seemed to love you much,   60
    Now in his majesty he leaves those looks,
    Those words of favour, and those comfortings,
    And gives no more than common courtesies.
Zenocrate. Thence rise the tears that so distain my cheeks,
    Fearing his love through my unworthiness.   65
       TAMBURLAINE *goes to her, and takes her away lovingly by*
       the hand, looking wrathfully on Agydas, and says nothing.
                    [Exeunt all except AGYDAS.]
Agydas. Betrayed by fortune and suspicious love,
    Threatened with frowning wrath and jealousy,
    Surprised with fear of hideous revenge,
    I stand aghast; but most astonièd
    To see his choler shut in secret thoughts   70
    And wrapped in silence of his angry soul.
    Upon his brows was portrayed ugly death,
    And in his eyes the fury of his heart
    That shine as comets, menacing revenge,
    And casts a pale complexion on his cheeks.   75

52.] Minerva (Athena) strove to outdo Neptune (Poseidon) in bidding to rule Attica; her superior gift (wisdom) led to Athens being named after her.

53. *estimate*] sense of my own worth; reputation.

57.] *the young Arabian*] Alcidamus, betrothed to Zenocrate.

59–60.] i.e. When first made King of Persia, Tamburlaine was close enough to his lowly origins to show his love for you.

64. *distain*] stain.

65. *Fearing*] doubting.

69. *astonièd*] dismayed, astounded.

70. *choler*] anger.

72.] As description of Tamburlaine, cf. *One* 2.1.21. With *ugly death*, cf. *Two* 2.4.14; 'ugly' associates with Marlowe's 'Virgilian' imagery of hell.

    portrayed] first syllable stressed.

74–5.] i.e. his eyes shine with fury, a passion which brings pallor to his face.

As when the seaman sees the Hyades
Gather an army of Cimmerian clouds
(Auster and Aquilon with wingèd steeds
All sweating, tilt about the wat'ry heavens
With shivering spears enforcing thunderclaps,   80
And from their shields strike flames of lightning),
All fearful folds his sails, and sounds the main,
Lifting his prayers to the heavens for aid
Against the terror of the winds and waves—
So fares Agydas for the late-felt frowns   85
That sent a tempest to my daunted thoughts
And makes my soul divine her overthrow.

Enter TECHELLES *with a naked dagger.*

Techelles. [*Giving the dagger*] See you, Agydas, how the King
    salutes you.
He bids you prophesy what it imports.   *Exit.*
Agydas. I prophesied before and now I prove   90
    The killing frowns of jealousy and love.
He needed not with words confirm my fear,
For words are vain where working tools present
The naked action of my threatened end.
It says, Agydas, thou shalt surely die,   95
And of extremities elect the least:
More honour and less pain it may procure
To die by this resolvèd hand of thine
Than stay the torments he and heaven have sworn.
Then haste, Agydas, and prevent the plagues   100

---

76. *Hyades*] seven stars in the constellation Taurus, traditionally seen as causing bad weather; they rise and set at rainy times of the year. The Cimmerii in classical fable lived in perpetual darkness: cf. *One* 5.1.234, *Two* 5.3.8.

78. *Auster and Aquilon*] the south wind and the north-east wind. Thunder was often explained as clouds colliding.

79. *tilt*] joust.

82. *sounds the main*] takes soundings of the sea's depths.

87. *divine*] have presentiment of.

90. *prove*] find by experience, suffer.

91. *jealousy*] suspicion.

96. *extremities*] extreme suffering; or, dire choices. (A proverbial saying.)

99. *stay*] await.

Which thy prolongèd fates may draw on thee.
Go wander free from fear of tyrant's rage,
Removèd from the torments and the hell
Wherewith he may excruciate thy soul;
And let Agydas by Agydas die,   105
And with this stab slumber eternally.

[He stabs himself and dies.]

[Enter TECHELLES *and* USUMCASANE.]

Techelles. Usumcasane, see how right the man
      Hath hit the meaning of my lord the King.
Usumcasane. Faith, and, Techelles, it was manly done;
      And since he was so wise and honourable   110
      Let us afford him now the bearing hence
      And crave his triple-worthy burial.
Techelles. Agreed, Casane, we will honour him.

[Exeunt, bearing out the body.]

SCENE 3

[*Enter*] TAMBURLAINE, TECHELLES, USUMCASANE,
THERIDAMAS, BASSO, ZENOCRATE, [ANIPPE,] *with others*
[*bearing a throne*].

Tamburlaine. Basso, by this thy lord and master knows
      I mean to meet him in Bithynia—
      See how he comes! Tush, Turks are full of brags,
      And menace more than they can well perform.
      He meet me in the field and fetch thee hence!   5
      Alas, poor Turk, his fortune is too weak
      T'encounter with the strength of Tamburlaine.

---

104. *excruciate*] torture.
109. *Faith*] in faith. (A mild oath.)
112.] and call for the noble funeral he has amply merited.

3.3. Location: in Scythia.
1. *this*] this time.
2. *Bithynia*] an ancient country on the shores of the Black Sea.
3. *See how he comes!*] i.e. He has not appeared.
5.] Tamburlaine ridicules Bajazeth's threat to confront him in battle. Cf.
One 3.1.40.

View well my camp, and speak indifferently:
Do not my captains and my soldiers look
As if they meant to conquer Africa?   10
Basso. Your men are valiant but their number few,
And cannot terrify his mighty host.
My lord, the great commander of the world,
Besides fifteen contributory kings
Hath now in arms ten thousand janizaries   15
Mounted on lusty Mauritanian steeds
Brought to the war by men of Tripoli;
Two hundred thousand footmen that have served
In two set battles fought in Graecia;
And for the expedition of this war,   20
If he think good, can from his garrisons
Withdraw as many more to follow him.
Techelles. The more he brings the greater is the spoil;
For, when they perish by our warlike hands,
We mean to seat our footmen on their steeds   25
And rifle all those stately janizars.
Tamburlaine. But will those kings accompany your lord?
Basso. Such as His Highness please, but some must stay
To rule the provinces he late subdued.
Tamburlaine. [*To his followers*] Then fight courageously, their
    crowns are yours;   30
This hand shall set them on your conquering heads
That made me emperor of Asia.
Usumcasane. Let him bring millions infinite of men,
Unpeopling Western Africa and Greece,
Yet we assure us of the victory.   35

---

8. *indifferently*] without bias.
14. *contributory*] tributary.
15. *janizaries*] Turkish troops, Sultan's guardsmen.
16. *lusty*] spirited.
Mauritanian steeds] famous horses from north-west Africa.
19. *set*] pitched.
20. *expedition*] prompt waging.
26. *rifle*] plunder.
29. *late*] lately.
34. *Unpeopling*] The word conveys the huge scale, and also the grotesque
human cost, of the conflicts.
35. *assure us*] feel certain.

Theridamas. Even he, that in a trice vanquished two kings
    More mighty than the Turkish emperor,
    Shall rouse him out of Europe and pursue
    His scattered army till they yield or die.
Tamburlaine. Well said, Theridamas! Speak in that mood,   40
    For 'will' and 'shall' best fitteth Tamburlaine,
    Whose smiling stars gives him assurèd hope
    Of martial triumph ere he meet his foes.
    I that am termed the scourge and wrath of God,
    The only fear and terror of the world,   45
    Will first subdue the Turk, and then enlarge
    Those Christian captives which you keep as slaves,
    Burdening their bodies with your heavy chains
    And feeding them with thin and slender fare
    That naked row about the Terrene sea;   50
    And when they chance to breathe and rest a space
    Are punished with bastones so grievously
    That they lie panting on the galley's side
    And strive for life at every stroke they give.
    These are the cruel pirates of Argier,   55
    That damnèd train, the scum of Africa,
    Inhabited with straggling runagates,
    That make quick havoc of the Christian blood.
    But, as I live, that town shall curse the time
    That Tamburlaine set foot in Africa.   60

Enter BAJAZETH *with his* Bassoes *and contributory* Kings
[*of* FEZ, MOROCCO, *and* ARGIER], [ZABINA *and* EBEA].
[*A throne is brought on.*]

---

38. *rouse*] cause (game) to rise from cover.
him] Bajazeth.
41.] recalling Bajazeth in *One* 3.1.27.
44.] The first reference in the play to Tamburlaine as the scourge of God identifies him as inflicting Christian vengeance on the Turks, a concept recalled at *Two* 2.1.53.
46. *enlarge*] set free.
47–55.] Tamburlaine's anger generates a vivid picture of cruelty, in the course of which the Turks change grammatical identity from 'you' to 'These', perhaps by way of an ambiguity in 'every stroke they give', which can refer equally to the galley oarsmen and to their captors.
52. *bastones*] cudgels.
57. *runagates*] vagabonds or apostates.

Bajazeth. Bassoes and janizaries of my guard,
    Attend upon the person of your lord,
    The greatest potentate of Africa.
Tamburlaine. Techelles and the rest, prepare your swords.
    I mean t'encounter with that Bajazeth.   65
Bajazeth. Kings of Fez, Moroccus, and Argier,
    He calls me Bajazeth, whom you call lord!
    Note the presumption of this Scythian slave.—
    I tell thee, villain, those that lead my horse
    Have to their names titles of dignity;   70
    And dar'st thou bluntly call me Bajazeth?
Tamburlaine. And know thou, Turk, that those which lead
    my horse
    Shall lead thee captive thorough Africa;
    And dar'st thou bluntly call me Tamburlaine?
Bajazeth. By Mahomet my kinsman's sepulchre   75
    And by the holy Alcoran I swear
    He shall be made a chaste and lustless eunuch
    And in my sarell tend my concubines;
    And all his captains that thus stoutly stand
    Shall draw the chariot of my emperess,   80
    Whom I have brought to see their overthrow.
Tamburlaine. By this my sword that conquered Persia,
    Thy fall shall make me famous through the world.
    I will not tell thee how I'll handle thee,
    But every common soldier of my camp   85
    Shall smile to see thy miserable state.
Fez. [*To Bajazeth*] What means the mighty Turkish
    emperor
    To talk with one so base as Tamburlaine?
Morocco. Ye Moors and valiant men of Barbary,
    How can ye suffer these indignities?   90
Argier. Leave words, and let them feel your lances' points,

---

70. *to*] added to.
73. *thorough*] through.
76. *Alcoran*] Koran.
78. *sarell*] seraglio, harem.
79. *stoutly*] bravely.
80. *emperess*] so spelled in the early texts, in conformity with the metre.
Cf. *One* 5.1.358, 369.

Which glided through the bowels of the Greeks.
Bajazeth. Well said, my stout contributory kings!
    Your threefold army and my hugy host
    Shall swallow up these base-born Persians.   95
Techelles. [*To Tamburlaine*] Puissant, renowned, and mighty
    Tamburlaine,
    Why stay we thus prolonging all their lives?
Theridamas. I long to see those crowns won by our swords,
    That we may reign as kings of Africa.
Usumcasane. What coward would not fight for such a prize?   100
Tamburlaine. Fight all courageously, and be you kings!
    I speak it, and my words are oracles.
Bajazeth. Zabina, mother of three braver boys
    Than Hercules, that in his infancy
    Did pash the jaws of serpents venomous,   105
    Whose hands are made to grip a warlike lance,
    Their shoulders broad, for complete armour fit,
    Their limbs more large and of a bigger size
    Than all the brats y-sprung from Typhon's loins;
    Who, when they come unto their father's age,   110
    Will batter turrets with their manly fists:
    Sit here upon this royal chair of state
    And on thy head wear my imperial crown,
    Until I bring this sturdy Tamburlaine
    And all his captains bound in captive chains.   115
Zabina. Such good success happen to Bajazeth!
        [*She ascends the Turkish throne and is crowned.*]
Tamburlaine. Zenocrate, the loveliest maid alive,
    Fairer than rocks of pearl and precious stone,
    The only paragon of Tamburlaine,
    Whose eyes are brighter than the lamps of heaven,   120

---

92. *glided through*] pierced.
    104–5.] Hera (Juno) sent two serpents to seek to kill baby Hercules, Jove's
bastard.
    109. *y-sprung*] sprung. (An archaic form.)
    Typhon] This frightful monster, son of Ge (Earth) and Tartarus, coupled
with the monster Echidna, to produce the Nemean lion, the dogs Orthrus
and Cerberus, the Chimaera, the Theban Sphinx, and the Lernaean Hydra.
    116. *success*] fortune.
    119. *paragon*] consort; with an implication of matchless excellence.

And speech more pleasant than sweet harmony;
That with thy looks canst clear the darkened sky
And calm the rage of thund'ring Jupiter:
Sit down by her, adornèd with my crown,
As if thou wert the empress of the world.   125

                   [*She ascends the Persian throne.*]

Stir not, Zenocrate, until thou see
Me march victoriously with all my men,
Triumphing over him and these his kings
Which I will bring as vassals to thy feet.
Till then, take thou my crown, vaunt of my worth,   130
And manage words with her as we will arms.

Zenocrate. And may my love, the King of Persia,
Return with victory, and free from wound!

                          [*She is crowned.*]

Bajazeth. [*To Tamburlaine*] Now shalt thou feel the force of
    Turkish arms
Which lately made all Europe quake for fear.   135
I have of Turks, Arabians, Moors, and Jews
Enough to cover all Bithynia.
Let thousands die; their slaughtered carcasses
Shall serve for walls and bulwarks to the rest;
And as the heads of Hydra, so my power,   140
Subdued, shall stand as mighty as before.
If they should yield their necks unto the sword,
Thy soldiers' arms could not endure to strike
So many blows as I have heads for thee.
Thou know'st not, foolish-hardy Tamburlaine,   145
What 'tis to meet me in the open field,
That leave no ground for thee to march upon.

Tamburlaine. Our conquering swords shall marshal us the
    way
We use to march upon the slaughtered foe,
Trampling their bowels with our horses' hoofs—   150

---

130. *vaunt of*] proudly proclaim.
131. *manage*] wield; a variant of the chivalric phrase 'manage arms'.
140. *Hydra*] one of Typhon's 'brats' (109 above); each of his nine heads,
if struck off, was replaced by two new ones.
142. *If they*] even if my troops.
148. *marshal . . . way*] guide us.

Brave horses, bred on the white Tartarian hills.
My camp is like to Julius Caesar's host,
That never fought but had the victory;
Nor in Pharsalia was there such hot war
As these my followers willingly would have.   155
Legions of spirits fleeting in the air
Direct our bullets and our weapons' points
And make your strokes to wound the senseless air;
And when she sees our bloody colours spread,
Then Victory begins to take her flight,   160
Resting herself upon my milk-white tent.
But come, my lords, to weapons let us fall.
The field is ours, the Turk, his wife, and all.
               Exit [TAMBURLAINE], *with his* followers.
Bajazeth. Come, kings and bassoes, let us glut our swords
    That thirst to drink the feeble Persians' blood.   165
               Exit [BAJAZETH], *with his* followers.
Zabina. [*To Zenocrate*] Base concubine, must thou be placed
    by me
    That am the empress of the mighty Turk?
Zenocrate. Disdainful Turkess and unreverend boss,
    Call'st thou me concubine, that am betrothed
    Unto the great and mighty Tamburlaine?   170
Zabina. To Tamburlaine the great Tartarian thief!
Zenocrate. Thou wilt repent these lavish words of thine
    When thy great basso-master and thyself
    Must plead for mercy at his kingly feet
    And sue to me to be your advocates.   175
Zabina. And sue to thee? I tell thee, shameless girl,

152.] My army rivals that of Julius Caesar.
153. *but had*] without achieving.
154.] Caesar defeated Pompey at Pharsalia in 482 B.C.
156. *fleeting*] gliding.
159. *colours*] ensigns, battle standards.
160. *take her flight*] spread her wings in triumph.
161. *Resting herself*] alighting.
168. *boss*] fat slut.
172. *lavish*] intemperate.
173. *basso-master*] a derisive taunt; cf. 212 below.
175. *sue to*] petition.
your advocates] advocate for you both.

Thou shalt be laundress to my waiting-maid.—
How lik'st thou her, Ebea, will she serve?
Ebea. Madam, she thinks perhaps she is too fine,
    But I shall turn her into other weeds   180
    And make her dainty fingers fall to work.
Zenocrate. Hear'st thou, Anippe, how thy drudge doth talk,
    And how my slave, her mistress, menaceth?
    Both, for their sauciness, shall be employed
    To dress the common soldiers' meat and drink,   185
    For we will scorn they should come near ourselves.
Anippe. Yet sometimes let Your Highness send for them
    To do the work my chambermaid disdains.
        They sound [trumpets to] the battle within, and stay.
Zenocrate. Ye gods and powers that govern Persia
    And made my lordly love her worthy king,   190
    Now strengthen him against the Turkish Bajazeth
    And let his foes, like flocks of fearful roes
    Pursued by hunters, fly his angry looks,
    That I may see him issue conqueror.
Zabina. Now, Mahomet, solicit God himself,   195
    And make him rain down murd'ring shot from heaven
    To dash the Scythians' brains and strike them dead
    That dare to manage arms with him
    That offered jewels to thy sacred shrine
    When first he warred against the Christians.   200
        [They sound trumpets within] to the battle again.
Zenocrate. By this the Turks lie welt'ring in their blood,
    And Tamburlaine is lord of Africa.
Zabina. Thou art deceived; I heard the trumpets sound
    As when my emperor overthrew the Greeks
    And led them captive into Africa.   205
    Straight will I use thee as thy pride deserves;
    Prepare thyself to live and die my slave.
Zenocrate. If Mahomet should come from heaven and swear
    My royal lord is slain or conquerèd,

---

179. *fine*] refined, dainty.
180. *weeds*] garments.
188.1.] The trumpet-signal to begin fighting offstage, and then to cease, is
sounded offstage.
201.] *this*] this time.

Yet should he not persuade me otherwise   210
But that he lives and will be conqueror.

> BAJAZETH *flies [across the stage], and he* [TAMBURLAINE]
> *pursues him [offstage]. The battle short, and they [re-]enter.*
> *Bajazeth is overcome.*

Tamburlaine. Now, king of bassoes, who is conqueror?
Bajazeth. Thou, by the fortune of this damnèd foil.
Tamburlaine. Where are your stout contributory kings?

> *Enter* TECHELLES, THERIDAMAS, USUMCASANE
> *[each bearing a crown].*

Techelles. We have their crowns; their bodies strew the field.   215
Tamburlaine. Each man a crown? Why, kingly fought, i'faith.
　　Deliver them into my treasury.
> *[They render up their crowns.]*
Zenocrate. Now let me offer to my gracious lord
　　His royal crown again, so highly won.
Tamburlaine. Nay, take the Turkish crown from her,
　　Zenocrate,   220
　　And crown me emperor of Africa.
Zabina. No, Tamburlaine, though now thou gat the best,
　　Thou shalt not yet be lord of Africa.
Theridamas. Give her the crown, Turkess, you were best.
> *He [Theridamas] takes it from her, and gives it [to]*
> *Zenocrate.*

Zabina. Injurious villains, thieves, runagates,   225
　　How dare you thus abuse my majesty?
Theridamas. [*To Zenocrate*] Here, madam, you are empress,
　　she is none.
Tamburlaine. Not now, Theridamas, her time is past.
　　The pillars that have bolstered up those terms
　　Are fall'n in clusters at my conquering feet.   230
Zabina. Though he be prisoner, he may be ransomed.
Tamburlaine. Not all the world shall ransom Bajazeth.

---

213. *foil*] defeat.
222. *gat the best*] got the upper hand.
228.] i.e. I agree, Theridamas; Zabina is no longer empress, her time
having passed.
229. *terms*] titles; also, statuary busts.

Bajazeth. Ah, fair Zabina, we have lost the field,
    And never had the Turkish emperor
    So great a foil by any foreign foe.   235
    Now will the Christian miscreants be glad,
    Ringing with joy their superstitious bells
    And making bonfires for my overthrow.
    But ere I die, those foul idolaters
    Shall make me bonfires with their filthy bones;   240
    For, though the glory of this day be lost,
    Afric and Greece have garrisons enough
    To make me sovereign of the earth again.
Tamburlaine. Those wallèd garrisons will I subdue,
    And write myself great lord of Africa: 245
    So from the east unto the furthest west
    Shall Tamburlaine extend his puissant arm.
    The galleys and those pilling brigantines
    That yearly sail to the Venetian gulf
    And hover in the straits for Christians' wrack,   250
    Shall lie at anchor in the Isle Asant
    Until the Persian fleet and men-of-war,
    Sailing along the oriental sea,
    Have fetched about the Indian continent,
    Even from Persepolis to Mexico,   255
    And thence unto the Straits of Jubalter,
    Where they shall meet and join their force in one,
    Keeping in awe the Bay of Portingale
    And all the ocean by the British shore;

---

236. *miscreants*] misbelievers.
248. *pilling brigantines*] plundering pirate craft.
250. *straits*] i.e. of Otranto.
for Christians' wrack] to the destruction of Christian ships.
251. *Asant*] Zacynthus in antiquity, Zante to the Venetians, modern Zacinthos.
253. *the oriental sea*] the Pacific.
254. *fetched about*] sailed round.
255. *Mexico*] Mexico presumably here includes what we know as Argentina and Chile. The journey goes from Persia to the Straits of Magellon, and thence to Gibraltar.
256. *Jubalter*] an alternative form of Gibraltar, which the early texts give as 'Gibraltar' at *Two* 1.3.80. Third syllable stressed.
258. *Bay of Portingale*] Bay of Biscay (Portugal).

And by this means I'll win the world at last.   260
Bajazeth. Yet set a ransom on me, Tamburlaine.
Tamburlaine. What, think'st thou Tamburlaine esteems thy
    gold?
    I'll make the kings of India, ere I die,
    Offer their mines, to sue for peace, to me,
    And dig for treasure to appease my wrath.—   265
    Come, bind them both, and one lead in the Turk.
    The Turkess let my love's maid lead away.
                  They bind them [Bajazeth and Zabina].
Bajazeth. Ah, villains, dare ye touch my sacred arms?
    O Mahomet, O sleepy Mahomet!
Zabina. O cursèd Mahomet that mak'st us thus   270
    The slaves to Scythians rude and barbarous!
Tamburlaine. Come, bring them in, and for this happy
    conquest
    Triumph, and solemnise a martial feast.
                          Exeunt.

        Finis Actus tertii.

267.] Let Anippe lead in Zabina.
269.] anticipating Tamburlaine's call to Mahomet, *Two* 5.1.186–98.
273. *Triumph*] hold a triumphal procession. Second syllable stressed.

Act 4

SCENE I

[Enter] SULTAN *of* EGYPT *with three or four* Lords,
CAPOLIN[, Messenger].

Sultan. Awake, ye men of Memphis, hear the clang
    Of Scythian trumpets, hear the basilisks
    That, roaring, shake Damascus' turrets down!
    The rogue of Volga holds Zenocrate,
    The Sultan's daughter, for his concubine,   5
    And with a troop of thieves and vagabonds
    Hath spread his colours to our high disgrace
    While you faint-hearted base Egyptians
    Lie slumb'ring on the flow'ry banks of Nile,
    As crocodiles that unaffrighted rest   10
    While thund'ring cannons rattle on their skins.
Messenger. Nay, mighty Sultan, did Your Greatness see
    The frowning looks of fiery Tamburlaine,
    That with his terror and imperious eyes
    Commands the hearts of his associates,   15
    It might amaze Your Royal Majesty.
Sultan. Villain, I tell thee, were that Tamburlaine

4.1. Location: at Memphis, the ancient centre of Lower Egypt.

1–3.] Damascus (in Syria) is far from Memphis (in Lower Egypt), but
Marlowe may have supposed them near to one another. See *One* 4.2.99 ff.,
where we learn that Tamburlaine and his forces are at Damascus still, shortly
after the battle at Memphis, and where Tamburlaine prepares to do battle
with the Sultan of Egypt. The Sultan seeks to raise the siege of Damascus
(*One* 4.3.17–18).

2. *basilisks*] brazen cannons.

4. *Volga*] Tamburlaine is here associated with the region of southern
Russia, though elsewhere in the play seen as from Samarkand, in eastern
Persia (Ellis-Fermor).

As monstrous as Gorgon, prince of hell,
The Sultan would not start a foot from him.
But speak, what power hath he?
Messenger.   Mighty lord,   20
Three hundred thousand men in armour clad
Upon their prancing steeds, disdainfully
With wanton paces trampling on the ground;
Five hundred thousand footmen threat'ning shot,
Shaking their swords, their spears and iron bills,   25
Environing their standard round, that stood
As bristle-pointed as a thorny wood.
Their warlike engines and munition
Exceed the forces of their martial men.
Sultan. Nay, could their numbers countervail the stars,   30
Or ever-drizzling drops of April showers,
Or withered leaves that Autumn shaketh down,
Yet would the Sultan by his conquering power
So scatter and consume them in his rage
That not a man should live to rue their fall.   35
Capolin. So might Your Highness, had you time to sort
Your fighting men and raise your royal host.
But Tamburlaine by expedition
Advantage takes of your unreadiness.
Sultan. Let him take all th'advantages he can.   40
Were all the world conspired to fight for him,
Nay, were he devil, as he is no man,

---

18. *monstrous*] unnatural, grotesque; frequently trisyllabic, and sometimes spelt 'monstruous'.
  Gorgon] Demogorgon, a prince of hell. Also, a monster; Medusa was a gorgon.
19. *start*] flinch.
23. *wanton*] frisky.
25. *bills*] spears, their long handles suggesting the apt image of 27.
26. *Environing . . . round*] grouped round their battle standard.
  that] referring to the spears.
28. *engines*] instruments of assault.
  munition] shot; four syllables.
30. *countervail*] rival.
36. *sort*] put into order.
38. *expedition*] speed; four syllables.

Yet in revenge of fair Zenocrate,
Whom he detaineth in despite of us,
This arm should send him down to Erebus   45
To shroud his shame in darkness of the night.
Messenger. Pleaseth Your Mightiness to understand,
His resolution far exceedeth all.
The first day, when he pitcheth down his tents,
White is their hue, and on his silver crest   50
A snowy feather spangled white he bears,
To signify the mildness of his mind
That, satiate with spoil, refuseth blood;
But when Aurora mounts the second time,
As red as scarlet is his furniture,   55
Then must his kindled wrath be quenched with blood,
Not sparing any that can manage arms;
But if these threats move not submission,
Black are his colours—black pavilion,
His spear, his shield, his horse, his armour, plumes, 60
And jetty feathers menace death and hell;
Without respect of sex, degree, or age,
He razeth all his foes with fire and sword.
Sultan. Merciless villain, peasant ignorant
Of lawful arms or martial discipline!   65
Pillage and murder are his usual trades;
The slave usurps the glorious name of war.
See Capolin, the fair Arabian king,
That hath been disappointed by this slave
Of my fair daughter and his princely love,   70
May have fresh warning to go war with us
And be revenged for her disparagement.   [*Exeunt.*]

---

45. *Erebus*] the gloomy underground region on whose 'blasted banks'
ghosts wait for the 'ugly ferryman' (*One* 5.1.243–7).
55. *furniture*] armour, accoutrements (listed in 59–61 below).
61. *jetty*] jet-black.
65. *lawful arms*] military codes of honour.
68. *See*] see that.
71. *warning*] notification.
with] in alliance with.
72. *disparagement*] indignity, disgrace.

SCENE 2

[A throne is brought on.] *[Enter]* TAMBURLAINE *[all in white],*
TECHELLES, THERIDAMAS, USUMCASANE, ZENOCRATE,
ANIPPE, *two* Moors *drawing* BAJAZETH *in his cage, and
his wife* [ZABINA] *following him.*

Tamburlaine. Bring out my footstool.
      They [the two Moors] take him [Bajazeth] out of the cage.
Bajazeth. Ye holy priests of heavenly Mahomet,
      That, sacrificing, slice and cut your flesh,
      Staining his altars with your purple blood,
      Make heaven to frown and every fixèd star   5
      To suck up poison from the moorish fens
      And pour it in this glorious tyrant's throat!
Tamburlaine. The chiefest God, first mover of that sphere
      Enchased with thousands ever-shining lamps,
      Will sooner burn the glorious frame of heaven   10
      Than it should so conspire my overthrow.
      But, villain, thou that wishest this to me,
      Fall prostrate on the low disdainful earth
      And be the footstool of great Tamburlaine,
      That I may rise into my royal throne.   15
Bajazeth. First shalt thou rip my bowels with thy sword
      And sacrifice my heart to death and hell,
      Before I yield to such a slavery.
Tamburlaine. Base villain, vassal, slave to Tamburlaine,
      Unworthy to embrace or touch the ground   20
      That bears the honour of my royal weight,
      Stoop, villain, stoop, stoop, for so he bids
      That may command thee piecemeal to be torn,

4.2. Location: at the siege of Damascus (capital of Syria).

0.1. *in white*] Tamburlaine is wearing a silver crest and white feather, and
other accoutrements, perhaps pennons and a tent, may be brought on stage:
it is the first day of the siege, as we are reminded at 111–12, and 4.1.49–51
provides a producer with clear instructions.

2–3.] Cf. *One* 4.4.43–5.

5–6. *star . . . poison*] Vapours sucked up by sun or stars from fens would
carry the infections thought to lie there (Kocher).

7. *glorious*] vainglorious, boastful.

8. *first mover*] primum mobile: in classical cosmology, a transparent
sphere jewelled with fixed stars, revolving round the world.

Or scattered like the lofty cedar trees
Struck with the voice of thund'ring Jupiter.   25
Bajazeth. Then, as I look down to the damnèd fiends,
    Fiends, look on me, and thou dread god of hell,
    With ebon sceptre strike this hateful earth
    And make it swallow both of us at once!
      He [Tamburlaine] gets up upon him [Bajazeth] to his chair.
Tamburlaine. Now clear the triple region of the air   30
    And let the majesty of heaven behold
    Their scourge and terror tread on emperors.
    Smile, stars that reigned at my nativity
    And dim the brightness of their neighbour lamps!
    Disdain to borrow light of Cynthia,   35
    For I, the chiefest lamp of all the earth,
    First rising in the east with mild aspect
    But fixèd now in the meridian line,
    Will send up fire to your turning spheres
    And cause the sun to borrow light of you.   40
    My sword struck fire from his coat of steel
    Even in Bithynia, when I took this Turk;
    As when a fiery exhalation
    Wrapt in the bowels of a freezing cloud,
    Fighting for passage, makes the welkin crack,   45
    And casts a flash of lightning to the earth.
    But ere I march to wealthy Persia
    Or leave Damascus and th'Egyptian fields,
    As was the fame of Clymen's brain-sick son

---

27. *dread god of hell*] Pluto.

30. *triple region of the air*] the received cosmology: fire, the highest region, a middle region of cold, and the region close to earth, warmed by sun.

33.] The antitype of this line opens the laments over Tamburlaine's fatal sickness, in *Two* 5.3.2: 'Fall, stars that govern his nativity'.

37. *aspect*] both astrological disposition and human appearance.

38. *meridian line*] 'the great circle (of the celestial sphere) which passes though the celestial poles and the zenith of any place on the earth's surface' (*OED*). Tamburlaine claims to have attained a perpetual noon.

43–6.] In classical cosmology, lightning was caused by compressed fire escaping through cloud.

49. *Clymen's . . . son*] Phaethon, child of Clymene and Apollo, the sun god, caused his father's chariot to career wildly off course, and was killed. Cf. *Two* 5.3.230–4.

That almost brent the axletree of heaven,   50
So shall our swords, our lances, and our shot
Fill all the air with fiery meteors;
Then, when the sky shall wax as red as blood,
It shall be said I made it red myself,
To make me think of naught but blood and war.   55
Zabina. Unworthy king, that by thy cruelty
Unlawfully usurp'st the Persian seat,
Dar'st thou, that never saw an emperor
Before thou met my husband in the field,
Being thy captive, thus abuse his state,   60
Keeping his kingly body in a cage
That roofs of gold and sun-bright palaces
Should have prepared to entertain His Grace?
And treading him beneath thy loathsome feet
Whose feet the kings of Africa have kissed?   65
Techelles. [*To Tamburlaine*] You must devise some torment
        worse, my lord,
To make these captives rein their lavish tongues.
Tamburlaine. Zenocrate, look better to your slave.
Zenocrates. She is my handmaid's slave, and she shall look
That these abuses flow not from her tongue.—   70
Chide her, Anippe.
Anippe. [*To Zabina*] Let these be warnings for you then, my
        slave,
How you abuse the person of the King,
Or else I swear to have you whipped stark naked.
Bajazeth. Great Tamburlaine, great in my overthrow,   75
Ambitious pride shall make thee fall as low

---

50. *brent*] burned.
    the axletree of heaven] the celestial diameter, axis of the heavens, running
through the earth at its centre.
    51–2.] Among the fiery impressions known to Renaissance meteorology
were 'burning spears', which are perhaps suggested here as specific meteors
caused by the shining weapons of Tamburlaine's army.
    52. *fiery meteors*] covering a multitude of phenomena associated with
exhalations: lightning, fiery impressions, blazing stars.
    53.] Cf. the imagery of Apocalypse in Joel 2.30 and Revelation 6.12,
including the turning of the moon to blood.
    63. *entertain*] receive.
    69. *look*] see to it.

For treading on the back of Bajazeth
That should be horsèd on four mighty kings.
Tamburlaine. Thy names and titles and thy dignities
 Are fled from Bajazeth and remain with me,   80
 That will maintain it against a world of kings.—
 Put him in again.
     [*The two Moors put Bajazeth into the cage.*]
Bajazeth. Is this a place for mighty Bajazeth?
 Confusion light on him that helps thee thus!
Tamburlaine. There, whiles he lives, shall Bajazeth be kept, 85
 And where I go be thus in triumph drawn;
 And thou, his wife, shalt feed him with the scraps
 My servitors shall bring thee from my board.
 For he that gives him other food than this
 Shall sit by him and starve to death himself.   90
 This is my mind, and I will have it so.
 Not all the kings and emperors of the earth,
 If they would lay their crowns before my feet,
 Shall ransom him or take him from his cage.
 The ages that shall talk of Tamburlaine,   95
 Even from this day to Plato's wondrous year,
 Shall talk how I have handled Bajazeth.
 These Moors that drew him from Bithynia
 To fair Damascus, where we now remain,
 Shall lead him with us wheresoe'er we go.   100
 Techelles and my loving followers,
 Now may we see Damascus' lofty towers,
 Like to the shadows of Pyramides
 That with their beauties graced the Memphian fields;
 The golden statue of their feathered bird   105
 That spreads her wings upon the city walls

78.] anticipating Tamburlaine's triumphal entry in *Two* 4.3.

86. *in triumph*] on show in triumphal procession.

96. *Plato's wondrous year*] when time would be consummated in the return of the planets to their original positions in the celestial cycle; cf. *Timaeus* 39D.

99.] See note at *One* 4.1.1–3.

103. *Like to the shadows*] like copies.

Pyramides] four syllables here, second one stressed.

105. *bird*] the ibis, invoked as sacred by Tamburlaine's opponent.

Shall not defend it from our battering shot.
The townsmen mask in silk and cloth of gold,
And every house is as a treasury.
The men, the treasure, and the town is ours.   110
Theridamas. Your tents of white now pitched before the gates,
    And gentle flags of amity displayed,
    I doubt not but the governor will yield,
    Offering Damascus to Your Majesty.
Tamburlaine. So shall he have his life, and all the rest.   115
    But if he stay until the bloody flag
    Be once advanced on my vermilion tent,
    He dies, and those that kept us out so long.
    And when they see me march in black array,
    With mournful streamers hanging down their heads,   120
    Were in that city all the world contained,
    Not one should 'scape, but perish by our swords.
Zenocrate. Yet would you have some pity for my sake,
    Because it is my country's, and my father's.
Tamburlaine. Not for the world, Zenocrate, if I have
    sworn.—   125
    Come, bring in the Turk.
          Exeunt [with the two Moors *drawing the cage].*

Scene 3

[Enter] Sultan, Arabia, Capolin, *with streaming
colours, and* Soldiers.

Sultan. Methinks we march as Meleager did,
    Environèd with brave Argolian knights,
    To chase the savage Calydonian boar;

---

108. *mask*] dress richly, as in masquerade.
115. *all the rest*] i.e. all the rest shall have their lives.
117. *advanced*] raised aloft.
120. *streamers . . . heads*] drooping pennons.

4.3. Location: at the siege of Damascus still. The Sultan and his forces are preparing to fight the besieger.
1–3.] Meleager, a prince of Calydon, joined with warriors of Argolis, in Greece, in hunting the wild boar sent by Artemis to ravage the land, and killed it.

Or Cephalus with lusty Theban youths,
Against the wolf that angry Themis sent   5
To waste and spoil the sweet Aonian fields.
A monster of five hundred thousand heads,
Compact of rapine, piracy, and spoil,
The scum of men, the hate and scourge of God,
Raves in Egyptia, and annoyeth us.   10
[To Arabia] My lord, it is the bloody Tamburlaine,
A sturdy felon and a base-bred thief
By murder raisèd to the Persian crown,
That dares control us in our territories.
To tame the pride of this presumptuous beast,   15
Join your Arabians with the Sultan's power;
Let us unite our royal bands in one
And hasten to remove Damascus' siege.
It is a blemish to the majesty
And high estate of mighty emperors   20
That such a base usurping vagabond
Should brave a king or wear a princely crown.
Arabia. Renownèd Sultan, have ye lately heard
The overthrow of mighty Bajazeth
About the confines of Bithynia?   25
The slavery wherewith he persecutes
The noble Turk and his great emperess?
Sultan. I have, and sorrow for his bad success.
But, noble lord of great Arabia,
Be so persuaded that the Sultan is   30

4–6.] Cephalus was implicated in the hunting of the Teumessian Fox, sent by Themis to avenge the death of the sphinx. His hound and the fox were turned to marble by Zeus.

6. *Aonian fields*] the district of Thebes and Mount Helicon.

8. *Compact of*] made entirely of.

9. *scourge of God*] The Sultan sees Tamburlaine as impiously opposing God, not—the usual sense of the phrase—as God's vengeful instrument.

10. *Raves*] rages, roves.

Egyptia] Marlowe evidently considers Damascus as part of Egypt; see *One* 4.1.1–3n and 14 below, 'in our territories'.

14. *control*] challenge.

22. *brave*] insult, challenge.

25. *About the confines*] in the border regions.

28. *his bad success*] Bajazeth's disastrous fortune.

No more dismayed with tidings of his fall
Than in the haven when the pilot stands
And views a stranger's ship rent in the winds
And shiverèd against a craggy rock.
Yet, in compassion of his wretched state,   35
A sacred vow to heaven and him I make,
Confirming it with Ibis' holy name,
That Tamburlaine shall rue the day, the hour,
Wherein he wrought such ignominious wrong
Unto the hallowed person of a prince,   40
Or kept the fair Zenocrate so long
As concubine, I fear, to feed his lust.
Arabia. Let grief and fury hasten on revenge!
    Let Tamburlaine for his offences feel
    Such plagues as heaven and we can pour on him.   45
    I long to break my spear upon his crest
    And prove the weight of his victorious arm,
    For Fame I fear hath been too prodigal
    In sounding through the world his partial praise.
Sultan. Capolin, hast thou surveyed our powers?   50
Capolin. Great emperors of Egypt and Arabia,
    The number of your hosts united is
    A hundred and fifty thousand horse,
    Two hundred thousand foot, brave men-at-arms,
    Courageous and full of hardiness,   55
    As frolic as the hunters in the chase
    Of savage beasts amid the desert woods.
Arabia. My mind presageth fortunate success;
    And, Tamburlaine, my spirit doth foresee
    The utter ruin of thy men and thee.   60
Sultan. Then rear your standards! Let your sounding drums
    Direct our soldiers to Damascus' walls.   [*Drums sound.*]

---

47. *prove*] try, test.
49. *his partial praise*] praise founded on prejudice in Tamburlaine's
favour.
56. *frolic*] sportive, exuberant.
58. *success*] outcome.
62.] The soldiers are to defend the walls of Damascus against the besieg-
ing Tamburlaine. Perhaps the intention is that the Sultan aids the city from
outside the walls.

Now, Tamburlaine, the mighty Sultan comes
And leads with him the great Arabian king
To dim thy baseness and obscurity,   65
Famous for nothing but for theft and spoil,
To raze and scatter thy inglorious crew
Of Scythians and slavish Persians.   *Exeunt.*

SCENE 4

The banquet [is brought on], and to it cometh TAMBURLAINE
all in scarlet, [ZENOCRATE,] THERIDAMAS, TECHELLES,
USUMCASANE, *the Turk* [BAJAZETH *drawn in his cage* by *the
two* Moors, ZABINA], *with others.*

Tamburlaine. Now hang our bloody colours by Damascus,
    Reflexing hues of blood upon their heads
    While they walk quiv'ring on their city walls,
    Half dead for fear before they feel my wrath.
    Then let us freely banquet and carouse   5
    Full bowls of wine unto the god of war
    That means to fill your helmets full of gold
    And make Damascus' spoils as rich to you
    As was to Jason Colchos' golden fleece.
    And now, Bajazeth, hast thou any stomach?   10
Bajazeth. Ay, such a stomach, cruel Tamburlaine, as I could
    willingly feed upon thy blood-raw heart.
Tamburlaine. Nay, thine own is easier to come by. Pluck out
    that and 'twill serve thee and thy wife.—Well, Zenocrate,
    Techelles, and the rest, fall to your victuals.   15
Bajazeth. Fall to, and never may your meat digest!
    Ye Furies, that can mask invisible,
    Dive to the bottom of Avernus' pool

4.4. Location: at Damascus, second (red) day of the siege.

5. *carouse*] drink heartily.

9. *Jason*] His journey to recover the Golden Fleece took him with his
Argonauts from Greece to Colchis, at the eastern end of the Black Sea.

10. *stomach*] The word taunts Bajazeth to register not just hunger, but
resistance to cruelty.

16. *digest*] be digested, or digestible.

17. *mask*] lurk in darkness.

18–19.] See *One* 1.2.159, 160n.

And in your hands bring hellish poison up
And squeeze it in the cup of Tamburlaine!   20
Or, wingèd snakes of Lerna, cast your stings,
And leave your venoms in this tyrant's dish!
Zabina. And may this banquet prove as ominous
    As Procne's to th'adulterous Thracian king
    That fed upon the substance of his child!   25
Zenocrate. My lord, how can you suffer these outrageous
    curses by these slaves of yours?
Tamburlaine. To let them see, divine Zenocrate,
    I glory in the curses of my foes,
    Having the power from th'empyreal heaven   30
    To turn them all upon their proper heads.
Techelles. I pray you give them leave, madam. This speech is
    a goodly refreshing to them.
Theridamas. But if His Highness would let them be fed, it
    would do them more good.   35
Tamburlaine. [*To Bajazeth*] Sirrah, why fall you not to? Are
    you so daintily brought up you cannot eat your own flesh?
Bajazeth. First, legions of devils shall tear thee in pieces.
Usumcasane. Villain, knowest thou to whom thou speakest?
Tamburlaine. Oh, let him alone.—Here, eat, sir, take it from   40
    my sword's point, or I'll thrust it to thy heart.
        He [Bajazeth] takes it [the meat] and stamps upon it.
Theridamas. He stamps it under his feet, my lord.
Tamburlaine. [*To Bajazeth*] Take it up, villain, and eat it, or
    I will make thee slice the brawns of thy arms into
    carbonadoes and eat them.   45
Usumcasane. Nay, 'twere better he killed his wife, and then

---

21. *Lerna*] Hercules' arrows bore lethal poison from the gall of the
Lernaean hydra.
24–5.] Tereus, married to Procne, raped her sister Philomela and tried to
conceal it by cutting out her tongue. In revenge, Procne killed her son Itys
and served up his flesh to Tereus.
31. *proper*] own.
32–3. *This . . . to them*] i.e. Their talk gives them comfort. A sardonic
twisting of the fact of their hunger.
36. *Sirrah*] an insulting form of address, used towards social inferiors.
44. *brawns*] muscles.
45. *carbonadoes*] strips of meat.

she shall be sure not to be starved, and he be provided for
a month's victual beforehand.

Tamburlaine. [*To Bajazeth*] Here is my dagger. Dispatch her
    while she is fat, for if she live but a while longer, she will   50
    fall into a consumption with fretting, and then she will
    not be worth the eating.

Theridamas. [*Sardonically*] Dost thou think that Mahomet
    will suffer this?

Techelles. 'Tis like he will, when he cannot let it.   55

Tamburlaine. Go to, fall to your meat. What, not a bit?
    Belike he hath not been watered today; give him some
    drink.

       They [*the two Moors*] *give him water to drink, and he*
                 flings it on the ground.

    Fast and welcome, sir, while hunger make you eat.—
    How now, Zenocrate, doth not the Turk and his wife   60
    make a goodly show at a banquet?

Zenocrate. Yes, my lord.

Theridamas. Methinks 'tis a great deal better than a consort of
    music.

Tamburlaine. Yet music would do well to cheer up Zenocrate.   65
    [*To Zenocrate*] Pray thee tell, why art thou so sad? If thou
    wilt have a song, the Turk shall strain his voice. But why
    is it?

Zenocrate. My lord, to see my father's town besieged,
    The country wasted where myself was born—   70
    How can it but afflict my very soul?
    If any love remain in you, my lord,
    Or if my love unto Your Majesty
    May merit favour at Your Highness' hands,
    Then raise your siege from fair Damascus' walls   75
    And with my father take a friendly truce.

---

55. *like*] likely.
let] hinder.
57. *Belike*] perhaps.
watered] i.e. like an animal.
59. *Fast and welcome*] i.e. Go ahead and starve yourself if you like.
while] until.
63. *consort*] harmonious combination of voices or instruments; also,
spouse.
67. *strain*] tax (to the full).
75. *raise*] cease.

Tamburlaine. Zenocrate, were Egypt Jove's own land,
    Yet would I with my sword make Jove to stoop!
    I will confute those blind geographers
    That make a triple region in the world,   80
    Excluding regions which I mean to trace,
    And with this pen reduce them to a map,
    Calling the provinces, cities, and towns
    After my name and thine, Zenocrate.
    Here at Damascus will I make the point   85
    That shall begin the perpendicular.
    And wouldst thou have me buy thy father's love
    With such a loss? Tell me, Zenocrate.
Zenocrate. Honour still wait on happy Tamburlaine!
    Yet give me leave to plead for him, my lord.   90
Tamburlaine. Content thyself, his person shall be safe,
    And all the friends of fair Zenocrate,
    If with their lives they will be pleased to yield
    Or may be forced to make me emperor;
    For Egypt and Arabia must be mine.   95
    [*To Bajazeth*] Feed, you slave; thou mayst think thyself
    happy to be fed from my trencher.
Bajazeth. My empty stomach, full of idle heat,
    Draws bloody humours from my feeble parts,
    Preserving life by hasting cruel death.   100
    My veins are pale, my sinews hard and dry,
    My joints benumbed; unless I eat, I die.

---

80. *triple region*] Asia, Europe, and Africa. The cartographer of Marlowe's day had a wide choice of *perpendicular* or meridian of longtitude. But if the reference is to the old-fashioned T-in-O maps (i.e. a T inside an O, thus dividing the area into three sections), Tamburlaine is arbitrarily making Damascus, not Jerusalem, the *point* at which the *perpendicular* (Mediterranean) meets the horizontal arms of the 'T', the rivers Nile and Tanais (Don).

81. *trace*] travel, and chart.

82. *this pen*] i.e. my sword. The word-play carries through to 'the point', 85.

reduce them to] bring them to the form of, subjugate.

89. *still*] for ever.

92. *friends*] near relatives.

97. *trencher*] plate, platter.

99. *bloody humours*] one of the four chief fluids of the body—blood, phlegm, choler, melancholy—whose relative proportion determined a person's constitution and character.

Zabina. Eat, Bajazeth. Let us live in spite of them, looking
    some happy power will pity and enlarge us.
Tamburlaine. [*Offering Bajazeth an empty plate*] Here, Turk,   105
    wilt thou have a clean trencher?
Bajazeth. Ay, tyrant, and more meat.
Tamburlaine. Soft, sir, you must be dieted; too much eating
    will make you surfeit.
Theridamas. So it would, my lord, specially having so small a   110
    walk and so little exercise.

           Enter a second course of crowns.

Tamburlaine. Theridamas, Techelles, and Casane, here are
    the cates you desire to finger, are they not?
Theridamas. Ay, my lord, but none save kings must feed with
    these.   115
Techelles. 'Tis enough for us to see them and for Tamburlaine
    only to enjoy them.
Tamburlaine. [*Proposing a toast*] Well, here is now to the
    Sultan of Egypt, the King of Arabia, and the Governor of
    Damascus. Now take these three crowns, and pledge me,   120
    my contributory kings.   [*He presents the crowns in turn.*]
    I crown you here, Theridamas, King of Argier, Techelles,
    King of Fez, and Usumcasane, King of Moroccus. How
    say you to this, Turk? These are not your contributory
    kings!   125
Bajazeth. Nor shall they long be thine, I warrant them.
Tamburlaine. Kings of Argier, Moroccus, and of Fez,
    You that have marched with happy Tamburlaine
    As far as from the frozen plage of heaven
    Unto the wat'ry morning's ruddy bower,   130
    And thence by land unto the torrid zone,

---

103. *looking*] expecting; hoping.
104. *happy power*] lucky intervention (human or divine).
    enlarge] liberate.
108. *Soft*] steady, not so fast.
111.1. *of crowns*] Perhaps the banquet itself included crowns made of
sweetmeats, echoing the crowns bestowed on Tamburlaine's three subordi-
nate generals.
113. *cates*] dainties.
129. *plage*] region; here, the far north.
130.] i.e. into the extreme east, where the sun rises over the ocean.

Deserve these titles I endow you with,
By valour and by magnanimity.
Your births shall be no blemish to your fame,
For virtue is the fount whence honour springs,   135
And they are worthy she investeth kings.
Theridamas. And since Your Highness hath so well
    vouchsafed,
If we deserve them not with higher meeds
Than erst our states and actions have retained,
Take them away again and make us slaves.   140
Tamburlaine. Well said, Theridamas! When holy Fates
Shall 'stablish me in strong Egyptia,
We mean to travel to th'Antarctic Pole,
Conquering the people underneath our feet,
And be renowned as never emperors were.   145
Zenocrate, I will not crown thee yet,
Until with greater honours I be graced.

>   [*Exeunt, with* BAJAZETH *in his cage.*]
>
>   *Finis Actus quarti.*

---

133. *magnanimity*] fortitude, loftiness of purpose.
134. *births*] humble origins.
135. *virtue*] nobility and power.
136. *they*] those who.
137. *so well vouchsafed*] so graciously granted (i.e. these titles).
138. *deserve*] earn.
meeds] merit, worth.
139. *erst*] erstwhile, before now.
states] ranks.
141. *holy Fates*] blending Christian and pagan resonances (Ellis-Fermor).
144. *underneath our feet*] in the southern hemisphere; and trampled upon
in conquest.

Act 5

[Enter] The GOVERNOR *of* DAMASCUS, *with three or four*
Citizens, *and four* Virgins *with branches of laurel
in their hands.*

Governor. Still doth this man or rather god of war
    Batter our walls and beat our turrets down;
    And to resist with longer stubbornness
    Or hope of rescue from the Sultan's power
    Were but to bring our wilful overthrow   5
    And make us desperate of our threatened lives.
    We see his tents have now been alterèd
    With terrors to the last and cruellest hue;
    His coal-black colours everywhere advanced
    Threaten our city with a general spoil;   10
    And if we should with common rites of arms
    Offer our safeties to his clemency,
    I fear the custom proper to his sword,
    Which he observes as parcel of his fame,
    Intending so to terrify the world,   15
    By any innovation or remorse
    Will never be dispensed with till our deaths.
    Therefore, for these our harmless virgins' sakes,

5.1. Location: at Damascus, final (black) day of siege.

6. *desperate*] despair.

8. *With terrors*] terrifyingly; among other terrible portents.

9. *advanced*] raised aloft.

13. *proper*] peculiar.

14. *parcel*] an essential part of.

16–17.] (His fearful purpose) will never be satisfied with any change in his customs or through pity until we have all been killed. *Remorse* associates persistently in this scene with 'ruth' and 'pity', against 'wrath' and against Tamburlaine's self-styled 'honour'.

18. *harmless*] causing no harm; or, innocent.

113

Whose honours and whose lives rely on him,
Let us have hope that their unspotted prayers,   20
Their blubbered cheeks and hearty humble moans
Will melt his fury into some remorse,
And use us like a loving conqueror.
First Virgin. If humble suits or imprecations—
    Uttered with tears of wretchedness and blood   25
    Shed from the heads and hearts of all our sex,
    Some made your wives, and some your children—
    Might have entreated your obdurate breasts
    To entertain some care of our securities
    Whiles only danger beat upon our walls,   30
    These more than dangerous warrants of our death
    Had never been erected as they be,
    Nor you depend on such weak helps as we.
Governor. Well, lovely virgins, think our country's care,
    Our love of honour, loath to be enthralled   35
    To foreign powers and rough imperious yokes,
    Would not with too much cowardice or fear,
    Before all hope of rescue were denied,
    Submit yourselves and us to servitude.
    Therefore, in that your safeties and our own,   40
    Your honours, liberties, and lives, were weighed
    In equal care and balance with our own,
    Endure as we the malice of our stars,
    The wrath of Tamburlaine and power of wars—
    Or be the means the overweighing heavens   45

---

21. *blubbered*] flooded with tears.
hearty] heartfelt.
23.] and (cause him to) treat us as a loving conqueror would.
24. *imprecations*] prayers.
25–6. *blood . . . hearts*] 'Each sigh was thought to cost the heart a drop of blood' (Bevington); cf. 85 below, and *Two* 5.3.215.
27. *made*] being.
29. *securities*] safety; or protection.
30. *danger*] i.e. menace, not certain destruction.
31. *warrants*] assurances (the 'coal-black colours' of 9 above).
35. *enthralled*] enslaved.
40. *in that*] since.
45. *overweighing*] overruling.

> Have kept to qualify these hot extremes,
> And bring us pardon in your cheerful looks.

Second Virgin. Then here, before the majesty of heaven
> And holy patrons of Egyptia,
> With knees and hearts submissive we entreat   50
> Grace to our words and pity to our looks,
> That this device may prove propitious,
> And through the eyes and ears of Tamburlaine
> Convey events of mercy to his heart;
> Grant that these signs of victory we yield   55
> May bind the temples of his conquering head
> To hide the folded furrows of his brows
> And shadow his displeasèd countenance
> With happy looks of ruth and lenity.
> Leave us, my lord, and loving countrymen;   60
> What simple virgins may persuade, we will

Governor. Farewell, sweet virgins, on whose safe return
> Depends our city, liberty, and lives.

>   *Exeunt [all except the* Virgins].

>   *[Enter]* TAMBURLAINE, TECHELLES, THERIDAMAS,
>   USUMCASANE, *with others:* TAMBURLAINE *all in black,
>   and very melancholy.*

Tamburlaine. What, are the turtles frayed out of their nests?
> Alas, poor fools, must you be first shall feel   65
> The sworn destruction of Damascus?
> They know my custom. Could they not as well
> Have sent ye out when first my milk-white flags
> Through which sweet Mercy threw her gentle beams,

---

46. *kept*] kept in reserve, as a last-minute expedient.
qualify] mitigate.
54. *Convey . . . mercy*] suggest a merciful outcome.
55. *these . . . yield*] i.e. the branches of laurel we present.
58. *shadow*] screen; soften propitiously.
59. *happy . . . ruth . . . lenity*] propitious . . . pity . . . mercy.
64. *turtles*] turtledoves.
frayed] frightened.
65. *fools*] innocents, and victims of the governor's delay.
68. *when . . . flags*] i.e. when they first appeared.

Reflexing them on your disdainful eyes,   70
As now when fury and incensèd hate
Flings slaught'ring terror from my coal-black tents
And tells for truth submissions comes too late?
First Virgin. Most happy king and emperor of the earth,
Image of honour and nobility,   75
For whom the powers divine have made the world,
And on whose throne the holy Graces sit;
In whose sweet person is comprised the sum
Of nature's skill and heavenly majesty:
Pity our plights, oh, pity poor Damascus!   80
Pity old age, within whose silver hairs
Honour and reverence evermore have reigned!
Pity the marriage bed, where many a lord
In prime and glory of his loving joy
Embraceth now with tears of ruth and blood   85
The jealous body of his fearful wife,
Whose cheeks and hearts, so punished with conceit
To think thy puissant never-stayèd arm
Will part their bodies and prevent their souls
From heavens of comfort yet their age might bear,   90
Now wax all pale and withered to the death—
As well for grief our ruthless governor
Have thus refused the mercy of thy hand
(Whose sceptre angels kiss and Furies dread)
As for their liberties, their loves, or lives.   95
Oh then, for these, and such as we ourselves,
For us, for infants, and for all our bloods,
That never nourished thought against thy rule,

---

70. *Reflexing them on*] directing them to.
your] Tamburlaine addresses the virgins here; the 'They' of 67 refers to
the governors of Damascus.
73. *submissions*] the act of yielding.
85.] Cf. *Two* 5.3.162–3 and 215.
86. *jealous*] anxious for the beloved's well-being.
87. *punished with conceit*] racked with anticipation.
88. *never-stayèd*] never halted.
89–90. *prevent . . . From*] deprive . . . of.
90. *age*] old age.
92. *grief*] i.e. grief because.
97. *bloods*] lives.

Pity, oh pity, sacred emperor,
The prostrate service of this wretched town!   100
And take in sign thereof this gilded wreath
Whereto each man of rule hath given his hand
And wished, as worthy subjects, happy means
To be investers of thy royal brows,
Even with the true Egyptian diadem.   105
                    [*She offers the laurel wreath.*]
Tamburlaine. Virgins, in vain ye labour to prevent
     That which mine honour swears shall be performed.
     Behold my sword. What see you at the point?
Virgins. Nothing but fear and fatal steel, my lord.
Tamburlaine. Your fearful minds are thick and misty, then,   110
     For there sits Death, there sits imperious Death,
     Keeping his circuit by the slicing edge.
     But I am pleased you shall not see him there;
     He now is seated on my horsemen's spears,
     And on their points his fleshless body feeds.   115
     Techelles, straight go charge a few of them
     To charge these dames, and show my servant Death,
     Sitting in scarlet on their armèd spears.
Omnes. Oh pity us!
Tamburlaine. Away with them, I say, and show them Death.   120
          They [TECHELLES *and others*] *take them away.*
     I will not spare these proud Egyptians,
     Nor change my martial observations
     For all the wealth of Gihon's golden waves,
     Or for the love of Venus, would she leave

---

100. *service*] homage.

103. *happy means*] fortunate opportunity (to crown Tamburlaine, as symbolised by the wreath).

104. *investers*] those who ceremonially adorn.

109. *fatal*] deadly, inevitable.

112. *his circuit*] i.e. a judge's circuit, and the swathe of a sword.

116–17.] Note the sardonic wordplay on *charge*.

117–18.] Cf. Theridamas's vision of Tamburlaine at *Two* 3.4.54–5: 'On whom Death and the Fatal Sisters wait / With naked swords and scarlet liveries'.

118. *armèd*] ready.

122. *observations*] rituals.

123. *Gihon's golden waves*] one of Eden's rivers (Genesis 2.13); the Nile.

The angry god of arms and lie with me.   125
They have refused the offer of their lives,
And know my customs are as peremptory
As wrathful planets, death, or destiny.

                    Enter TECHELLES.

What, have your horsemen shown the virgins Death?
Techelles. They have, my lord, and on Damascus' walls   130
   Have hoisted up their slaughtered carcasses.
Tamburlaine. A sight as baneful to their souls, I think,
   As are Thessalian drugs or mithridate.
   But go, my lords, put the rest to the sword.
                    Exeunt [all except TAMBURLAINE].
Ah, fair Zenocrate, divine Zenocrate,   135
Fair is too foul an epithet for thee,
That in thy passion for thy country's love,
And fear to see thy kingly father's harm,
With hair dishevelled wip'st thy wat'ry cheeks;
And like to Flora in her morning's pride,   140
Shaking her silver tresses in the air,
Rain'st on the earth resolvèd pearl in showers
And sprinklest sapphires on thy shining face
Where Beauty, mother to the Muses, sits
And comments volumes with her ivory pen,   145
Taking instructions from thy flowing eyes—
Eyes, when that Ebena steps to heaven
In silence of thy solemn evening's walk,

---

    125. *god of arms*] Mars.
    127. *peremptory*] final, fixed, precluding all doubt or hesitation. First
syllable stressed.
    133.] Thessaly was renowned for witchcraft and exotic drugs. *Mithridate*
was famed as an antidote to every poison; here, a poison in itself.
    140. *Flora*] Roman goddess of flowers.
    142. *resolvèd*] dissolved. Zenocrate weeps tears like jewelled dew.
    145. *comments*] expounds (the beauty of Zenocrate's distress).
    147–50.] i.e. eyes whose heavenly gleams resemble the rich mantle of light
shed by the moon, the planets, and meteors in the quiet of evening.
    147. *when that*] when.
    Ebena] Night—the colour of ebony. Zenocrate's eyes light up the night
sky.

Making the mantle of the richest night,
The moon, the planets, and the meteors, light.   150
There angels in their crystal armours fight
A doubtful battle with my tempted thoughts
For Egypt's freedom and the Sultan's life—
His life that so consumes Zenocrate,
Whose sorrows lay more siege unto my soul   155
Than all my army to Damascus' walls;
And neither Persia's sovereign nor the Turk
Troubled my senses with conceit of foil
So much by much as doth Zenocrate.
What is beauty, saith my sufferings, then?   160
If all the pens that ever poets held
Had fed the feeling of their masters' thoughts
And every sweetness that inspired their hearts,
Their minds and muses on admired themes;
If all the heavenly quintessence they still   165
From their immortal flowers of poesy,
Wherein as in a mirror we perceive
The highest reaches of a human wit;
If these had made one poem's period,
And all combined in beauty's worthiness,   170
Yet should there hover in their restless heads
One thought, one grace, one wonder at the least,
Which into words no virtue can digest.
But how unseemly is it for my sex,
My discipline of arms and chivalry,   175
My nature, and the terror of my name,
To harbour thoughts effeminate and faint!
Save only that in beauty's just applause,

---

158. *conceit of foil*] anticipation of defeat.

165. *still*] produce by distillation.

169. *period*] end to be attained; also, complete rhetorical structure, uniting all the ideal resources of poetry in iconic homage to beauty.

171. *their*] the poets'.

173. *virtue . . . digest*] creative power can distil, assimilate.

178 ff.] The main thread of Tamburlaine's meditative discourse seems to be 'Save only that . . . I thus conceiving and subduing . . . Shall give the world to note'. In this reading, the impulse to assert mastery over a troubled sensitivity to Beauty struggles through two keenly-felt parentheses which recognise that such sensitivity is indispensable even to a warrior (180–2) and

With whose instinct the soul of man is touched—
And every warrior that is rapt with love   180
Of fame, of valour, and of victory,
Must needs have beauty beat on his conceits—
I thus conceiving and subduing, both,
That which hath stopped the tempest of the gods,
Even from the fiery spangled veil of heaven,   185
To feel the lovely warmth of shepherds' flames
And march in cottages of strewèd weeds,
Shall give the world to note, for all my birth,
That virtue solely is the sum of glory
And fashions men with true nobility.—   190
Who's within there?

Enter two or three [Attendants].

Hath Bajazeth been fed today?
Attendant. Ay, my lord.

---

that Beauty itself is powerful enough to cause gods to abandon wrath in
favour of human love, in particular the love of the artless poor (184–7). The
syntactical complexity registers Tamburlaine's perplexity in a fully dramatic
fashion, and issues in his affirming a compound sense of 'virtue' as an ardent
discipline of powerful feelings which are mutually opposed though they have
the same stimulus: beauty incites man to valorous action, on the one hand;
on the other, it dissuades him from violence, in the name of human love and
pity. As an incitement, beauty has been an insistent theme in the play; as a
dissuasion, it was associated with Zenocrate in *One* 3.3.122–3, and she is
greeted by Tamburlaine in the truce at the end of this Part as 'She that hath
calmed the fury of my sword' (438). On the conjunction of Jupiter and
Venus, see *Two* 3.5.79–82. Poetry is like Zenocrate in that its beauty is finally
inexpressible, mysterious.

179. *instinct*] second syllable stressed.
180. *rapt*] smitten.
182. *beat on . . . conceits*] impinge on his thoughts.
183.] I who both conceive in my thoughts what beauty is and conquer it
by making it mine.
184.] beauty, something that even stops the anger of the gods.
186–7.] Jove and Mercury, disguised as humans, found all doors closed to
them except the humble cottage of Baucis and Philemon.
187. *march in*] enter.
strewèd weeds] common vegetation strewing the floor.
188. *my birth*] my lowly birth.
189. *virtue*] nobility, *virtù* (depending not on birth, but military prowess).
190. *fashions*] forms, moulds.

Tamburlaine. Bring him forth, and let us know if the town
    be ransacked.   [*Exeunt* Attendants.]   195

   Enter TECHELLES, THERIDAMAS, USUMCASANE, *and others.*

Techelles. The town is ours, my lord, and fresh supply
    Of conquest and of spoil is offered us.
Tamburlaine. That's well, Techelles, what's the news?
Techelles. The Sultan and the Arabian king together
    March on us with such eager violence   200
    As if there were no way but one with us.
Tamburlaine. No more there is not, I warrant thee, Techelles.

       They [Moors *and* Attendants] *bring in the Turk*
       [BAJAZETH *in his cage, and* ZABINA].

Theridamas. We know the victory is ours, my lord,
    But let us save the reverend Sultan's life
    For fair Zenocrate that so laments his state.   205
Tamburlaine. That will we chiefly see unto, Theridamas,
    For sweet Zenocrate, whose worthiness
    Deserves a conquest over every heart.
    [*To Bajazeth*] And now, my footstool, if I lose the field,
    You hope of liberty and restitution.—   210
    Here let him stay, my masters, from the tents,
    Till we have made us ready for the field.—
    Pray for us, Bajazeth, we are going.
           Exeunt [*all except* BAJAZETH *and* ZABINA].
Bajazeth. Go, never to return with victory!
    Millions of men encompass thee about   215
    And gore thy body with as many wounds!
    Sharp, forkèd arrows light upon thy horse!

---

   201. *no way but one*] proverbial. Techelles notes the Egyptians' menacing
resolve, and Tamburlaine reverses the fatal menace at his enemies' cost (in
202).

   203–8.] Theridamas prompts Tamburlaine to reaffirm his readiness to
spare Zenocrate's father, first expressed (with conditions) at *One* 4.4.91–4.
That Zenocrate's beauty merits this 'conquest' over him returns our attention to the theme of 'conceiving and subduing, both' (183); here, beauty is
allowed to deflect the will to destroy.

   211. *my masters*] good sirs. (Said to the attendants.)

   215. *Millions*] may millions.

Furies from the black Cocytus lake
Break up the earth, and with their firebrands
Enforce thee run upon the baneful pikes!   220
Volleys of shot pierce through thy charmèd skin,
And every bullet dipped in poisoned drugs;
Or roaring cannons sever all thy joints,
Making thee mount as high as eagles soar!

Zabina. Let all the swords and lances in the field   225
Stick in his breast as in their proper rooms;
At every pore let blood come dropping forth,
That ling'ring pains may massacre his heart
And madness send his damnèd soul to hell!

Bajazeth. Ah, fair Zabina, we may curse his power,   230
The heavens may frown, the earth for anger quake,
But such a star hath influence in his sword
As rules the skies and countermands the gods
More than Cimmerian Styx or Destiny.
And then shall we in this detested guise,   235
With shame, with hunger, and with horror aye
Griping our bowels with retorquèd thoughts,
And have no hope to end our ecstasies.

Zabina. Then is there left no Mahomet, no God,
No fiend, no Fortune, nor no hope of end   240
To our infamous, monstrous slaveries?
Gape, earth, and let the fiends infernal view
A hell as hopeless and as full of fear
As are the blasted banks of Erebus,

---

218. *Cocytus*] a river of Hades.
220. *baneful*] harmful, poisonous.
224.] i.e. blasting you into the sky.
226. *their proper rooms*] i.e. where they belong.
233. *countermands*] goes counter to.
234. *Cimmerian Styx*] The chief river of Hades 'was the deity by which the most solemn oaths were sworn' (Ellis-Fermor). For *Cimmerian*, cf. *One* 3.2.76n.
235-7.] We may understand 'live' after 'shall we' in 235.
237. *retorquèd*] turned back on themselves.
238. *ecstasies*] extreme anguish.
240. *fiend*] devil, who might avenge them on Tamburlaine.
241. *infamous*] second syllable stressed (as in 392, 405).
244. *Erebus*] the Underworld; cf. *One* 4.1.45n.

Where shaking ghosts with ever-howling groans   245
Hover about the ugly ferryman
To get a passage to Elysium!
Why should we live, oh, wretches, beggars, slaves,
Why live we, Bajazeth, and build up nests
So high within the region of the air,   250
By living long in this oppression,
That all the world will see and laugh to scorn
The former triumphs of our mightiness
In this obscure infernal servitude?

Bajazeth. O life more loathsome to my vexèd thoughts   255
Than noisome parbreak of the Stygian snakes
Which fills the nooks of hell with standing air,
Infecting all the ghosts with cureless griefs!
O dreary engines of my loathèd sight
That sees my crown, my honour, and my name   260
Thrust under yoke and thraldom of a thief,
Why feed ye still on day's accursèd beams,
And sink not quite into my tortured soul?
You see my wife, my queen and emperess,
Brought up and proppèd by the hand of fame,   265
Queen of fifteen contributory queens,
Now thrown to rooms of black abjection,
Smearèd with blots of basest drudgery,
And villeiness to shame, disdain, and misery.
Accursèd Bajazeth, whose words of ruth,   270
That would with pity cheer Zabina's heart
And make our souls resolve in ceaseless tears,

---

246. *ugly ferryman*] Charon, ferrying souls across hell's river Styx.
247. *Elysium*] the classical heaven of the blessed.
249–50. *build . . . air*] subsist on false hopes.
256. *noisome parbreak*] stinking vomit. The snakes are perhaps those entwined in the Furies' hair.
257. *standing*] stagnant.
258. *cureless griefs*] irremediable sufferings.
259. *engines*] instruments: the eyes.
263. *quite*] totally. Bajazeth asks rhetorically why his tortured eyes do not simply give up seeing and drown in his tormented spirit.
267. *abjection*] degradation.
269. *villeiness*] servant, bondwoman.
272. *resolve*] dissolve.

Sharp hunger bites upon and gripes the root
From whence the issues of my thoughts do break.
O poor Zabina, O my queen, my queen,   275
Fetch me some water for my burning breast,
To cool and comfort me with longer date,
That, in the shortened sequel of my life,
I may pour forth my soul into thine arms
With words of love, whose moaning intercourse   280
Hath hitherto been stayed with wrath and hate
Of our expressless banned inflictions.

Zabina. Sweet Bajazeth, I will prolong thy life
  As long as any blood or spark of breath
  Can quench or cool the torments of my grief.   285

                                                She goes out.

Bajazeth. Now, Bajazeth, abridge thy baneful days
  And beat thy brains out of thy conquered head,
  Since other means are all forbidden me
  That may be ministers of my decay.
  O highest lamp of ever-living Jove,   290
  Accursèd day, infected with my griefs,
  Hide now thy stainèd face in endless night
  And shut the windows of the lightsome heavens!
  Let ugly Darkness with her rusty coach
  Engirt with tempests wrapped in pitchy clouds   295
  Smother the earth with never-fading mists,
  And let her horses from their nostrils breathe
  Rebellious winds and dreadful thunderclaps,
  That in this terror Tamburlaine may live,
  And my pined soul, resolved in liquid air,   300
  May still excruciate his tormented thoughts!
  Then let the stony dart of senseless cold

---

273. *gripes*] grasps, clutches. (Sharp hunger prevents Bajazeth from speaking to Zabina the words of comfort he feels in his heart.)

277. *date*] duration.

282. *banned*] accursed.

293. *lightsome*] luminous, radiant.

299.] that Tamburlaine may live in a state of constant terror.

300. *pined . . . resolved*] wasted away . . . dissolved.

301. *excruciate*] torture.

Pierce through the centre of my withered heart
And make a passage for my loathèd life.

He brains himself against the cage.

Enter ZABINA.

Zabina. What do mine eyes behold? My husband dead!   305
His skull all riven in twain, his brains dashed out!
The brains of Bajazeth, my lord and sovereign!
O Bajazeth, my husband and my lord,
O Bajazeth, O Turk, O emperor—give him his liquor?
Not I. Bring milk and fire, and my blood I bring him   310
again, tear me in pieces, give me the sword with a ball of
wild-fire upon it. Down with him, down with him! Go to
my child, away, away, away. Ah, save that infant, save
him, save him! I, even I, speak to her. The sun was down.
Streamers white, red, black, here, here, here. Fling the   315
meat in his face. Tamburlaine, Tamburlaine! Let the
soldiers be buried. Hell, death, Tamburlaine, hell! Make
ready my coach, my chair, my jewels, I come, I come, I
come!   *She runs against the cage and brains herself.*
[*Enter*] ZENOCRATE *with* ANIPPE.

Zenocrate. Wretched Zenocrate, that liv'st to see   320
Damascus' walls dyed with Egyptian blood,
Thy father's subjects and thy countrymen;
Thy streets strewed with disseevered joints of men
And wounded bodies gasping yet for life;
But most accurst, to see the sun-bright troop   325
Of heavenly virgins and unspotted maids,
Whose looks might make the angry god of arms
To break his sword and mildly treat of love,
On horsemen's lances to be hoisted up
And guiltlessly endure a cruel death!   330
For every fell and stout Tartarian steed
That stamped on others with their thund'ring hoofs,

---

312. *wild-fire*] incendiaries used in warfare.
315. *Streamers*] pennons.
322.] the blood of your father's subjects, your fellow Egyptians.
331. *fell and stout*] fierce and burly.

When all their riders charged their quiv'ring spears,
Began to check the ground and rein themselves,
Gazing upon the beauty of their looks.   335
Ah, Tamburlaine, wert thou the cause of this,
That term'st Zenocrate thy dearest love—
Whose lives were dearer to Zenocrate
Than her own life, or aught save thine own love?
                    [*She sees the dead Bajazeth and Zabina.*]
But see, another bloody spectacle!   340
Ah, wretched eyes, the enemies of my heart,
How are ye glutted with these grievous objects,
And tell my soul more tales of bleeding ruth!
See, see, Anippe, if they breathe or no.
Anippe. [*Examining the bodies*] No breath, nor sense, nor
        motion in them both.   345
    Ah, madam, this their slavery hath enforced,
    And ruthless cruelty of Tamburlaine.
Zenocrate. Earth, cast up fountains from thy entrails,
    And wet thy cheeks for their untimely deaths;
    Shake with their weight in sign of fear and grief!   350
    Blush, heaven, that gave them honour at their birth
    And let them die a death so barbarous!
    Those that are proud of fickle empery
    And place their chiefest good in earthly pomp,
    Behold the Turk and his great emperess!   355
    Ah, Tamburlaine my love, sweet Tamburlaine,
    That fight'st for sceptres and for slipp'ry crowns,
    Behold the Turk and his great emperess!
    Thou that in conduct of thy happy stars
    Sleep'st every night with conquest on thy brows   360

---

333. *charged*] levelled.
334. *check*] paw.
343. *bleeding ruth*] piteous atrocity.
345. *motion*] power of movement.
346.] i.e. their deaths were the result of their cruel enslavement.
348.] Fountains were thought to be cast up during earthquakes by the agency of subterranean wind.
350.] Zenocrate bids the earth shake in fear and grief at the momentousness of this tragic event.
353. *Those*] any persons.
359. *in conduct*] under the guidance.

And yet wouldst shun the wavering turns of war,
In fear and feeling of the like distress
Behold the Turk and his great emperess!
Ah, mighty Jove and holy Mahomet,
Pardon my love, Oh, pardon his contempt   365
Of earthly fortune and respect of pity,
And let not conquest ruthlessly pursued
Be equally against his life incensed
In this great Turk and hapless emperess!
And pardon me that was not moved with ruth   370
To see them live so long in misery.
Ah, what may chance to thee, Zenocrate?

Anippe. Madam, content yourself, and be resolved;
Your love hath Fortune so at his command
That she shall stay and turn her wheel no more   375
As long as life maintains his mighty arm
That fights for honour to adorn your head.

Enter [PHILEMUS,] *a* Messenger.

Zenocrate. What other heavy news now brings Philemus?
Philemus. Madam, your father and th'Arabian king,
The first affecter of your excellence,   380
Comes now as Turnus 'gainst Aeneas did,
Armèd with lance into th'Egyptian fields,
Ready for battle 'gainst my lord the King.
Zenocrate. Now shame and duty, love and fear, presents
A thousand sorrows to my martyred soul.   385
Whom should I wish the fatal victory,

---

362. *the like distress*] suffering like that of Bajazeth and Zabina.
366. *earthly fortune*] vicissitude.
respect of pity] regard for compassion.
368. *incensed*] inflamed.
369. *In*] as in.
370. *ruth*] pity.
373. *resolved*] convinced that.
375. *stay*] remain motionless.
380. *affecter*] lover.
381. *Turnus . . . Aeneas*] the defeated (Italian) and victorious (Trojan) competitors for the hand of Lavinia, in Virgil's *Aeneid*.
383. *the King*] i.e. Tamburlaine.
386. *fatal*] fated; momentous; mortally dangerous to the loser.

When my poor pleasures are divided thus
And racked by duty from my cursèd heart?
My father and my first betrothèd love
Must fight against my life and present love;   390
Wherein the change I use condemns my faith
And makes my deeds infamous through the world.
But as the gods, to end the Trojan's toil,
Prevented Turnus of Lavinia,
And fatally enriched Aeneas' love,   395
So, for a final issue to my griefs,
To pacify my country and my love,
Must Tamburlaine, by their resistless powers,
With virtue of a gentle victory
Conclude a league of honour to my hope;   400
Then, as the powers divine have pre-ordained,
With happy safety of my father's life
Send like defence of fair Arabia.

They sound [trumpets within] to the battle, and
TAMBURLAINE *enjoys the victory. After,* ARABIA
enters wounded.

Arabia. What cursèd power guides the murdering hands
Of this infamous tyrant's soldiers,   405
That no escape may save their enemies
Nor fortune keep themselves from victory?
Lie down, Arabia, wounded to the death,
And let Zenocrate's fair eyes behold
That, as for her thou bear'st these wretched arms,   410
Even so for her thou diest in these arms,

---

388. *racked*] torn apart (by having two lovers).

391. *change I use*] changefulness I commit.

393–5.] The 'enrichment' of Aeneas, in gaining Lavinia, was 'fatal' to Turnus. The allusion works itself out to Arabia's cost, within a few lines.

394. *Prevented*] deprived.

396. *issue . . . griefs*] resolution of my sufferings.

398. *by . . . powers*] considering their opposed irresistible armies.

399. *With virtue of*] in consequence of.

gentle] honourable.

400. *to*] in accordance with.

403.] provide a similar deliverance for Alcidamas, King of Arabia.

403.1. *to*] to begin.

Leaving thy blood for witness of thy love.
Zenocrate. Too dear a witness for such love, my lord.
    Behold Zenocrate, the cursed object
    Whose fortunes never masterèd her griefs!   415
    Behold her wounded in conceit for thee,
    As much as thy fair body is for me.
Arabia. Then shall I die with full contented heart,
    Having beheld divine Zenocrate
    Whose sight with joy would take away my life,   420
    As now it bringeth sweetness to my wound,
    If I had not been wounded as I am.
    Ah, that the deadly pangs I suffer now
    Would lend an hour's licence to my tongue,
    To make discourse of some sweet accidents   425
    Have chanced thy merits in this worthless bondage,
    And that I might be privy to the state
    Of thy deserved contentment and thy love!
    But, making now a virtue of thy sight
    To drive all sorrow from my fainting soul,   430
    Since death denies me further cause of joy,
    Deprived of care, my heart with comfort dies
    Since thy desirèd hand shall close mine eyes.

                                  [*He dies.*]

    Enter TAMBURLAINE *leading the* SULTAN; TECHELLES,
    THERIDAMAS, USUMCASANE, [*bearing the Persian crown*]
        with others. [*A throne is brought on.*]

Tamburlaine. Come, happy father of Zenocrate,
    A title higher than thy Sultan's name: 435
    Though my right hand have thus enthrallèd thee,
    Thy princely daughter here shall set thee free—
    She that hath calmed the fury of my sword,
    Which had ere this been bathed in streams of blood

---

413. *for such love*] for such an unworthy loved one (as I).
415.] whose seeming good fortune never outweighed her suffering.
416. *conceit*] imaginative sympathy.
425. *sweet accidents*] unexpected pleasant happenings.
426.] that have occurred according to your high deserts, during your degrading captivity.

As vast and deep as Euphrates or Nile.   440
Zenocrate. Oh, sight thrice welcome to my joyful soul,
    To see the King my father issue safe
    From dangerous battle of my conquering love!
Sultan. Well met, my only dear Zenocrate,
    Though with the loss of Egypt and my crown.   445
Tamburlaine. 'Twas I, my lord, that gat the victory;
    And therefore, grieve not at your overthrow,
    Since I shall render all into your hands
    And add more strength to your dominions
    Than ever yet confirmed th'Egyptian crown.   450
    The god of war resigns his room to me,
    Meaning to make me general of the world;
    Jove, viewing me in arms, looks pale and wan,
    Fearing my power should pull him from his throne;
    Where'er I come the Fatal Sisters sweat,   455
    And grisly Death, by running to and fro
    To do their ceaseless homage to my sword;
    And here in Afric where it seldom rains,
    Since I arrived with my triumphant host
    Have swelling clouds drawn from wide gasping wounds 460
    Been oft resolved in bloody purple showers,
    A meteor that might terrify the earth
    And make it quake at every drop it drinks;
    Millions of souls sit on the banks of Styx,
    Waiting the back return of Charon's boat;   465
    Hell and Elysium swarm with ghosts of men
    That I have sent from sundry foughten fields
    To spread my fame through hell and up to heaven.
    And see, my lord, a sight of strange import:
    Emperors and kings lie breathless at my feet!   470

---

440. *Euphrates*] first syllable stressed.

443. *of*] with.

450. *confirmed*] sustained, or was confirmed by.

454. *pull . . . throne*] as he had pulled Saturn. Cf. *One* 2.7.13–15.

455. *Fatal Sisters*] the Parcae, or Fates, Tamburlaine's menials here and at *Two* 3.4.54.

460–1.] It was believed that the sun could draw up blood from scenes of carnage, and distil it in bloody rain.

467. *foughten fields*] battlegrounds.

The Turk and his great empress, as it seems,
Left to themselves while we were at the fight,
Have desperately dispatched their slavish lives;
With them Arabia too hath left his life—
All sights of power to grace my victory;   475
And such are objects fit for Tamburlaine,
Wherein as in a mirror may be seen
His honour, that consists in shedding blood
When men presume to manage arms with him.
Sultan. Mighty hath God and Mahomet made thy hand,   480
Renownèd Tamburlaine, to whom all kings
Of force must yield their crowns and emperies;
And I am pleased with this my overthrow
If, as beseems a person of thy state,
Thou hast with honour used Zenocrate.   485
Tamburlaine. Her state and person wants no pomp, you see,
And for all blot of foul inchastity,
I record heaven, her heavenly self is clear.
Then let me find no further time to grace
Her princely temples with the Persian crown;   490
But here these kings, that on my fortunes wait
And have been crowned for provèd worthiness
Even by this hand that shall establish them,
Shall now, adjoining all their hands with mine,
Invest her here my Queen of Persia.   495
What saith the noble Sultan and Zenocrate?
Sultan. I yield, with thanks and protestations
Of endless honour to thee for her love.
Tamburlaine. Then doubt I not but fair Zenocrate
Will soon consent to satisfy us both.   500
Zenocrate. Else should I much forget myself, my lord.
Theridamas. Then let us set the crown upon her head
That long hath lingered for so high a seat.

---

475. *of power to*] able to.
482. *Of force*] of necessity.
484. *beseems*] befits (cf. 532).
487. *for*] as for.
488. *record*] call to witness; first syllable stressed.
489. *find . . . further*] seek no more distant.
498. *her love*] your love of her.

Techelles. My hand is ready to perform the deed,
   For now her marriage time shall work us rest.   505
Usumcasane. And here's the crown, my lord; help set it on.
Tamburlaine. Then sit thou down, divine Zenocrate,
                        [She ascends the throne.]
   And here we crown thee Queen of Persia
   And all the kingdoms and dominions
   That late the power of Tamburlaine subdued.   510
   As Juno, when the giants were suppressed
   That darted mountains at her brother Jove,
   So looks my love, shadowing in her brows
   Triumphs and trophies for my victories;
   Or as Latona's daughter bent to arms,   515
   Adding more courage to my conquering mind.
   To gratify thee, sweet Zenocrate,
   Egyptians, Moors, and men of Asia,
   From Barbary unto the Western Indie,
   Shall pay a yearly tribute to thy sire;   520
   And from the bounds of Afric to the banks
   Of Ganges shall his mighty arm extend.
   And now, my lords and loving followers,
   That purchased kingdoms by your martial deeds,
   Cast off your armour, put on scarlet robes,   525
   Mount up your royal places of estate,
   Environèd with troops of noble men,
   And there make laws to rule your provinces;
   Hang up your weapons on Alcides' post,
   For Tamburlaine takes truce with all the world.   530
   [To Zenocrate] Thy first betrothèd love, Arabia,
   Shall we with honour, as beseems, entomb,
   With this great Turk and his fair emperess;

511–12.] Cf. *One* 2.3.18–21n., 2.6.2–6n.
512. *darted*] hurled.
513. *shadowing*] harbouring, or depicting.
515. *Latona's daughter*] Diana (Artemis), patroness of hunting.
bent to arms] devoted to the hunt.
524. *purchased*] won.
525. *scarlet robes*] i.e. of peaceful lawgivers.
526. *Mount up*] rise up to the full height of.
529. *Alcides' post*] the door-post of Hercules' (Alcides') temple.

Then after all these solemn exequies
We will our rites of marriage solemnise.   535
　　　[*Exeunt, bearing the bodies in solemn procession.*]

　　Finis Actus quinti & ultimi huius primae partis.

535.2] End of Act 5 and of the last Act of Part One.

Part Two

THE SECOND PART OF
The bloody Conquests
of mighty Tamburlaine.

With his impassionate fury for the death of
his Lady and love, fair Zenocrate, his form
of exhortation and discipline to his three
sons, and the manner of his own death.

[DRAMATIS PERSONAE

The Prologue.
ORCANES, *King of Natolia.*
GAZELLUS, *Viceroy of Byron.*
URIBASSA, *attending on Orcanes.*
SIGISMOND, *King of Hungary.*   5
FREDERICK, *lord of Buda.*
BALDWIN, *lord of Bohemia.*
CALLAPINE, *son of Bajazeth and prisoner of Tamburlaine.*
ALMEDA, *his keeper.*
TAMBURLAINE, *King of Persia.*   10
ZENOCRATE, *Queen of Persia, wife of Tamburlaine.*

CALYPHAS
AMYRAS   } *his sons.*
CELEBINUS

THERIDAMAS, *King of Argier.*   15
TECHELLES, *King of Fez.*
USUMCASANE, *King of Morocco.*
KING OF TREBIZOND.
KING OF SORIA.
KING OF JERUSALEM.   20
KING OF AMASIA.
CAPTAIN OF BALSERA.
OLYMPIA, *his wife.*
SON *of the Captain and Olympia.*
PERDICAS.   25
GOVERNOR OF BABYLON.
MAXIMUS.

A Captain, Messengers, Attendants, Physicians, Soldiers,
   Pioners, Citizens, Lords, Turkish Concubines.]

---

5. *SIGISMOND*] Hungarian king contemporary with Tamburlaine.
Marlowe involves him unhistorically, in place of Vladislaus, in the events that
led up to the battle of Varna in 1444.
   12–14.] Whetstone mentions only two sons of Tamburlaine.
   19. *SORIA*] See *Two* 1.1.63n.
   21. *AMASIA*] a province in northern Asia Minor.

The Prologue

The general welcomes Tamburlaine received
When he arrivèd last upon our stage
Hath made our poet pen his second part,
Where death cuts off the progress of his pomp
And murd'rous Fates throws all his triumphs down.   5
But what became of fair Zenocrate,
And with how many cities' sacrifice
He celebrated her sad funeral,
Himself in presence shall unfold at large.

---

2. *last*] recently.
5. *Fates*] Clotho, Lachesis, Atropos. Cf. *One* 1.2.173 and note.
throws] normal third-person plural form in Elizabethan grammar.

Act 1

SCENE I

[*Enter*] ORCANES *King of* NATOLIA, GAZELLUS *Viceroy of*
BYRON, URIBASSA, *and their* train,
with drums and trumpets.

Orcanes. Egregious viceroys of these eastern parts,
    Placed by the issue of great Bajazeth
    And sacred lord, the mighty Callapine,
    Who lives in Egypt prisoner to that slave
    Which kept his father in an iron cage: 5
    Now have we marched from fair Natolia
    Two hundred leagues, and on Danubius' banks
    Our warlike host in complete armour rest,
    Where Sigismond the King of Hungary
    Should meet our person to conclude a truce.   10
    What, shall we parley with the Christian,
    Or cross the stream and meet him in the field?
Gazellus. King of Natolia, let us treat of peace;
    We all are glutted with the Christians' blood,
    And have a greater foe to fight against—   15
    Proud Tamburlaine, that now in Asia
    Near Guyron's head doth set his conquering feet

1.1. Location: on the banks of the Danube.
0.1. NATOLIA] Asia Minor; roughly, modern Turkey.
0.2. BYRON] a town not far from Babylon.
1. *Egregious*] outstanding, remarkable.
2. *Placed . . . issue*] appointed by the offspring.
4. *slave*] wretch.
8. *complete*] first syllable stressed.
10. *Should . . . our person*] is scheduled to meet me.
13. *treat of*] discuss, negotiate.
17. *Guyron*] The 'Guiron' of Ortelius's maps is a town on the Upper
Euphrates.

138

And means to fire Turkey as he goes.
'Gainst him, my lord, must you address your power.
Uribassa. Besides, King Sigismond hath brought from
    Christendom   20
    More than his camp of stout Hungarians,
    Slavonians, Almains, rutters, Muffs, and Danes,
    That with the halberd, lance, and murdering axe
    Will hazard that we might with surety hold.
Orcanes. Though from the shortest northern parallel,   25
    Vast Gruntland, compassed with the frozen sea,
    Inhabited with tall and sturdy men,
    Giants as big as hugy Polypheme,
    Millions of soldiers cut the Arctic line,
    Bringing the strength of Europe to these arms,   30
    Our Turkey blades shall glide through all their throats
    And make this champian mead a bloody fen;
    Danubius' stream, that runs to Trebizond,
    Shall carry wrapped within his scarlet waves,
    As martial presents to our friends at home,   35
    The slaughtered bodies of these Christians;
    The Terrene main, wherein Danubius falls,
    Shall by this battle be the bloody sea.
    The wand'ring sailors of proud Italy
    Shall meet those Christians fleeting with the tide,   40

---

18. *fire*] burn down.
19. *address your power*] prepare, dispatch, your army.
21. *stout*] hearty, brave.
22. *Almains, rutters, Muffs*] Germans, cavalry, Swiss.
24.] will put at risk what we might otherwise certainly defend.
25. *shortest northern parallel*] most northerly circle of latitude.
26. *Gruntland*] Greenland.
compassed with] encircled by.
28. *Polypheme*] Polyphemus, the one-eyed giant in the *Odyssey*.
29. *cut the Arctic line*] cross the Arctic Circle southwards.
30. *these arms*] i.e. Tamburlaine's army.
32. *champian mead*] open plain.
33–41.] Marlowe 'sees the waters of the Danube sweeping from the river
mouths in two strong currents, the one racing across the Black Sea to
Trebizond, the other swirling southward to the Bosphorus, and so onward to
the Hellespont and the Aegean. Both currents bear the slaughtered bodies of
Christian soldiers, the one to bring proof of victory to the great Turkish
town, the other to strike terror to the Italian merchants cruising round the
Isles of Greece' (Seaton).

Beating in heaps against their argosies,
And make fair Europe, mounted on her bull,
Trapped with the wealth and riches of the world,
Alight and wear a woeful mourning weed.
Gazellus. Yet, stout Orcanes, prorex of the world,   45
Since Tamburlaine hath mustered all his men,
Marching from Cairon northward with his camp
To Alexandria and the frontier towns,
Meaning to make a conquest of our land,
'Tis requisite to parley for a peace   50
With Sigismond the King of Hungary,
And save our forces for the hot assaults
Proud Tamburlaine intends Natolia.
Orcanes. Viceroy of Byron, wisely hast thou said.
My realm, the centre of our empery,   55
Once lost, all Turkey would be overthrown;
And for that cause the Christians shall have peace.
Slavonians, Almains, rutters, Muffs, and Danes
Fear not Orcanes, but great Tamburlaine—
Nor he, but Fortune that hath made him great.   60
We have revolted Grecians, Albanese,
Sicilians, Jews, Arabians, Turks, and Moors,
Natolians, Sorians, black Egyptians,
Illyrians, Thracians, and Bithynians,

---

37. *Terrene main*] Mediterranean Sea.
40. *fleeting*] floating.
41. *argosies*] large merchant ships.
42.] Europa was abducted by Zeus, disguised as a bull.
43. *Trapped*] adorned.
44. *weed*] robe.
45. *prorex*] viceroy.
47. *Cairon*] Cairo.
50. *parley for*] negotiate.
60.] Orcanes is awed, not by Tamburlaine, but by the favouring Fortune
to whom Tamburlaine owes his power.
61. *Albanese*] Albanians.
63. *Sorians*] 'Egyptia in Part I includes Siria, for Damascus is Egyptian; in
Part 2, Egypt is distinct from Soria, and its capital is Cairo, named for the
first time' (Seaton).
64. *Illyrians*] inhabitants of part of the Balkan peninsula.
Bithynians] from the north-west of Asia Minor.

Enough to swallow forceless Sigismond,   65
Yet scarce enough t'encounter Tamburlaine;
He brings a world of people to the field.
From Scythia to the oriental plage
Of India, where raging Lantchidol
Beats on the regions with his boist'rous blows,   70
That never seaman yet discoverèd,
All Asia is in arms with Tamburlaine.
Even from the midst of fiery Cancer's tropic
To Amazonia under Capricorn,
And thence as far as Archipelago,   75
All Afric is in arms with Tamburlaine.
Therefore, viceroys, the Christians must have peace.

[Enter] SIGISMOND, FREDERICK, BALDWIN, *and their* train,
with drums and trumpets.

Sigismond. Orcanes, as our legates promised thee,
We with our peers have crossed Danubius' stream
To treat of friendly peace or deadly war.   80
Take which thou wilt, for as the Romans used
I here present thee with a naked sword.
              [He hands his sword formally to Orcanes.]
Wilt thou have war, then shake this blade at me;
If peace, restore it to my hands again,
And I will sheathe it to confirm the same.   85
Orcanes. Stay, Sigismond. Forgett'st thou I am he
That with the cannon shook Vienna walls,
And made it dance upon the continent,
As when the massy substance of the earth
Quiver about the axletree of heaven?   90

---

65. *forceless*] weak.
66. *encounter*] face up to.
68. *plage*] region.
69. *Lantchidol*] the Indian Ocean.
73–6.] The geography runs from the intersection of the meridian with the
tropic of Cancer, south to *Amazonia* (in Africa, west of Mozambique), and
north again to *Archipelago*, the islands of the Aegean.
81. *used*] used to do.
88. *continent*] solid land.
90. *the axletree of heaven*] the axis of the celestial sphere, running through
the earth at the centre.

Forgett'st thou that I sent a shower of darts
Mingled with powdered shot and feathered steel
So thick upon the blink-eyed burghers' heads
That thou thyself, then County Palatine,
The King of Boheme, and the Austric Duke   95
Sent heralds out, which basely on their knees
In all your names desired a truce of me?
Forgett'st thou that, to have me raise my siege,
Waggons of gold were set before my tent,
Stamped with the princely fowl that in her wings   100
Carries the fearful thunderbolts of Jove?
How canst thou think of this and offer war?
Sigismond. Vienna was besieged, and I was there,
Then County Palatine, but now a king;
And what we did was in extremity.   105
But now, Orcanes, view my royal host
That hides these plains and seems as vast and wide
As doth the desert of Arabia
To those that stand on Baghdad's lofty tower,
Or as the ocean to the traveller   110
That rests upon the snowy Apennines,
And tell me whether I should stoop so low,
Or treat of peace with the Natolian king!
Gazellus. Kings of Natolia and of Hungary,
We came from Turkey to confirm a league,   115
And not to dare each other to the field.
A friendly parley might become ye both.
Frederick. And we from Europe to the same intent,
Which, if your general refuse or scorn,
Our tents are pitched, our men stand in array,   120
Ready to charge you ere you stir your feet.
Orcanes. So prest are we, but yet if Sigismond

---

91. *darts*] spears.
92. *feathered steel*] arrows.
93. *blink-eyed*] shutting their eyes continually in recoil.
94. *then County Palatine*] at that time Palatinate Lord.
95. *Austric*] Austrian.
100. *princely fowl*] eagle, 'thought to be invulnerable to lightning, and hence the armour-bearer to Jove' (Heninger).
119. *your general*] i.e. Orcanes.
122. *prest*] ready, eager.

Speak as a friend, and stand not upon terms,
Here is his sword; let peace be ratified
On these conditions specified before,   125
Drawn with advice of our ambassadors.

Sigismond. [*Receiving back his sword*] Then here I sheathe it,
    and give thee my hand
Never to draw it out or manage arms
Against thyself or thy confederates,
But whilst I live will be at truce with thee.   130

Orcanes. But, Sigismond, confirm it with an oath,
And swear in sight of heaven and by thy Christ.

Sigismond. By Him that made the world and saved my soul,
The son of God and issue of a maid,
Sweet Jesus Christ, I solemnly protest   135
And vow to keep this peace inviolable.

Orcanes. By sacred Mahomet, the friend of God,
Whose holy Alcoran remains with us,
Whose glorious body, when he left the world
Closed in a coffin, mounted up the air   140
And hung on stately Mecca's temple roof,
I swear to keep this truce inviolable;
Of whose conditions and our solemn oaths
Signed with our hands, each shall retain a scroll
As memorable witness of our league.   145
Now, Sigismond, if any Christian king
Encroach upon the confines of thy realm,
Send word Orcanes of Natolia
Confirmed this league beyond Danubius' stream,
And they will, trembling, sound a quick retreat—   150
So am I feared among all nations.

Sigismond. If any heathen potentate or king
Invade Natolia, Sigismond will send
A hundred thousand horse trained to the war
And backed by stout lancers of Germany,   155

---

123. *stand not upon terms*] does not take too firm a line upon conditions.
134. *issue*] offspring.
135. *protest*] swear.
138. *Alcoran*] Koran.
147. *confines*] borders.
155. *lancers*] second syllable stressed (cf. 'lanciers').

The strength and sinews of th'imperial seat.
Orcanes. I thank thee, Sigismond, but when I war
All Asia Minor, Africa, and Greece
Follow my standard and my thund'ring drums.
Come, let us go and banquet in our tents.   160
I will dispatch chief of my army hence
To fair Natolia and to Trebizond,
To stay my coming 'gainst proud Tamburlaine.
Friend Sigismond, and peers of Hungary,
Come banquet and carouse with us a while,   165
And then depart we to our territories.   *Exeunt.*

SCENE 2

[*Enter*] CALLAPINE *with* ALMEDA, *his keeper.*

Callapine. Sweet Almeda, pity the ruthful plight
Of Callapine, the son of Bajazeth,
Born to be monarch of the western world,
Yet here detained by cruel Tamburlaine.
Almeda. My lord, I pity it, and with my heart   5
Wish your release; but he whose wrath is death,
My sovereign lord, renownèd Tamburlaine,
Forbids you further liberty than this.
Callapine. Ah, were I now but half so eloquent
To paint in words what I'll perform in deeds,   10
I know thou wouldst depart from hence with me!
Almeda. Not for all Afric; therefore move me not.
Callapine. Yet hear me speak, my gentle Almeda.
Almeda. No speech to that end, by your favour, sir.
Callapine. By Cairo runs—   15
Almeda. No talk of running, I tell you, sir.
Callapine. A little further, gentle Almeda.

---

156. *seat*] throne, and seat of power.
161. *chief*] the greater part.
163. *stay*] await.

1.2. Location: in Egypt.
3. *the western world*] the Turkish empire, as seen from Asia.
5–7. *lord . . . sovereign lord*] Almeda's double servility is pointedly graded.
14. *by your favour*] if you please.

Almeda. Well sir, what of this?

Callapine. By Cairo runs to Alexandria Bay
    Darote's streams, wherein at anchor lies   20
    A Turkish galley of my royal fleet,
    Waiting my coming to the river side,
    Hoping by some means I shall be released,
    Which when I come aboard will hoist up sail
    And soon put forth into the Terrene sea,   25
    Where 'twixt the isles of Cyprus and of Crete
    We quickly may in Turkish seas arrive.
    Then shalt thou see a hundred kings and more
    Upon their knees, all bid me welcome home.
    Amongst so many crowns of burnished gold   30
    Choose which thou wilt; all are at thy command.
    A thousand galleys manned with Christian slaves
    I freely give thee, which shall out the Straits
    And bring armadoes from the coasts of Spain,
    Fraughted with gold of rich America.   35
    The Grecian virgins shall attend on thee,
    Skilful in music and in amorous lays,
    As fair as was Pygmalion's ivory girl
    Or lovely Io metamorphosèd.
    With naked negroes shall thy coach be drawn,   40
    And as thou rid'st in triumph through the streets,
    The pavement underneath thy chariot wheels
    With Turkey carpets shall be coverèd,
    And cloth of arras hung about the walls,
    Fit objects for thy princely eye to pierce.   45
    A hundred bassoes clothed in crimson silk

---

20. *Darote's streams*] Ortelius shows Darote or Derote as 'a town at the bend of the westernmost arm of the Nile delta, that is, on the river-way from Cairo to Alexandria' (Seaton).

25. *Terrene*] Mediterranean.

33. *Straits*] Straits of Gibraltar.

34. *armadoes*] large war-vessels.

35. *Fraughted*] freighted, laden.

38–9.] Venus brought to life a statue made by *Pygmalion*. *Io* was turned into a white heifer by Jove.

44. *cloth of arras*] rich tapestry.

46. *bassoes*] bashaws, pashas.

Shall ride before thee on Barbarian steeds;
And when thou goest, a golden canopy
Enchased with precious stones which shine as bright
As that fair veil that covers all the world   50
When Phoebus leaping from his hemisphere
Descendeth downward to th'Antipodes—
And more than this, for all I cannot tell.

Almeda. How far hence lies the galley, say you?

Callapine. Sweet Almeda, scarce half a league from hence.   55

Almeda. But need we not be spied going aboard?

Callapine. Betwixt the hollow hanging of a hill
And crooked bending of a craggy rock,
The sails wrapped up, the mast and tacklings down,
She lies so close that none can find her out.   60

Almeda. I like that well; but tell me, my lord, if I should let
you go, would you be as good as your word? Shall I be
made a king for my labour?

Callapine. As I am Callapine the Emperor,
And by the hand of Mahomet I swear,   65
Thou shalt be crowned a king and be my mate.

Almeda. Then here I swear, as I am Almeda,
Your keeper under Tamburlaine the Great—
For that's the style and title I have yet—
Although he sent a thousand armèd men   70
To intercept this haughty enterprise,
Yet would I venture to conduct Your Grace
And die before I brought you back again.

Callapine. Thanks, gentle Almeda. Then let us haste,
Lest time be past, and ling'ring let us both.   75

---

47. *Barbarian steeds*] Barbary horses.
49. *Enchased*] set.
50. *fair veil*] moonlight, the 'shining veil of Cynthia' (*Two* 2.2.47), perhaps 'enchased' with stars.
51. *Phoebus*] the sun.
56. *need we not*] shall we not inevitably.
60. *close*] well concealed.
66. *mate*] equal.
69. *style*] official designation.
yet] as yet.
71. *haughty*] lofty.
75. *let*] hinder.

Almeda. When you will, my lord, I am ready.

Callapine. Even straight; and farewell, cursèd Tamburlaine!
  Now go I to revenge my father's death.   *Exeunt.*

SCENE 3

[*Enter*] TAMBURLAINE *with* ZENOCRATE, *and his three sons,*
CALYPHAS, AMYRAS, *and* CELEBINUS, *with drums and trumpets.*
[*A throne is brought on.*]

Tamburlaine. Now bright Zenocrate, the world's fair eye
  Whose beams illuminate the lamps of heaven,
  Whose cheerful looks do clear the cloudy air
  And clothe it in a crystal livery,
  Now rest thee here on fair Larissa plains   5
  Where Egypt and the Turkish empire parts,
  Between thy sons that shall be emperors
  And every one commander of a world.
Zenocrate. Sweet Tamburlaine, when wilt thou leave these
      arms
  And save thy sacred person free from scathe   10
  And dangerous chances of the wrathful war?
Tamburlaine. When heaven shall cease to move on both the
      poles,
  And when the ground whereon my soldiers march
  Shall rise aloft and touch the hornèd moon,
  And not before, my sweet Zenocrate.   15
  Sit up and rest thee like a lovely queen.
                        [*She ascends the throne.*]
  So, now she sits in pomp and majesty
  When these my sons, more precious in mine eyes
  Than all the wealthy kingdoms I subdued,

---

77. *straight*] straightway.

1.3. Location: near Larissa (see 5n).
2. *illuminate*] light up.
5. *Larissa*] modern El Arish, near Egypt's border with Israel.
6. *parts*] are divided.
9. *these arms*] the weaponry of war.
10. *scathe*] harm.
12.] Cf. the 'axletree of heaven', at *One* 4.2.50n.

Placed by her side, look on their mother's face.   20
But yet methinks their looks are amorous,
Not martial as the sons of Tamburlaine;
Water and air, being symbolised in one,
Argue their want of courage and of wit;
Their hair as white as milk and soft as down—   25
Which should be like the quills of porcupines,
As black as jet, and hard as iron or steel—
Bewrays they are too dainty for the wars.
Their fingers made to quaver on a lute,
Their arms to hang about a lady's neck,   30
Their legs to dance and caper in the air,
Would make me think them bastards, not my sons,
But that I know they issued from thy womb
That never looked on man but Tamburlaine.
Zenocrate. My gracious lord, they have their mother's looks,   35
But when they list, their conquering father's heart.
[*Indicating Celebinus*] This lovely boy, the youngest of
the three,
Not long ago bestrid a Scythian steed,
Trotting the ring, and tilting at a glove,
Which when he tainted with his slender rod,   40
He reined him straight and made him so curvet
As I cried out for fear he should have fall'n.
Tamburlaine. [*To Celebinus*] Well done, my boy. Thou shalt
have shield and lance,

---

22. *as*] as would befit.
23–4.] 'The moist and cold qualities of water (corresponding to the phleg-
matic humour) and the moist and hot qualities of air (corresponding to the
sanguine humour) argue ill for the temperament which is over-balanced in
these directions and lacks the firmness and fierceness due to a just admixture
of the bile and choler (earth and fire)' (Ellis-Fermor).
23. *symbolised*] mixed.
28. *Bewrays*] reveals (that).
39. *Trotting the ring*] riding in the equestrian schooling ring.
tilting . . . glove] jousting at a mark—here, a glove.
40. *tainted*] hit; a technical term from tilting.
41. *curvet*] an accomplished skill from the *manège*: to raise a horse's forelegs and execute a spring from the hindlegs before the forelegs touch the
ground.
42. *As*] that.

Armour of proof, horse, helm, and curtle-axe,
And I will teach thee how to charge thy foe   45
And harmless run among the deadly pikes.
If thou wilt love the wars and follow me,
Thou shalt be made a king and reign with me,
Keeping in iron cages emperors.
If thou exceed thy elder brothers' worth   50
And shine in complete virtue more than they,
Thou shalt be king before them, and thy seed
Shall issue crownèd from their mother's womb.
Celebinus. Yes, father, you shall see me, if I live,
Have under me as many kings as you,   55
And march with such a multitude of men
As all the world shall tremble at their view.
Tamburlaine. These words assure me, boy, thou art my son.
When I am old and cannot manage arms,
Be thou the scourge and terror of the world.   60
Amyras. Why may not I, my lord, as well as he,
Be termed the scourge and terror of the world?
Tamburlaine. Be all a scourge and terror to the world,
Or else you are not sons of Tamburlaine.
Calyphas. But while my brothers follow arms, my lord,   65
Let me accompany my gracious mother.
They are enough to conquer all the world,
And you have won enough for me to keep.
Tamburlaine. Bastardly boy, sprung from some coward's loins
And not the issue of great Tamburlaine,   70
Of all the provinces I have subdued
Thou shalt not have a foot unless thou bear
A mind courageous and invincible;
For he shall wear the crown of Persia
Whose head hath deepest scars, whose breast most
     wounds,   75

---

44. *Armour of proof*] armour of tried strength, proof-armour.
46. *harmless*] unharmed.
49.] alluding to the imprisonment of Bajazeth in Part One, which is also recalled at *Two* 5.2.19–20.
51. *in complete virtue*] in full manliness, valour; first syllable of *complete* stressed.
52–3. *thy seed . . . womb*] i.e. your children will inherit the kingdom, being named as heirs at birth.

Which, being wroth, sends lightning from his eyes,
And in the furrows of his frowning brows
Harbours revenge, war, death and cruelty.
For in a field whose superficies
Is covered with a liquid purple veil   80
And sprinkled with the brains of slaughtered men,
My royal chair of state shall be advanced;
And he that means to place himself therein
Must armèd wade up to the chin in blood.
Zenocrate. My lord, such speeches to our princely sons   85
　　Dismays their minds before they come to prove
　　The wounding troubles angry war affords.
Celebinus. No, madam, these are speeches fit for us,
　　For if his chair were in a sea of blood
　　I would prepare a ship and sail to it   90
　　Ere I would lose the title of a king.
Amyras. And I would strive to swim through pools of blood
　　Or make a bridge of murdered carcasses
　　Whose arches should be framed with bones of Turks,
　　Ere I would lose the title of a king.   95
Tamburlaine. Well, lovely boys, you shall be emperors both,
　　Stretching your conquering arms from east to west.
　　[*To Calyphas*] And, sirrah, if you mean to wear a crown,
　　When we shall meet the Turkish deputy
　　And all his viceroys, snatch it from his head   100
　　And cleave his pericranion with thy sword.
Calyphas. If any man will hold him, I will strike,
　　And cleave him to the channel with my sword.
Tamburlaine. Hold him and cleave him too, or I'll cleave thee,
　　For we will march against them presently.   105
　　Theridamas, Techelles, and Casane

---

79. *superficies*] surface; five syllables.
80. *purple*] i.e. blood-red.
82. *advanced*] lifted high.
86. *prove*] find by experience.
89. *if*] even if.
98. *sirrah*] a condescending form of address, used to subordinates and children.
101. *pericranion*] the skull, in Tamburlaine's mock-pedantic jest; technically, the pericranium is the membrane enveloping the skull.
103. *channel*] neck, throat.

Promised to meet me on Larissa plains
With hosts apiece against this Turkish crew,
For I have sworn by sacred Mahomet
To make it parcel of my empery.   110
The trumpets sound, Zenocrate! They come.

Enter THERIDAMAS *and his* train, *with drums and trumpets.*

Welcome, Theridamas, King of Argier.
Theridamas. My lord the great and mighty Tamburlaine,
Arch-monarch of the world, I offer here
My crown, myself, and all the power I have,   115
In all affection at thy kingly feet.
                              [*He presents his crown.*]
Tamburlaine. Thanks, good Theridamas.
Theridamas. Under my colours march ten thousand Greeks,
And of Argier and Afric's frontier towns
Twice twenty thousand valiant men-at-arms,   120
All which have sworn to sack Natolia;
Five hundred brigantines are under sail,
Meet for your service on the sea, my lord,
That, launching from Argier to Tripoli,
Will quickly ride before Natolia   125
And batter down the castles on the shore.
Tamburlaine. Well said, Argier; receive thy crown again.
                              [*He returns the crown.*]

Enter TECHELLES *and* USUMCASANE *together.*

Kings of Moroccus and of Fez, welcome.
Usumcasane. Magnificent and peerless Tamburlaine,
I and my neighbour King of Fez have brought,   130
To aid thee in this Turkish expedition,
A hundred thousand expert soldiers;

---

107. *Larissa plains*] Cf. 5n, above.
108. *hosts*] armies.
110. *parcel*] part.
122. *brigantines*] small ships.
123. *Meet*] fit.
125. *ride*] ride at anchor.
130. *King of Fez*] i.e. Techelles.
132. *expert*] tried, proved in battle.

From Azamor to Tunis near the sea
Is Barbary unpeopled for thy sake,
And all the men in armour under me,   135
Which with my crown I gladly offer thee.
                              [*He presents his crown.*]
Tamburlaine. Thanks, King of Moroccus; take your crown
       again.   [*He returns the crown.*]
Techelles. And, mighty Tamburlaine, our earthly god,
       Whose looks make this inferior world to quake,
       I here present thee with the crown of Fez,   140
                              [*He presents his crown.*]
And with an host of Moors trained to the war,
Whose coal-black faces make their foes retire
And quake for fear, as if infernal Jove,
Meaning to aid thee in these Turkish arms,
Should pierce the black circumference of hell   145
With ugly Furies bearing fiery flags
And millions of his strong tormenting spirits.
From strong Tesella unto Biledull
All Barbary is unpeopled for thy sake.
Tamburlaine. Thanks, King of Fez; take here thy crown
       again.   [*He returns the crown.*]   150
Your presence, loving friends and fellow kings,
Makes me to surfeit in conceiving joy.
If all the crystal gates of Jove's high court
Were opened wide, and I might enter in
To see the state and majesty of heaven,   155
It could not more delight me than your sight.
Now will we banquet on these plains a while
And after march to Turkey with our camp,
In number more than are the drops that fall
When Boreas rents a thousand swelling clouds,   160

---

133. *Azamor*] Azimur, town on the Atlantic coast of Morocco.
139. *inferior*] below the heavens.
143. *infernal Jove*] i.e. the ruler of Hades.
148. *Tesella*] south of Oran.
Biledull] Ortelius's Biledulgerid, a district in north Africa.
152.] fills me to the brim with present and future joy.
158. *camp*] army.
160. *Boreas*] the north wind.
rents] tears apart.

And proud Orcanes of Natolia
With all his viceroys shall be so afraid
That though the stones, as at Deucalion's flood,
Were turned to men, he should be overcome.
Such lavish will I make of Turkish blood   165
That Jove shall send his wingèd messenger
To bid me sheathe my sword and leave the field.
The sun, unable to sustain the sight,
Shall hide his head in Thetis' watery lap
And leave his steeds to fair Boötes' charge;   170
For half the world shall perish in this fight.
But now, my friends, let me examine ye.
How have ye spent your absent time from me?
Usumcasane. My lord, our men of Barbary have marched
Four hundred miles with armour on their backs   175
And lain in leaguer fifteen months and more.
For, since we left you at the Sultan's court,
We have subdued the southern Guallatia
And all the land unto the coast of Spain.
We kept the narrow Strait of Gibraltar   180
And made Canaria call us kings and lords;
Yet never did they recreate themselves
Or cease one day from war and hot alarms;
And therefore let them rest a while, my lord.
Tamburlaine. They shall, Casane, and 'tis time, i'faith.   185
Techelles. And I have marched along the river Nile

163–4. *stones . . . turned to men*] Men were reborn from stones thrown by
Deucalion and Pyrrha after the flood: cf. Ovid, *Metamorphoses*, I.318 ff.
    165. *lavish*] prodigal spilling.
    166. *his wingèd messenger*] Mercury.
    169. *Thetis*] a Nereid or sea-maiden, the sea personified.
    170. *Boötes*] a northern constellation, traditionally depicted as a driver of
oxen.
    176. *lain in leaguer*] encamped to besiege.
    178. *Guallatia*] Ortelius's 'Gualata', in the Libyan desert.
    180. *kept*] controlled; or sailed through.
    Gibraltar] stressed on first and third syllables.
    181. *Canaria*] the Canary Islands.
    182. *they recreate*] my soldiers refresh.
    186–205.] Marlowe constructs from Ortelius a route for Techelles's
conquests. He explores the Nile as far as Machda in Abyssinia where he
subdues the legendary Prester John. Then he follows the Nile to Cazates,

To Machda, where the mighty Christian priest
Called John the Great sits in a milk-white robe,
Whose triple mitre I did take by force
And made him swear obedience to my crown.   190
From thence unto Cazates did I march,
Where Amazonians met me in the field,
With whom, being women, I vouchsafed a league,
And with my power did march to Zanzibar,
The western part of Afric, where I viewed   195
The Ethiopian sea, rivers and lakes—
But neither man nor child in all the land!
Therefore I took my course to Manico,
Where, unresisted, I removed my camp.
And by the coast of Byather at last   200
I came to Cubar, where the negroes dwell,
And conquering that, made haste to Nubia.
There, having sacked Borno, the kingly seat,
I took the King and led him bound in chains
Unto Damasco, where I stayed before.   205
Tamburlaine. Well done, Techelles. What saith Theridamas?
Theridamas. I left the confines and the bounds of Afric
And made a voyage into Europe,
Where by the river Tyros I subdued
Stoka, Padalia, and Codemia;   210
Then crossed the sea and came to Oblia,
And Nigra Silva, where the devils dance,
Which in despite of them I set on fire.
From thence I crossed the gulf called by the name
Mare Maggiore of th'inhabitants.   215

---

near its source; he invades the huge Southern African province of Zanzibar
(as distinct from the island), then marches north to Manicongo (Byather
province), to Borno, near Tamburlaine's 'Borno lake' (*Two* 5.3.137).

189. *triple mitre*] papal tiara.

192. *Amazonians*] legendary female warriors of Scythia and elsewhere.

199. *removed*] located, having moved it from a previous place.

202. *Nubia*] south of Egypt.

209–15.] Stoko (Stoka) and Codemia are close to the Tyros (Dnieper), the
boundary of the province Podalia (Padalia). The dangers of the Black Forest
(Nigra Silva, 212), between Codemia and Olbia (Oblia), may have neces-
sitated an otherwise unnecessary sea-journey.

215. *Mare Maggiore*] the Black Sea.

Yet shall my soldiers make no period
Until Natolia kneel before your feet.
Tamburlaine. Then will we triumph, banquet, and carouse;
    Cooks shall have pensions to provide us cates
    And glut us with the dainties of the world.   220
    Lacryma Christi and Calabrian wines
    Shall common soldiers drink in quaffing bowls—
    Ay, liquid gold when we have conquered him,
    Mingled with coral and with orient pearl.
    Come, let us banquet and carouse the whiles.   *Exeunt.*   225

Finis Actus primi.

---

216. *period*] end, stop.
219. *pensions*] payments.
cates] delicacies.
221. *Lacryma Christi*] sweet red Italian wine; literally, 'Christ's tears'.
Calabrian] from Calabria, in Italy.
224. *orient pearl*] pearl from the Indian seas, brilliant pearl.

Act 2

[*Enter*] SIGISMOND, FREDERICK, BALDWIN, *with their* train.

Sigismond. Now say, my lords of Buda and Bohemia,
 What motion is it that inflames your thoughts
 And stirs your valours to such sudden arms?
Frederick. Your Majesty remembers, I am sure,
 What cruel slaughter of our Christian bloods   5
 These heathenish Turks and pagans lately made
 Betwixt the city Zula and Danubius;
 How through the midst of Varna and Bulgaria
 And almost to the very walls of Rome
 They have, not long since, massacred our camp.   10
 It resteth now, then, that Your Majesty
 Take all advantages of time and power,
 And work revenge upon these infidels.
 Your Highness knows for Tamburlaine's repair,
 That strikes a terror to all Turkish hearts,   15
 Natolia hath dismissed the greatest part
 Of all his army, pitched against our power
 Betwixt Cutheia and Orminius' mount,

2.1. Location: Buda, in Hungary, the old Magyar capital.

2. *motion*] impulse, emotion.

5. *bloods*] lives, people.

7. *Zula*] north of the Danube.

8. *Varna*] a Bulgarian seaport, evidently taken here as a region.

9. *Rome*] Romania.

11. *resteth*] remains to be done.

14. *for Tamburlaine's repair*] because of Tamburlaine's imminent approach.

16–17.] Orcanes has redeployed most of his troops from Eastern Europe to Turkey.

18. *Cutheia*] Kütalya, a region of Turkey.

Orminius' mount] See *Two* 2.2 location note.

And sent them marching up to Belgasar,
Acantha, Antioch, and Caesaria,   20
To aid the Kings of Soria and Jerusalem.
Now then, my lord, advantage take hereof,
And issue suddenly upon the rest,
That, in the fortune of their overthrow,
We may discourage all the pagan troop   25
That dare attempt to war with Christians.

Sigismond. But calls not, then, Your Grace to memory
The league we lately made with King Orcanes,
Confirmed by oath and articles of peace,
And calling Christ for record of our truths?   30
This should be treachery and violence
Against the grace of our profession.

Baldwin. No whit, my lord, for with such infidels,
In whom no faith nor true religion rests,
We are not bound to those accomplishments   35
The holy laws of Christendom enjoin;
But as the faith which they profanely plight
Is not by necessary policy
To be esteemed assurance for ourselves,
So what we vow to them should not infringe   40
Our liberty of arms and victory.

Sigismond. Though I confess the oaths they undertake
Breed little strength to our security,
Yet those infirmities that thus defame
Their faiths, their honours, and their religion   45
Should not give us presumption to the like.

19–20. *Belgasar, Acantha*] marked by Ortelius as Beglasar and Acanta, in
Natolia.

20. *Caesaria*] Caesarea, on the coast of present-day Israel, north of
Jerusalem.

30. *record . . . truths*] witness of our good faith.

31. *should be*] would be.

32. *profession*] religious beliefs. The proverbial 'No faith with heretics' was
detested by Protestants as one aspect of Roman Catholic 'equivocation'.

35. *accomplishments*] fulfilments of sworn promises.

38. *policy*] prudent statecraft—'Machiavellian' cant for political cunning
and treachery.

39. *assurance*] a trustworthy pledge.

Our faiths are sound, and must be consummate,
Religious, righteous, and inviolate.
Frederick. Assure Your Grace, 'tis superstition
    To stand so strictly on dispensive faith;   50
    And should we lose the opportunity
    That God hath given to venge our Christians' death
    And scourge their foul blasphemous paganism?
    As fell to Saul, to Balaam, and the rest
    That would not kill and curse at God's command,   55
    So surely will the vengeance of the Highest,
    And jealous anger of His fearful arm,
    Be poured with rigour on our sinful heads
    If we neglect this offered victory.
Sigismond. Then arm, my lords, and issue suddenly,   60
    Giving commandment to our general host
    With expedition to assail the pagan
    And take the victory our God hath given.   *Exeunt.*

SCENE 2

[*Enter*] ORCANES, GAZELLUS, URIBASSA, *with their* train.

Orcanes. Gazellus, Uribassa, and the rest,
    Now will we march from proud Orminius' mount
    To fair Natolia, where our neighbour kings
    Expect our power and our royal presence,
    T'encounter with the cruel Tamburlaine   5

---

47. *consummate*] perfect.
50. *dispensive faith*] pledge that can be broken at will.
53. *scourge*] In seeking to act as scourge for the Christian God, Frederick recalls Tamburlaine's first appeal to the concept at *One* 3.3.44.
54–9.] Saul loses the kingdom of Israel for disobeying God's command to destroy all the Amalekites. It is actually the Lord, speaking through Balaam's ass, and the angel rebuking him, that deters Balaam as he is about to curse the Israelites. See 1 Samuel 15, and Numbers 22 and 23.
62. *expedition*] haste.

2.2. Location: near Mount Orminius, in Transylvania (region of modern Romania). Orcanes has redeployed most of his troops to Turkey, with the result that he is under strength here. Orcanes himself is about to head for Natolia (3–5), to join in the fight against Tamburlaine.
4. *Expect our power*] await our army.

That nigh Larissa sways a mighty host,
And with the thunder of his martial tools
Makes earthquakes in the hearts of men and heaven.
Gazellus. And now come we to make his sinews shake
With greater power than erst his pride hath felt.   10
An hundred kings by scores will bid him arms,
And hundred thousands subjects to each score—
Which, if a shower of wounding thunderbolts
Should break out of the bowels of the clouds
And fall as thick as hail upon our heads   15
In partial aid of that proud Scythian,
Yet should our courages and steelèd crests
And numbers more than infinite of men
Be able to withstand and conquer him.
Uribassa. Methinks I see how glad the Christian king   20
Is made for joy of your admitted truce,
That could not but before be terrified
With unacquainted power of our host.

                    Enter a Messenger.

Messenger. Arm, dread sovereign and my noble lords!
The treacherous army of the Christians,   25
Taking advantage of your slender power,
Comes marching on us, and determines straight
To bid us battle for our dearest lives.
Orcanes. Traitors, villains, damnèd Christians!
Have I not here the articles of peace   30
And solemn covenants we have both confirmed,
He by his Christ, and I by Mahomet?
Gazellus. Hell and confusion light upon their heads

---

6. *sways*] commands.
10. *erst*] until now.
11. *by scores*] twenty at a time.
bid him arms] challenge him to combat.
12.] with a hundred thousand troops to each score of kings.
16. *partial*] biased.
21. *admitted*] granted.
23. *unacquainted*] unexampled.
24–6.] The contrast is sharp with Tamburlaine's assault on Cosroe's army immediately after joining forces with him: 'We will not steal upon him cowardly, / But give him warning and more warriors' (*One* 2.5.102–3).

That with such treason seek our overthrow
And cares so little for their prophet, Christ!   35
Orcanes. Can there be such deceit in Christians,
        Or treason in the fleshly heart of man,
        Whose shape is figure of the highest God?
        Then if there be a Christ, as Christians say—
        But in their deeds deny him for their Christ—   40
        If he be son to everliving Jove
        And hath the power of his outstretched arm,
        If he be jealous of his name and honour
        As is our holy prophet Mahomet,
        Take here these papers as our sacrifice   45
        And witness of Thy servant's perjury!
                [He tears to pieces the articles of peace.]
        Open, thou shining veil of Cynthia,
        And make a passage from th'empyreal heaven,
        That He that sits on high and never sleeps
        Nor in one place is circumscriptible,   50
        But everywhere fills every continent
        With strange infusion of His sacred vigour,
        May in His endless power and purity
        Behold and venge this traitor's perjury!
        Thou Christ, that art esteemed omnipotent,   55
        If thou wilt prove thyself a perfect God
        Worthy the worship of all faithful hearts,
        Be now revenged upon this traitor's soul
        And make the power I have left behind
        (Too little to defend our guiltless lives)   60
        Sufficient to discomfit and confound

---

38. *figure*] the likeness. Genesis 1.26: 'And God said, Let us make man in our image . . .'

42–3.] Cf. Exodus 7.5: 'And the Egyptians shall know that I am the Lord, when I stretch forth mine hand upon Egypt,' and 20.5: 'I the Lord thy God am a jealous God'.

47. *shining veil of Cynthia*] moonlit sky.

48. *empyreal heaven*] the empyrean; see *One* 2.7.15n.

50.] i.e. God cannot be limited to any one place.

59. *power*] army.

left behind] still remaining with me, not yet gone to Turkey (see headnote to scene).

61. *confound*] destroy.

The trustless force of those false Christians.
To arms, my lords! On Christ still let us cry!
If there be Christ, we shall have victory.   [*Exeunt.*]

[SCENE 3]

Sound [trumpets] to the battle [within], and SIGISMOND
comes out wounded.

Sigismond. Discomfited is all the Christian host,
     And God hath thundered vengeance from on high
     For my accurst and hateful perjury.
     O just and dreadful punisher of sin,
     Let the dishonour of the pains I feel   5
     In this my mortal well-deservèd wound
     End all my penance in my sudden death;
     And let this death wherein to sin I die
     Conceive a second life in endless mercy.   [*He dies.*]

          Enter ORCANES, GAZELLUS, URIBASSA, *with others.*

Orcanes. Now lie the Christians bathing in their bloods,   10
     And Christ or Mahomet hath been my friend.
Gazellus. See here the perjured traitor Hungary,
     Bloody and breathless for his villainy!
Orcanes Now shall his barbarous body be a prey
     To beasts and fowls, and all the winds shall breathe   15
     Through shady leaves of every senseless tree
     Murmurs and hisses for his heinous sin.
     Now scalds his soul in the Tartarian streams
     And feeds upon the baneful tree of hell,
     That Zoacum, that fruit of bitterness,   20

---

62. *trustless*] treacherous.
63. *still*] continually.

2.3. Location: as in 2.2.
8. *wherein . . . I die*] by which I cease to be capable of sinning.
9. *Conceive*] bring about.
18. *Tartarian*] in Tartarus, an abyss of Hades reserved for evildoers.
19. *baneful*] poisonous, deadly.
19–23.] The Koran tells of this mythical tree. Marlowe follows the
detailed description given in Lonicerus' Latin *Chronicorum Turcorum* (1578).

That in the midst of fire is ingraft,
Yet flourisheth as Flora in her pride,
With apples like the heads of damnèd fiends.
The devils there in chains of quenchless flame
Shall lead his soul through Orcus' burning gulf   25
From pain to pain, whose change shall never end.
What say'st thou yet, Gazellus, to his foil,
Which we referred to justice of his Christ
And to His power, which here appears as full
As rays of Cynthia to the clearest sight?   30
Gazellus. 'Tis but the fortune of the wars, my lord,
   Whose power is often proved a miracle.
Orcanes. Yet in my thoughts shall Christ be honourèd,
   Not doing Mahomet an injury,
   Whose power had share in this our victory;   35
   And since this miscreant hath disgraced his faith
   And died a traitor both to heaven and earth,
   We will both watch and ward shall keep his trunk
   Amidst these plains for fowls to prey upon.
   Go, Uribassa, give it straight in charge.   40
Uribassa. I will, my lord.
                  Exit URIBASSA [*and others, with the body*].
Orcanes. And now, Gazellus, let us haste and meet
   Our army, and our brother of Jerusalem,
   Of Soria, Trebizond, and Amasia,
   And happily with full Natolian bowls   45

---

22. *Flora*] the Roman goddess of flowers.

25. *Orcus'*] hell's.

26. *whose . . . end*] i.e. the torment will vary endlessly but will itself be endless.

27. *foil*] overthrow; disgrace.

30. *Cynthia*] the moon.

32. *proved a miracle*] offered as demonstration of miraculous agency, the fortunes of war being unforeseeable.

36. *miscreant*] heretic, misbeliever.

38.] I order continuous lookout and guard so that his corpse remains here.

40. *give . . . charge*] see to it immediately.

43. *Our army*] i.e. the main part of the army that Orcanes has sent ahead against Tamburlaine; see headnote to this scene.

brother] fellow-kings. A typical plural form.

44. *Amasia*] a province in northern Asia Minor.

Of Greekish wine now let us celebrate
Our happy conquest, and his angry fate.   *Exeunt.*

SCENE 4

The arras is drawn, and ZENOCRATE *lies in her bed of
state,* TAMBURLAINE *sitting by her; three* Physicians *about
her bed, tempering potions.* THERIDAMAS, TECHELLES,
USUMCASANE, *and the* three sons [CALYPHAS, AMYRAS,
CELEBINUS].

Tamburlaine. Black is the beauty of the brightest day!
    The golden ball of heaven's eternal fire,
    That danced with glory on the silver waves,
    Now wants the fuel that inflamed his beams,
    And all with faintness and for foul disgrace   5
    He binds his temples with a frowning cloud,
    Ready to darken earth with endless night.
    Zenocrate, that gave him light and life,
    Whose eyes shot fire from their ivory bowers
    And tempered every soul with lively heat,   10
    Now by the malice of the angry skies,
    Whose jealousy admits no second mate,
    Draws in the comfort of her latest breath
    All dazzled with the hellish mists of death.
    Now walk the angels on the walls of heaven,   15
    As sentinels to warn th'immortal souls

---

47. *his*] Sigismond's.

2.4. Location: near Larissa (El Arish).

0.1. The arras is drawn] i.e. a curtain is drawn open across the discovery
space, or some removable curtained booth.

0.3. *tempering*] concocting, mixing.

2.] i.e. the sun.

4. *wants*] lacks.

9. *bowers*] i.e. eye-sockets.

10. *tempered*] refreshed, gave health to. Cf. 0.3. The word suggests
alchemical mystery.

12. *admits . . . mate*] allows no rival to the power of the gods.

13.] draws comfort from her final mortal breath.

14. *dazzled with*] overcome by.

To entertain divine Zenocrate.
Apollo, Cynthia, and the ceaseless lamps
That gently looked upon this loathsome earth
Shine downwards now no more, but deck the heavens   20
To entertain divine Zenocrate.
The crystal springs whose taste illuminates
Refinèd eyes with an eternal sight
Like trièd silver runs through Paradise
To entertain divine Zenocrate.   25
The cherubins and holy seraphins
That sing and play before the King of Kings
Use all their voices and their instruments
To entertain divine Zenocrate.
And in this sweet and curious harmony   30
The God that tunes this music to our souls
Holds out his hand in highest majesty
To entertain divine Zenocrate.
Then let some holy trance convey my thoughts
Up to the palace of th'empyreal heaven,   35
That this my life may be as short to me
As are the days of sweet Zenocrate.—
Physicians, will no physic do her good?
Physician. My lord, Your Majesty shall soon perceive;
An if she pass this fit, the worst is past.   40
Tamburlaine. [*To Zenocrate*] Tell me, how fares my fair
    Zenocrate?

---

17. *entertain*] receive, welcome.

18.] sun, moon, and stars.

22–5.] principally invoking Revelation 22.1: 'And he showed me a pure river of water of life, clear as a crystal, proceeding out of the throne of God and of the Lamb'. Celebrating eloquence and harmony, the lines may also allude to Aganippe, the fountain on Mount Helicon, sacred to the Muses.

24. *trièd*] purified, refined. The springs of vision which purge mortal sight are crystal, like Zenocrate herself in love's eyes, and they share beneficent virtue with the pure fire of her spirit (9–10), and with the paradisal music— metaphysical and actual—which is tuned to the human spirit. Harmony, beauty, 'measure', health, are all in creative relation.

30. *curious*] exquisite, elaborately wrought, associating with the 'en-chased' gems and embroideries of actual and metaphoric artistry.

38. *physic*] medicine.

40. *An if*] if.

fit] severe period of illness, crisis.

Zenocrate. I fare, my lord, as other empresses,
    That, when this frail and transitory flesh
    Hath sucked the measure of that vital air
    That feeds the body with his dated health,   45
    Wanes with enforced and necessary change.
Tamburlaine. May never such a change transform my love,
    In whose sweet being I repose my life,
    Whose heavenly presence, beautified with health,
    Gives light to Phoebus and the fixèd stars,   50
    Whose absence makes the sun and moon as dark
    As when, opposed in one diameter,
    Their spheres are mounted on the Serpent's head
    Or else descended to his winding train.
    Live still, my love, and so conserve my life,   55
    Or, dying, be the author of my death.
Zenocrate. Live still, my lord, Oh, let my sovereign live,
    And sooner let the fiery element
    Dissolve, and make your kingdom in the sky,
    Than this base earth should shroud your majesty!   60
    For, should I but suspect your death by mine,
    The comfort of my future happiness
    And hope to meet Your Highness in the heavens,
    Turned to despair, would break my wretched breast,
    And fury would confound my present rest.   65
    But let me die, my love, yet let me die;
    With love and patience let your true love die.
    Your grief and fury hurts my second life.
    Yet let me kiss my lord before I die,
    And let me die with kissing of my lord.   [*They kiss.*]   70

---

45. *dated*] having a fixed period.

52–6.] a standard description of lunar eclipse: when the sun and moon are diametrically opposed on two sides of the earth, as the ascending moon crosses the ecliptic at the Serpent's head, or else in its descending mode at the Serpent's tail. The *Serpent* is probably the constellation Scorpio, in the Zodiac, but it could be Hydra, or Serpens, which is divided into *Serpens Caput* and *Serpens Cauda*, head and tail.

58–9. *let . . . sky*] may the sphere of fire, which encloses the regions of the air, come to an end, and may you make your kingdom among the heavenly spheres which lie beyond it.

61. *by*] would be caused by.

68. *second life*] immortal life after death.

But since my life is lengthened yet a while,
Let me take leave of these my loving sons
And of my lords, whose true nobility
Have merited my latest memory.
Sweet sons, farewell! In death resemble me,   75
And in your lives your father's excellency.—
Some music, and my fit will cease, my lord.

They call [*for*] *music.*

Tamburlaine. Proud fury and intolerable fit
That dares torment the body of my love
And scourge the scourge of the immortal God!   80
Now are those spheres where Cupid used to sit,
Wounding the world with wonder and with love,
Sadly supplied with pale and ghastly Death
Whose darts do pierce the centre of my soul.
Her sacred beauty hath enchanted heaven,   85
And, had she lived before the siege of Troy,
Helen, whose beauty summoned Greece to arms
And drew a thousand ships to Tenedos,
Had not been named in Homer's Iliads;
Her name had been in every line he wrote.   90
Or had those wanton poets, for whose birth
Old Rome was proud, but gazed a while on her,
Nor Lesbia nor Corinna had been named;
Zenocrate had been the argument
Of every epigram or elegy.   95

The music sounds, and she dies.

What, is she dead? Techelles, draw thy sword,
And wound the earth, that it may cleave in twain,

---

74. *latest memory*] last act of remembering.
81. *those spheres*] i.e. her eyes.
84. *Whose darts*] i.e. Death's, in place of those which Cupid once fired
from Zenocrate's eyes.
87–8.] recalled in Faustus's praise of Helen of Troy: *Dr Faustus*, A-text,
5.1.90–1.
88. *Tenedos*] base of the Greek fleet for the Trojan war.
90. *Her*] Zenocrate's.
91. *wanton*] lascivious, sensual.
92. *but*] only.
93. *Nor*] neither.
Lesbia . . . Corinna] in the 'wanton' poetry of Catullus and Ovid.

And we descend into th'infernal vaults
To hale the Fatal Sisters by the hair
And throw them in the triple moat of hell,   100
For taking hence my fair Zenocrate.
Casane and Theridamas, to arms!
Raise cavalieros higher than the clouds,
And with the cannon break the frame of heaven,
Batter the shining palace of the sun   105
And shiver all the starry firmament;
For amorous Jove hath snatched my love from hence,
Meaning to make her stately queen of heaven.
[*To Zenocrate's body*] What god soever holds thee in his
    arms,
Giving thee nectar and ambrosia,   110
Behold me here, divine Zenocrate,
Raving, impatient, desperate and mad,
Breaking my steelèd lance with which I burst
The rusty beams of Janus' temple doors,
Letting out death and tyrannising war,   115
To march with me under this bloody flag;
And if thou pitiest Tamburlaine the Great,
Come down from heaven and live with me again!
Theridamas. Ah, good my lord, be patient. She is dead,
And all this raging cannot make her live.   120
If words might serve, our voice hath rent the air;
If tears, our eyes have watered all the earth;
If grief, our murdered hearts have strained forth blood.
Nothing prevails, for she is dead, my lord.
Tamburlaine. 'For she is dead!' Thy words do pierce my soul. 125
Ah, sweet Theridamas, say so no more.
Though she be dead, yet let me think she lives,
And feed my mind that dies for want of her.

---

98. *And we*] and so that we may.

99. *Fatal Sisters*] the Fates; cf. *One* 5.1.455n.

100. *triple moat*] Lethe, Styx and Phlegethon, the rivers of Hades.

103. *cavalieros*] commanding redoubts in a fortress.

114. *rusty*] Cf. the 'rusty coach' of Darkness at *One* 5.1.294, and the 'rusty gates of hell' at *Two* 5.1.96.

Janus' temple doors] The temple of Janus, god of doorways, in the Roman Forum, stood open in time of war, and was closed in peacetime.

Where'er her soul be, [*Turning to address her body*] thou
   shalt stay with me,
Embalmed with cassia, ambergris, and myrrh,   130
Not lapped in lead, but in a sheet of gold,
And till I die thou shalt not be interred.
Then, in as rich a tomb as Mausolus',
We both will rest and have one epitaph
Writ in as many several languages   135
As I have conquered kingdoms with my sword.
This cursèd town will I consume with fire
Because this place bereft me of my love;
The houses, burnt, will look as if they mourned,
And here will I set up her statua   140
And march about it with my mourning camp,
Drooping and pining for Zenocrate.

                   The arras is drawn. [*Exeunt.*]

          [*Finis Actus secundi.*]

---

    129. *her . . . thou*] a telling shift of focus, as Tamburlaine turns to address
his dead queen.

    130. *cassia*] fragrant plant.

    133. *Mausolus'*] The tomb of Mausolus, King of Caria, fourth century
B.C., was one of the seven wonders of the world. Timur's own mausoleum
survives in Samarkand.

    135. *several*] different.

    140. *statua*] effigy.

Act 3

Enter the Kings of TREBIZOND *and* SORIA, *one bringing a*
sword, and another a sceptre; next [ORCANES *of*]
NATOLIA and JERUSALEM *with the imperial crown; after,*
CALLAPINE, *and after him other* Lords [*and* ALMEDA.]
Orcanes and Jerusalem crown him [*Callapine*], *and the*
other[*s*] *give him the sceptre.*

Orcanes. Callapinus Cyricelibes, otherwise Cybelius, son and
successive heir to the late mighty emperor Bajazeth, by
the aid of God and his friend Mahomet Emperor of
Natolia, Jerusalem, Trebizond, Soria, Amasia, Thracia,
Illyria, Carmonia, and all the hundred and thirty king-   5
doms late contributory to his mighty father: long live
Callapinus, Emperor of Turkey!
Callapine. Thrice worthy Kings of Natolia, and the rest,
I will requite your royal gratitudes
With all the benefits my empire yields;   10
And were the sinews of th'imperial seat
So knit and strengthened as when Bajazeth
My royal lord and father filled the throne,
Whose cursèd fate hath so dismembered it,
Then should you see this thief of Scythis,   15
This proud usurping King of Persia,
Do us such honour and supremacy,
Bearing the vengeance of our father's wrongs,

3.1. Location: at the Turkish court.

5. *Carmonia*] Carmania, on the borders of Natolia and Syria.

17.] acknowledge us with honour as supreme.

18.] either: (1) we bearing the obligation to avenge the wrong done to
Bajazeth; or (2) Tamburlaine, undergoing punishment in revenge for his
abuse of Bajazeth.

As all the world should blot our dignities
Out of the book of baseborn infamies.   20
And now I doubt not but your royal cares
Hath so provided for this cursèd foe
That, since the heir of mighty Bajazeth
(An emperor so honoured for his virtues)
Revives the spirits of true Turkish hearts   25
In grievous memory of his father's shame,
We shall not need to nourish any doubt
But that proud Fortune, who hath followed long
The martial sword of mighty Tamburlaine,
Will now retain her old inconstancy   30
And raise our honours to as high a pitch
In this our strong and fortunate encounter.
For so hath heaven provided my escape
From all the cruelty my soul sustained,
By this my friendly keeper's happy means,   35
That Jove, surcharged with pity of our wrongs,
Will pour it down in showers on our heads,
Scourging the pride of cursèd Tamburlaine.
Orcanes. I have a hundred thousand men in arms—
Some that, in conquest of the perjured Christian,   40
Being a handful to a mighty host,
Think them in number yet sufficient
To drink the river Nile or Euphrates,
And, for their power, enough to win the world.
Jerusalem. And I as many from Jerusalem,   45
Judaea, Gaza, and Scalonia's bounds,
That on Mount Sinai with their ensigns spread
Look like the parti-coloured clouds of heaven

19–20.] i.e. so that the world would delete our exalted names from the roll
of infamy (on which the ill-usage of Bajazeth had inscribed them).

30.] i.e. Fortune, notorious in her inconstancy, will now change and
favour us.

32. *fortunate*] engineered by Fortune; a stronger sense than our 'lucky'.

36. *surcharged*] filled to the brim.

37. *it*] pity.

40–1.] the small army that scourged Sigismond's 'mighty host' in *Two* 2.3.

42. *them*] themselves.

46. *Scalonia*] Ascalon, on the coast of present-day Israel, south of Jaffa.

That show fair weather to the neighbour morn.
Trebizond. And I as many bring from Trebizond,   50
    Chio, Famastro, and Amasia,
    All bord'ring on the Mare-Major sea,
    Riso, Sancina, and the bordering towns,
    That touch the end of famous Euphrates,
    Whose courages are kindled with the flames   55
    The cursèd Scythian sets on all their towns,
    And vow to burn the villain's cruel heart.
Soria. From Soria with seventy thousand strong,
    Ta'en from Aleppo, Soldino, Tripoli,
    And so unto my city of Damasco,   60
    I march to meet and aid my neighbour kings,
    All which will join against this Tamburlaine
    And bring him captive to Your Highness' feet.
Orcanes. Our battle, then, in martial manner pitched,
    According to our ancient use shall bear   65
    The figure of the semicircled moon,
    Whose horns shall sprinkle through the tainted air
    The poisoned brains of this proud Scythian.
Callapine. Well then, my noble lords, for this my friend
    That freed me from the bondage of my foe,   70
    I think it requisite and honourable
    To keep my promise and to make him king,
    That is a gentleman, I know, at least.
Almeda. That's no matter, sir, for being a king,
    For Tamburlaine came up of nothing.   75

50–4. *from   Trebizond... Euphrates*] 'For   the   king   of   Trebizond,
Marlowe's finger traces from west to east the northern seaboard of Asia
Minor: Chia, Famastro, Riso, Sanzina' (Seaton). *Euphrates* is accented on the
first syllable.

52. *the Mare-Major sea*] the Black Sea.

55–6.] whose valour is kindled by the burning of their towns.

58–60.] 'For the king of Soria, Marlowe passes from Aleppo south-
westward to the sea-coast near Cyprus, and chooses Soldino and Tripoli, and
so inland again to Damasco' (Seaton).

64–6.] i.e. Our armies will adopt a crescent formation.

69. *for*] as for.

74.] i.e. promoting Callapine to be king is a relatively easy matter.

74–80.] The skilfully-phased decline into banality and prosaic rhythms
recalls aptly the scenes featuring Mycetes in Part One.

Jerusalem. Your Majesty may choose some 'pointed time,
  Performing all your promise to the full.
  'Tis nought for Your Majesty to give a kingdom.
Callapine. Then will I shortly keep my promise, Almeda.
Almeda. Why, I thank Your Majesty.   *Exeunt.*   80

SCENE 2

[*Enter*] TAMBURLAINE [*bearing a portrait of Zenocrate*] *with*
USUMCASANE, *and his three* sons [CALYPHAS, AMYRAS,
CELEBINUS, *bearing a memorial pillar, a black pennon, and
an inscribed tablet*]; *four* [Soldiers] *bearing the hearse of
Zenocrate, and the drums sounding a doleful march,
the town burning.*

Tamburlaine. So burn the turrets of this cursèd town!
  Flame to the highest region of the air
  And kindle heaps of exhalations
  That, being fiery meteors, may presage
  Death and destruction to th'inhabitants.   5
  Over my zenith hang a blazing star
  That may endure till heaven be dissolved,
  Fed with the fresh supply of earthly dregs,
  Threat'ning a death and famine to this land.
  Flying dragons, lightning, fearful thunderclaps,   10
  Singe these fair plains, and make them seem as black
  As is the island where the Furies mask,
  Compassed with Lethe, Styx, and Phlegethon,
  Because my dear Zenocrate is dead.
Calyphas. This pillar placed in memory of her,   15
  Where in Arabian, Hebrew, Greek, is writ,

3.2. Location: near Larissa.

1. *this ... town*] i.e. Larissa.

2. *Flame*] burn, blaze (a verb, not a noun).

2–10.] The *exhalations*, lighter than 'vapours', are, in standard Renaissance meteorology, drawn up to the highest region and ignited by the
neighbouring element of fire, and manifest themselves to the eye as dragons,
spears, etc.

6.] may a comet hang over my point of dominant astrological influence.

12. *mask*] lurk unseen.

13.] encompassed or surrounded by Hades's three rivers.

> *This town being burnt by Tamburlaine the Great*
> *Forbids the world to build it up again.*

Amyras. And here this mournful streamer shall be placed,
　　Wrought with the Persian and Egyptian arms　　　　20
　　To signify she was a princess born
　　And wife unto the monarch of the East.
Celebinus. And here this table as a register
　　Of all her virtues and perfections.
Tamburlaine. And here the picture of Zenocrate,　　　25
　　To show her beauty which the world admired—
　　Sweet picture of divine Zenocrate
　　That, hanging here, will draw the gods from heaven
　　And cause the stars fixed in the southern arc,
　　Whose lovely faces never any viewed　　　　30
　　That have not passed the centre's latitude,
　　As pilgrims travel to our hemisphere
　　Only to gaze upon Zenocrate.
　　[*To the hearse*] Thou shalt not beautify Larissa plains,
　　But keep within the circle of mine arms!　　　　35
　　At every town and castle I besiege
　　Thou shalt be set upon my royal tent,
　　And when I meet an army in the field
　　Those looks will shed such influence in my camp
　　As if Bellona, goddess of the war,　　　　40
　　Threw naked swords and sulphur balls of fire
　　Upon the heads of all our enemies.
　　And now, my lords, advance your spears again.
　　Sorrow no more, my sweet Casane, now;
　　Boys, leave to mourn. This town shall ever mourn,　　　45
　　Being burnt to cinders for your mother's death.
Calyphas. If I had wept a sea of tears for her,
　　It would not ease the sorrow I sustain.
Amyras. As is that town, so is my heart consumed

---

　20. *Wrought*] decorated.
　23. *table*] memorial tablet.
　29–33.] The stars of the southern hemisphere (*arc*) will become visible in northern latitudes when they cross the Equator as pilgrims to gaze on the portrait of Zenocrate.
　43. *advance*] raise aloft.
　45. *leave*] cease.

With grief and sorrow for my mother's death.   50
Celebinus. My mother's death hath mortified my mind,
    And sorrow stops the passage of my speech.
Tamburlaine. But now, my boys, leave off and list to me,
    That mean to teach you rudiments of war.
    I'll have you learn to sleep upon the ground,   55
    March in your armour thorough watery fens,
    Sustain the scorching heat and freezing cold,
    Hunger and thirst—right adjuncts of the war;
    And after this, to scale a castle wall,
    Besiege a fort, to undermine a town,   60
    And make whole cities caper in the air.
    Then next, the way to fortify your men;
    In champian grounds what figure serves you best,
    For which the quinque-angle form is meet,
    Because the corners there may fall more flat   65
    Whereas the fort may fittest be assailed,
    And sharpest where th'assault is desperate.
    The ditches must be deep, the counterscarps
    Narrow and steep, the walls made high and broad,
    The bulwarks and the rampiers large and strong,   70

55–92.] Marlowe draws directly on the technical information in Paul Ive's
Practise of Fortification, 19. In the National Theatre production of 1976, this
densely technical speech was given authentic human point by its being
spoken very rapidly, up to a moment of breathlessness, as if Tamburlaine
knew it by heart and now recited it to allay grief over the death of Zenocrate.

56. *thorough*] through.

58. *right*] fit.

61. *caper*] i.e. having been blown up.

63. *champian*] level and open.

figure] lay-out of fortification.

64–7.] i.e. in country *other than* level and open, where the star-shape is
best suited because its strong and weak points may be placed so as to take
advantage of the inequalities of the terrain, which render some sections more
assailable than others (Kocher).

66. *Whereas*] where.

68–9. *counterscarps . . . steep.*] The outermost ring of defence (detailed in
75 below) must have earthworks that are *steep* and a covered way that is
narrow.

70. *bulwarks*] earthworks projecting outward from the fort at each angle
as artillery bases.

rampiers] ramparts supporting the walls from behind.

With cavalieros and thick counterforts,
And room within to lodge six thousand men.
It must have privy ditches, countermines,
And secret issuings to defend the ditch;
It must have high argins and covered ways   75
To keep the bulwark fronts from battery,
And parapets to hide the musketeers,
Casemates to place the great artillery,
And store of ordnance, that from every flank
May scour the outward curtains of the fort,   80
Dismount the cannon of the adverse part,
Murder the foe, and save the walls from breach.
When this is learned for service on the land,
By plain and easy demonstration
I'll teach you how to make the water mount,   85
That you may dry-foot march through lakes and pools,
Deep rivers, havens, creeks, and little seas,
And make a fortress in the raging waves,
Fenced with the concave of a monstrous rock,
Invincible by nature of the place.   90
When this is done, then are ye soldiers,
And worthy sons of Tamburlaine the Great.
Calyphas. My lord, but this is dangerous to be done.
   We may be slain or wounded ere we learn.
Tamburlaine. Villain, art thou the son of Tamburlaine,   95
   And fear'st to die, or with a curtle-axe

---

71. *cavalieros*] commanding artillery platforms within a fortification.
counterforts] braces strengthening the walls on the inside.
73. *privy ditches*] deeper ditches set into the main ditch.
countermines] tunnels used to counter enemy mining operations.
74. *secret issuings*] small doorways to permit defensive sallies.
75. *argins*] earthworks shielding ('covering') infantry.
76.] to protect the earthworks from enemy artillery.
77. *parapets*] defences formed by the difference in height between wall
and rampart.
78. *Casemates*] vaults within the ramparts.
80. *curtains*] fortified walls.
81. *Dismount*] throw down from their carriages.
adverse part] enemy.
85. *mount*] rise (by damming).
86. *That*] so that.

To hew thy flesh and make a gaping wound?
Hast thou beheld a peal of ordnance strike
A ring of pikes, mingled with shot and horse,
Whose shattered limbs, being tossed as high as heaven,   100
Hang in the air as thick as sunny motes,
And canst thou, coward, stand in fear of death?
Hast thou not seen my horsemen charge the foe,
Shot through the arms, cut overthwart the hands,
Dyeing their lances with their streaming blood,   105
And yet at night carouse within my tent,
Filling their empty veins with airy wine
That, being concocted, turns to crimson blood—
And wilt thou shun the field for fear of wounds?
View me, thy father, that hath conquered kings   110
And with his host marched round about the earth
Quite void of scars and clear from any wound,
That by the wars lost not a dram of blood,
And see him lance his flesh to teach you all.

He cuts his arm.

A wound is nothing, be it ne'er so deep.   115
Blood is the god of war's rich livery.
Now look I like a soldier, and this wound
As great a grace and majesty to me
As if a chair of gold enamellèd,
Enchased with diamonds, sapphires, rubies,   120
And fairest pearl of wealthy India,
Were mounted here under a canopy,
And I sat down, clothed with the massy robe
That late adorned the Afric potentate
Whom I brought bound unto Damascus' walls.   125

---

98. *peal*] volley, discharge (of cannon).
99.] a defensive ring of pikemen, supported by infantry with small fire-arms, and closely flanked by cavalry (an orthodox military disposition).
104. *overthwart*] across.
107. *airy*] elementally hot and moist, like blood.
107–8.] an elaboration of the commonplace 'Good wine makes good blood'.
114. *lance*] gash.
120. *Enchased*] set.
124. *late*] lately.
the Afric potentate] Bajazeth, conqueror of Africa.

Come, boys, and with your fingers search my wound
And in my blood wash all your hands at once,
While I sit smiling to behold the sight.

                                      [*They touch his wound.*]

　　Now, my boys, what think you of a wound?

Calyphas. I know not what I should think of it.　　　　130
　　Methinks 'tis a pitiful sight.

Celbinus. 'Tis nothing. Give me a wound, father.

Amyras. And me another, my lord.

Tamburlaine. [*To Celebinus*] Come, sirrah, give me your arm.

Celebinus. Here, father, cut it bravely as you did your own.　　135

Tamburlaine. It shall suffice thou dar'st abide a wound.
　　My boy, thou shalt not lose a drop of blood
　　Before we meet the army of the Turk;
　　But then, run desperate through the thickest throngs,
　　Dreadless of blows, of bloody wounds and death;　　140
　　And let the burning of Larissa walls,
　　My speech of war, and this my wound you see,
　　Teach you, my boys, to bear courageous minds
　　Fit for the followers of great Tamburlaine.
　　Usumcasane, now come let us march　　　　145
　　Towards Techelles and Theridamas,
　　That we have sent before to fire the towns,
　　The towers and cities of these hateful Turks,
　　And hunt that coward, faint-heart, runaway,
　　With that accursèd traitor Almeda,　　　　150
　　Till fire and sword have found them at a bay.

Usumcasane. I long to pierce his bowels with my sword
　　That hath betrayed my gracious sovereign,
　　That curst and damnèd traitor Almeda.

Tamburlaine. Then let us see if coward Callapine　　155
　　Dare levy arms against our puissance,
　　That we may tread upon his captive neck
　　And treble all his father's slaveries.　　　　*Exeunt.*

---

126. *search*] probe.
135. *bravely*] well, boldly.
149. *coward . . . runaway*] i.e. Callapine.
151. *at a bay*] at bay.
156. *puissance*] power; trisyllabic.

SCENE 3

[*Enter*] TECHELLES, THERIDAMAS, *and their* train
[Soldiers *and* Pioners].

Theridamas. Thus have we marched northward from
    Tamburlaine
    Unto the frontier point of Soria;
    And this is Balsera, their chiefest hold,
    Wherein is all the treasure of the land.
Techelles. Then let us bring our light artillery,   5
    Minions, falc'nets, and sakers, to the trench,
    Filling the ditches with the walls' wide breach,
    And enter in to seize upon the gold.
    How say ye, soldiers, shall we not?
Soldiers. Yes, my lord, yes! Come, let's about it.   10
Theridamas. But stay a while. Summon a parley, drum.
    It may be they will yield it quietly,
    Knowing two kings, the friends to Tamburlaine,
    Stand at the walls with such a mighty power.

    Summon the battle [*with a drum*]. [*Enter above, on the fortress
    walls,*] Captain *with his wife* [OLYMPIA] *and* son.

Captain. What require you, my masters?   15
Theridamas. Captain, that thou yield up thy hold to us.
Captain. To you! Why, do you think me weary of it?
Techelles. Nay, captain, thou art weary of thy life
    If thou withstand the friends of Tamburlaine.
Theridamas. These pioners of Argier in Africa   20
    Even in the cannon's face shall raise a hill
    Of earth and faggots higher than thy fort,

3.3. Location: at Balsera, a town not clearly identified, on the Natolian
frontier of Soria.
    3. *hold*] stronghold, as in 48 below.
    6. *Minions . . . sakers*] small cannon of various types and sizes.
    14.1. *the battle*] to the conflict. The *battle* is the armed forces.
    14.1–2. Enter . . . son] The besieged Captain speaks from 'the walls' down
to the main stage.
    16. *hold*] inner fortress, as in 24 below.
    20. *pioners*] sappers, tunnel-diggers.
    21. *Even . . . face*] right under enemy fire.
    22. *faggots*] bundles of tree-branches.

And over thy argins and covered ways
Shall play upon the bulwarks of thy hold
Volleys of ordnance till the breach be made   25
That with his ruin fills up all the trench;
And when we enter in, not heaven itself
Shall ransom thee, thy wife, and family.

Techelles. Captain, these Moors shall cut the leaden pipes
That bring fresh water to thy men and thee,   30
And lie in trench before thy castle walls,
That no supply of victual shall come in,
Nor any issue forth but they shall die.
And therefore, captain, yield it quietly.

Captain. Were you that are the friends of Tamburlaine   35
Brothers to holy Mahomet himself,
I would not yield it. Therefore, do your worst:
Raise mounts, batter, intrench, and undermine,
Cut off the water, all convoys that can,
Yet I am resolute; and so, farewell.   *Exeunt [above].*   40

Theridamas. Pioners, away! And where I stuck the stake,
Intrench with those dimensions I prescribed.
Cast up the earth towards the castle wall,
Which, till it may defend you, labour low,
And few or none shall perish by their shot.   45

Pioners. We will, my lord.   *Exeunt [Pioners].*

Techelles. A hundred horse shall scout about the plains
To spy what force comes to relieve the hold.
Both we, Theridamas, will intrench our men,
And with the Jacob's staff measure the height   50
And distance of the castle from the trench,
That we may know if our artillery

23–4. *argins and covered ways*] Cf. *Two* 3.2.75–6 and notes.
24. *bulwarks*] ramparts.
26. *his ruin*] its downfall.
31. *lie in trench*] lay siege while protected by a trench.
33. *any*] anyone.
38. *mounts*] earthworks.
39. *all . . . can*] what supply convoys you can.
44. *labour low*] i.e. keep low until your growing earthworks protect you.
49.] the two of us, Theridamas, will direct the digging and manning of trenches in front of the besieged stronghold.
50. *Jacob's staff*] a gunner's quadrant, used for range-finding.

Will carry full point-blank unto their walls.
Theridamas. Then see the bringing of our ordnance
    Along the trench into the battery,   55
    Where we will have gabions of six foot broad
    To save our cannoneers from musket shot,
    Betwixt which shall our ordnance thunder forth,
    And with the breach's fall, smoke, fire, and dust,
    The crack, the echo, and the soldiers' cry,   60
    Make deaf the air and dim the crystal sky.
Techelles. Trumpets and drums, alarum presently,
    And soldiers, play the men; the hold is yours!
                  [*Battle drums and trumpets. Exeunt.*]

[SCENE 4]

Enter the Captain *with his wife* [OLYMPIA] *and* Son.

Olympia. Come, good my lord, and let us haste from hence
    Along the cave that leads beyond the foe.
    No hope is left to save this conquered hold.
Captain. A deadly bullet gliding through my side
    Lies heavy on my heart; I cannot live.   5
    I feel my liver pierced, and all my veins
    That there begin and nourish every part
    Mangled and torn, and all my entrails bathed
    In blood that straineth from their orifex.
    Farewell, sweet wife! Sweet son, farewell! I die.   10
                  [*He dies.*]
Olympia. Death, whither art thou gone, that both we live?
    Come back again, sweet Death, and strike us both!
    One minute end our days, and one sepulchre
    Contain our bodies! Death, why com'st thou not?
               [*She draws a dagger.*]

---

53. *full point-blank*] horizontally, at close range.
54. *see*] see to.
56. *gabions*] shields made of earth packed into a 'wigwam' of stakes.
60. *crack*] explosion.
63. *play the men*] fight boldly.

3.4. Location: at Balsera.
9. *straineth*] bleeds, oozes.
orifex] orifice, wound.

Well, this must be the messenger for thee.   15
Now, ugly Death, stretch out thy sable wings,
And carry both our souls where his remains.—
Tell me, sweet boy, art thou content to die?
These barbarous Scythians, full of cruelty,
And Moors in whom was never pity found,   20
Will hew us piecemeal, put us to the wheel,
Or else invent some torture worse than that.
Therefore, die by thy loving mother's hand,
Who gently now will lance thy ivory throat,
And quickly rid thee both of pain and life.   25
Son. Mother, dispatch me, or I'll kill myself.
For think ye I can live, and see him dead?
Give me your knife, good mother, or strike home.
The Scythians shall not tyrannise on me.
Sweet mother, strike, that I may meet my father!   30
                          She stabs him.
Olympia. Ah, sacred Mahomet, if this be sin,
Entreat a pardon of the God of heaven,
And purge my soul before it come to thee!
                         [She burns the bodies.]

Enter THERIDAMAS, TECHELLES, *and all their* train. [*Olympia*
attempts to kill herself, but is prevented.]

Theridamas. How now, madam, what are you doing?
Olympia. Killing myself, as I have done my son,   35
Whose body with his father's I have burnt,
Lest cruel Scythians should dismember him.
Techelles. 'Twas bravely done, and like a soldier's wife.
Thou shalt with us to Tamburlaine the Great
Who, when he hears how resolute thou wert,   40
Will match thee with a viceroy or a king.
Olympia. My lord deceased was dearer unto me
Than any viceroy, king, or emperor,
And for his sake here will I end my days.
Theridamas. But lady, go with us to Tamburlaine,   45

---

21. *wheel*] torture-wheel.

30.1.] Cf. *Two* 4.1.120.1.

33.1.] Perhaps the staging is to provide some way in which the bodies of the Captain and the Son are seen as being burnt. See also 69–71 below.

And thou shalt see a man greater than Mahomet,
In whose high looks is much more majesty
Than from the concave superficies
Of Jove's vast palace, th'empyreal orb,
Unto the shining bower where Cynthia sits   50
Like lovely Thetis in a crystal robe;
That treadeth Fortune underneath his feet
And makes the mighty god of arms his slave;
On whom Death and the Fatal Sisters wait
With naked swords and scarlet liveries;   55
Before whom, mounted on a lion's back,
Rhamnusia bears a helmet full of blood
And strews the way with brains of slaughtered men;
By whose proud side the ugly Furies run,
Heark'ning when he shall bid them plague the world;   60
Over whose zenith, clothed in windy air,
And eagle's wings joined to her feathered breast,
Fame hovereth, sounding of her golden trump,
That to the adverse poles of that straight line
Which measureth the glorious frame of heaven   65
The name of mighty Tamburlaine is spread—
And him, fair lady, shall thy eyes behold. Come.

Olympia. [*Kneeling*] Take pity of a lady's ruthful tears,
That humbly craves upon her knees to stay
And cast her body in the burning flame   70
That feeds upon her son's and husband's flesh.

48–51.] i.e. than is to be found in the entire universe, from the outermost sphere of fire that forms the concave surface of Jove's palace to the innermost sphere of the moon.

51. *Thetis*] one of the Nereids. The moon is associated with the ocean tides.

52. *That*] he that (i.e. Tamburlaine).

54–5.] In *One* 5.1.117–18, Tamburlaine speaks of 'my servant Death, / Sitting in scarlet on their armèd spears'. For *Fatal Sisters*, see *One* 5.1.455n.

57. *Rhamnusia*] Nemesis: her temple was at Rhamnus.

59. *ugly*] occasioning dread and horror.

Furies] Cf. *One* 2.7.53n.

61. *zenith*] the highest point in Tamburlaine's career: alternatively, high in the heavens above the world.

63. *trump*] trumpet.

64. *that straight line*] i.e. heaven's 'axletree' (cf. *One* 4.2.50n).

Techelles. Madam, sooner shall fire consume us both
    Than scorch a face so beautiful as this,
    In frame of which Nature hath showed more skill
    Than when she gave eternal chaos form,   75
    Drawing from it the shining lamps of heaven.
Theridamas. Madam, I am so far in love with you
    That you must go with us—no remedy.
Olympia. Then carry me I care not where you will,
    And let the end of this my fatal journey   80
    Be likewise end to my accursèd life.
Techelles. No, madam, but the beginning of your joy.
    Come willingly, therefore.
Theridamas. Soldiers, now let us meet the general,
    Who by this time is at Natolia,   85
    Ready to charge the army of the Turk.
    The gold, the silver, and the pearl ye got
    Rifling this fort, divide in equal shares.
    This lady shall have twice so much again
    Out of the coffers of our treasury.   *Exeunt.*   90

SCENE 5

[*Enter*] CALLAPINE, ORCANES, JERUSALEM, TREBIZOND,
    SORIA, ALMEDA, *with their* train. [*To them enter a*
    Messenger.]

Messenger. Renownèd emperor, mighty Callapine,
    God's great lieutenant over all the world,
    Here at Aleppo with an host of men
    Lies Tamburlaine, this King of Persia—
    In number more than are the quiv'ring leaves   5
    Of Ida's forest, where Your Highness' hounds
    With open cry pursues the wounded stag—
    Who means to girt Natolia's walls with siege,

---

74. *In frame of*] in fashioning.
80. *fatal*] decreed by fate.

3.5. Location: near Aleppo, in Syria, to the south of the Turks, who are in
Asia Minor.
6. *Ida*] Mount Ida near Troy (?).
8. *Natolia*] commonly Asia Minor; here, confusingly, a city.

    Fire the town, and overrun the land.
Callapine. My royal army is as great as his,   10
    That from the bounds of Phrygia to the sea
    Which washeth Cyprus with his brinish waves
    Covers the hills, the valleys, and the plains.
    Viceroys and peers of Turkey, play the men!
    Whet all your swords to mangle Tamburlaine,   15
    His sons, his captains, and his followers.
    By Mahomet, not one of them shall live!
    The field wherein this battle shall be fought
    For ever term the Persians' sepulchre,
    In memory of this our victory.   20
Orcanes. Now he that calls himself the scourge of Jove,
    The emperor of the world, and earthly god,
    Shall end the warlike progress he intends
    And travel headlong to the lake of hell
    Where legions of devils, knowing he must die   25
    Here in Natolia by Your Highness' hands,
    All brandishing their brands of quenchless fire,
    Stretching their monstrous paws, grin with their teeth
    And guard the gates to entertain his soul.
Callapine. Tell me, viceroys, the number of your men,   30
    And what our army royal is esteemed.
Jerusalem. From Palestina and Jerusalem,
    Of Hebrews three score thousand fighting men
    Are come since last we showed Your Majesty.
Orcanes. So from Arabia desert, and the bounds   35
    Of that sweet land whose brave metropolis
    Re-edified the fair Semiramis,
    Came forty thousand warlike foot and horse

---

    11. *Phrygia*] country in western central Asia Minor.
    the sea] i.e. the Mediterranean.
    14. *play the men!*] be valiant!
    18. *The field wherein*] identified as 'Asphaltis' by Tamburlaine at *Two*
4.3.5: the bituminous lake near Babylon.
    27. *quenchless*] Cf. the 'quenchless flame' of hell at *Two* 2.3.24.
    29. *entertain*] receive.
    31. *esteemed*] estimated, numbered. (Also at 50.)
    34. *showed*] displayed before.
    36–7.] The legendary Semiramis rebuilt Babylon.

Since last we numbered to Your Majesty.
Trebizond. From Trebizond in Asia the Less,   40
  Naturalised Turks and stout Bithynians
  Came to my bands full fifty thousand more
  That, fighting, knows not what retreat doth mean,
  Nor e'er return but with the victory,
  Since last we numbered to Your Majesty.   45
Soria. Of Sorians from Halla is repaired,
  And neighbour cities of Your Highness' land,
  Ten thousand horse and thirty thousand foot
  Since last we numbered to Your Majesty;
  So that the army royal is esteemed   50
  Six hundred thousand valiant fighting men.
Callapine. Then welcome, Tamburlaine, unto thy death.
  Come, puissant viceroys, let us to the field—
  The Persians' sepulchre—and sacrifice
  Mountains of breathless men to Mahomet,   55
  Who now with Jove opens the firmament
  To see the slaughter of our enemies.

   [*Enter*] TAMBURLAINE *with his three* sons [CALYPHAS,
   AMYRAS, CELEBINUS], USUMCASANE, *with other*
      [Soldiers].

Tamburlaine. How now, Casane! See, a knot of kings,
  Sitting as if they were a-telling riddles.
Usumcasane. My lord, your presence makes them pale and
  wan.   60
  Poor souls, they look as if their deaths were near.
Tamburlaine. Why, so he is, Casane, I am here;
  But yet I'll save their lives and make them slaves.—
  Ye petty kings of Turkey, I am come
  As Hector did into the Grecian camp   65

---

39. *numbered to*] reckoned them for.
40. *Asia the Less*] Asia Minor.
43. *knows*] standard Elizabethan plural. (Not all examples of this form are noted in this edition.)
46–7.] i.e. Sorian soldiers have come from Halla and nearby cities.
52.] Callapine apostrophises the absent Tamburlaine.
65–8. *As Hector . . . fame*] an episode in post-Homeric narratives of the Trojan war.

To overdare the pride of Graecia
And set his warlike person to the view
Of fierce Achilles, rival of his fame.
I do you honour in the simile;
For if I should, as Hector did Achilles   70
(The worthiest knight that ever brandished sword),
Challenge in combat any of you all,
I see how fearfully ye would refuse,
And fly my glove as from a scorpion.

Orcanes. Now thou art fearful of thy army's strength,   75
Thou wouldst with overmatch of person fight.
But, shepherd's issue, baseborn Tamburlaine,
Think of thy end. This sword shall lance thy throat.

Tamburlaine. Villain, the shepherd's issue, at whose birth
Heaven did afford a gracious aspect   80
And joined those stars that shall be opposite
Even till the dissolution of the world,
And never meant to make a conqueror
So famous as is mighty Tamburlaine,
Shall so torment thee and that Callapine   85
That like a roguish runaway suborned
That villain there, that slave, that Turkish dog,
To false his service to his sovereign,
As ye shall curse the birth of Tamburlaine.

Callapine. Rail not, proud Scythian. I shall now revenge   90
My father's vile abuses and mine own.

Jerusalem. By Mahomet, he shall be tied in chains,

---

66. *overdare*] surpass in daring; daunt.

74. *fly my glove*] fly from the gauntlet I throw down in challenge.

75–6.] Now that you fear your army is not strong enough, you seek to rely
on your superiority in single combat.

77. *issue*] progeny, son.

78. *lance*] slash.

80. *a gracious aspect*] favourable astrological conjunction; the 'gracious
stars' of *One* 1.2.92.

81. *opposite*] (1) astrologically in opposition, that is, furthest opposite the
sun; (2) hostile.

87. *That villain*] i.e. Almeda.

88. *false his service*] break his allegiance.

89. *As*] that.

91. *abuses*] ill-usage.

Rowing with Christians in a brigantine
About the Grecian isles to rob and spoil
And turn him to his ancient trade again.   95
Methinks the slave should make a lusty thief!
Callapine. Nay, when the battle ends, all we will meet
And sit in council to invent some pain
That most may vex his body and his soul.
Tamburlaine. Sirrah Callapine, I'll hang a clog about your   100
neck for running away again. You shall not trouble me
thus to come and fetch you.
[*To Almeda*] But as for you, viceroy, you shall have bits
And, harnessed like my horses, draw my coach,
And, when ye stay, be lashed with whips of wire.   105
I'll have you learn to feed on provender
And in a stable lie upon the planks.
Orcanes. But, Tamburlaine, first thou shalt kneel to us
And humbly crave a pardon for thy life.
Trebizond. The common soldiers of our mighty host   110
Shall bring thee bound unto the general's tent.
Soria. And all have jointly sworn thy cruel death,
Or bind thee in eternal torment's wrath.
Tamburlaine. Well, sirs, diet yourselves; you know I shall have
occasion shortly to journey you.   115
Celebinus. See, father, how Almeda the jailer looks upon us!
Tamburlaine. [*To Almeda*] Villain, traitor, damnèd fugitive,
I'll make thee wish the earth had swallowed thee!
Seest thou not death within my wrathful looks?
Go, villain, cast thee headlong from a rock,   120
Or rip thy bowels and rend out thy heart
T'appease my wrath, or else I'll torture thee,

---

93. *brigantine*] small pirate craft.
94. *spoil*] plunder.
99. *vex*] afflict.
100. *clog*] heavy weight.
101. *for*] to prevent.
103. *have bits*] have bits thrust into your mouths.
105. *stay*] fail to move quickly enough.
111. *the general's*] Callapine's.
114. *diet yourselves*] get yourselves fit.
115. *journey*] drive.

Searing thy hateful flesh with burning irons
And drops of scalding lead, while all thy joints
Be racked and beat asunder with the wheel.   125
For, if thou liv'st, not any element
Shall shroud thee from the wrath of Tamburlaine.
Callapine. Well, in despite of thee he shall be king.—
Come, Almeda, receive this crown of me.
I here invest thee King of Ariadan,   130
Bordering on Mare Rosso near to Mecca.
  [*Callapine offers Almeda a crown, but Almeda hesitates,*
       looking fearfully at Tamburlaine.]
Orcanes. [*To Almeda*] What, take it, man!
Almeda. [*To Tamburlaine*] Good my lord, let me take it.
Callapine. [*To Almeda*] Dost thou ask him leave? Here, take it.
Tamburlaine. [*To Almeda*] Go to, sirrah, take your crown, and   135
  make up the half dozen. [*Almeda takes the crown.*]
  So, sirrah, now you are a king you must give arms.
Orcanes. So he shall, and wear thy head in his scutcheon.
Tamburlaine. No, let him hang a bunch of keys on his stan-
  dard, to put him in remembrance he was a jailer, that,   140
  when I take him, I may knock out his brains with them,
  and lock you in the stable when you shall come sweating
  from my chariot.
Trebizond. Away! Let us to the field, that the villain may be
  slain.   145
Tamburlaine. [*To a Soldier*] Sirrah, prepare whips, and bring
  my chariot to my tent, for as soon as the battle is done
  I'll ride in triumph through the camp.

   Enter THERIDAMAS, TECHELLES, *and their* train.

---

 125. *the wheel*] the torture-wheel.

 126. *not any element*] i.e. not earth, water, fire, or air.

 131. *Mare Rosso*] the Red Sea.

 133 ff.] This comic by-play recalls the scene between Tamburlaine and the cowardly Mycetes in *One* 2.4, a parallel explicitly invoked in 155–7 below.

 136. *make . . . half dozen*] i.e. swell the absurdly large number of Callapine's supposed kings to an even half dozen. (Said scornfully.)

 137. *give arms*] a pun: display a coat of arms, also give alms.

 138.] Orcanes jibes that Almeda will indeed 'give arms', by beheading Tamburlaine and 'wearing' his head in his escutcheon or armorial display.

How now, ye petty kings. Lo, here are bugs
Will make the hair stand upright on your heads,   150
And cast your crowns in slavery at their feet.
Welcome, Theridamas and Techelles both.
See ye this rout, and know ye this same king?
Theridamas. Ay, my lord, he was Callapine's keeper.
Tamburlaine. Well, now you see he is a king, look to him,   155
Theridamas, when we are fighting, lest he hide his crown
as the foolish King of Persia did.
Soria. No, Tamburlaine, he shall not be put to that exigent,
I warrant thee.
Tamburlaine. You know not, sir.   160
But now, my followers and my loving friends,
Fight as you ever did, like conquerors.
The glory of this happy day is yours.
My stern aspect shall make fair Victory,
Hovering betwixt our armies, light on me,   165
Loaden with laurel wreaths to crown us all.
Techelles. I smile to think how, when this field is fought
And rich Natolia ours, our men shall sweat
With carrying pearl and treasure on their backs.
Tamburlaine. You shall be princes all immediately.   170
Come, fight, ye Turks, or yield us victory.
Orcanes. No, we will meet thee, slavish Tamburlaine.
                                Exeunt [*in two separate armies*].

                    [*Finis Actus tertii.*]

---

149. *petty*] paltry.
bugs] bogeys (who).
153. *rout*] gang, mob.
160.] i.e. don't count on it.
164. *aspect*] countenance, expression; but also astrological *aspect*, the way
the heavenly bodies look down on the earth (here, dooming the Turks).
166. *Loaden*] laden.

Act 4

SCENE I

Alarm: AMYRAS *and* CELEBINUS *issue from the tent where*
CALYPHAS *sits asleep.*

Amyras. Now in their glories shine the golden crowns
Of these proud Turks, much like so many suns
That half dismay the majesty of heaven.
Now, brother, follow we our father's sword
That flies with fury swifter than our thoughts   5
And cuts down armies with his conquering wings.
Celebinus. Call forth our lazy brother from the tent,
For, if my father miss him in the field,
Wrath kindled in the furnace of his breast
Will send a deadly lightning to his heart.   10
Amyras. [*Calling*] Brother, ho! What, given so much to sleep
You cannot leave it when our enemies' drums
And rattling cannons thunder in our ears
Our proper ruin and our father's foil?
Calyphas. Away, ye fools! My father needs not me,   15
Nor you, in faith, but that you will be thought
More childish-valorous than manly-wise.
If half our camp should sit and sleep with me,
My father were enough to scare the foe.
You do dishonour to his majesty   20
To think our helps will do him any good.
Amyras. What, dar'st thou then be absent from the fight,

4.1. Location: near Aleppo.

0.1. *tent*] probably a movable property, perhaps set up at a stage door,
with Calyphas within sight of the audience.

14. *proper*] own.
foil] defeat.

20. *his majesty*] (1) his majestic standing; (2) His Majesty (an honorific
title, perhaps used irreverently here).

Knowing my father hates thy cowardice
And oft hath warned thee to be still in field
When he himself amidst the thickest troops   25
Beats down our foes, to flesh our taintless swords?
Calyphas. I know, sir, what it is to kill a man;
   It works remorse of conscience in me.
   I take no pleasure to be murderous,
   Nor care for blood when wine will quench my thirst.   30
Celebinus. O cowardly boy! Fie, for shame, come forth.
   Thou dost dishonour manhood and thy house.
Calyphas. Go, go, tall stripling, fight you for us both,
   And take my other toward brother here,
   For person like to prove a second Mars.   35
   'Twill please my mind as well to hear both you
   Have won a heap of honour in the field
   And left your slender carcasses behind
   As if I lay with you for company.
Amyras. You will not go, then?   40
Calyphas. You say true.
Amyras. Were all the lofty mounts of Zona Mundi
   That fill the midst of farthest Tartary
   Turned into pearl and proffered for my stay,
   I would not bide the fury of my father   45
   When, made a victor in these haughty arms,
   He comes and finds his sons have had no shares
   In all the honours he proposed for us.
Calyphas. Take you the honour; I will take my ease.
   My wisdom shall excuse my cowardice.   50
   I go into the field before I need?
        Alarm, and AMYRAS *and* CELEBINUS *run in.*

---

24. *still*] constantly.
26. *to flesh . . . swords*] to accustom, or incite, our unstained swords to killing.
32. *house*] family, race.
33. *tall*] bold, valiant; used here sneeringly.
34. *toward*] eager; presumptuous.
35. *like*] likely.
39.] as if I went along with you on the campaign.
42. *Zona Mundi*] mountains in north-west Asia (*Tartary*, 43).
46. *haughty arms*] exalted conquests.
51.1. *run in*] go offstage to the battle.

The bullets fly at random where they list,
And should I go and kill a thousand men
I were as soon rewarded with a shot,
And sooner far than he that never fights.   55
And should I go and do nor harm nor good
I might have harm, which all the good I have,
Joined with my father's crown, would never cure.
I'll to cards.—Perdicas!

[*Enter* PERDICAS.]

Perdicas. Here, my lord.   60
Calyphas. Come, thou and I will go to cards to drive away the
    time.
Perdicas. Content, my lord. But what shall we play for?
Calyphas. Who shall kiss the fairest of the Turks' concubines
    first, when my father hath conquered them.   65
Perdicas. Agreed, i'faith.   *They play* [*in the open tent*].
Calyphas. They say I am a coward, Perdicas, and I fear as
    little their *taratantaras*, their swords, or their cannons, as
    I do a naked lady in a net of gold, and for fear I should be
    afraid, would put it off and come to bed with me.   70
Perdicas. Such a fear, my lord, would never make ye retire.
Calyphas. I would my father would let me be put in the front
    of such a battle once, to try my valour!   *Alarm.*
    What a coil they keep! I believe there will be some hurt
    done anon amongst them.   75

Enter TAMBURLAINE, THERIDAMAS, TECHELLES,
USUMCASANE, AMYRAS, CELEBINUS, *leading the*
Turkish Kings [ORCANES *of* NATOLIA, JERUSALEM,
TREBIZOND, SORIA; *and* Soldiers].

Tamburlaine. See now, ye slaves, my children stoops your
    pride

---

56. *nor harm*] neither harm.
68. taratantaras] bugle calls.
69. *net*] veil, gown of fine mesh; with a suggestion of 'snare'.
and] i.e. and who.
73. *such a battle*] i.e. a love-encounter with a naked lady.
74. *coil they keep*] noisy fuss they are making.
76. *stoops*] humiliate, subdue; Elizabethan plural.

And leads your glories sheep-like to the sword.
Bring them, my boys, and tell me if the wars
Be not a life that may illustrate gods,
And tickle not your spirits with desire   80
Still to be trained in arms and chivalry?
Amyras. Shall we let go these kings again, my lord,
To gather greater numbers 'gainst our power,
That they may say it is not chance doth this
But matchless strength and magnanimity?   85
Tamburlaine. No, no, Amyras, tempt not Fortune so;
Cherish thy valour still with fresh supplies,
And glut it not with stale and daunted foes.
But where's this coward—villain, not my son,
But traitor to my name and majesty?   90
        He goes in [the tent] and brings him [CALYPHAS] *out.*
Image of sloth and picture of a slave,
The obloquy and scorn of my renown,
How may my heart, thus firèd with mine eyes,
Wounded with shame and killed with discontent,
Shroud any thought may hold my striving hands   95
From martial justice on thy wretched soul?
Theridamas. Yet pardon him, I pray Your Majesty.
Techelles and Usumcasane. Let all of us entreat Your
        Highness' pardon.   [*They kneel.*]
Tamburlaine. Stand up, ye base unworthy soldiers!
Know ye not yet the argument of arms?   100
        [*They stand. Amyras and Celebinus kneel.*]
Amyras. Good my lord, let him be forgiven for once,
And we will force him to the field hereafter.
Tamburlaine. Stand up, my boys, and I will teach ye arms
And what the jealousy of wars must do.   [*They stand.*]

---

79. *illustrate*] shed lustre on. Second syllable stressed.
85. *magnanimity*] courage.
87.] Feed your renown continually with new enemies.
92. *obloquy*] reproach, disgrace.
93. *firèd . . . eyes*] inflamed with what I see.
95. *Shroud*] harbour.
thought] i.e. thought which.
100. *argument of arms*] code of justice governing military conduct.
103. *arms*] how to fight.
104. *jealousy of wars*] zeal or vehemence of feeling for military values.

O Samarcanda, where I breathèd first,   105
And joyed the fire of this martial flesh,
Blush, blush, fair city, at thine honour's foil,
And shame of nature, which Jaertis' stream,
Embracing thee with deepest of his love,
Can never wash from thy distainèd brows!   110
Here, Jove, receive his fainting soul again—
A form not meet to give that subject essence
Whose matter is the flesh of Tamburlaine,
Wherein an incorporeal spirit moves,
Made of the mould whereof thyself consists,   115
Which makes me valiant, proud, ambitious,
Ready to levy power against thy throne,
That I might move the turning spheres of heaven;
For earth and all this airy region
Cannot contain the state of Tamburlaine.   120

                    [*He stabs Calyphas.*]

By Mahomet thy mighty friend I swear,
In sending to my issue such a soul,
Created of the massy dregs of earth,
The scum and tartar of the elements,
Wherein was neither courage, strength, or wit,   125
But folly, sloth, and damnèd idleness,
Thou hast procured a greater enemy
Than he that darted mountains at thy head,
Shaking the burden mighty Atlas bears,

---

106. *joyed*] delighted in.

107. *foil*] disgrace, stigma.

108. *Jaertis' stream*] the river Jaxartes, between Persia and India.

109. *thee*] i.e. Samarkand.

110. *distainèd*] dishonoured.

111–15.] i.e. Calyphas' spirit is unfit to embody Tamburlaine's godlike essence. The alchemist's application of these terms is found at *Two* 4.2.62–4.

118.] Cf. *One* 4.2.8n.

119–20.] Tamburlaine's brag impiously echoes 1 Kings 8.27: 'But will God indeed dwell on the earth? Behold, the heaven, and heaven of heavens cannot contain Thee.'

121. *thy*] still addressing Jove (111).

122. *to my issue*] to be my child.

124. *tartar*] chemical crust deposited in the fermenting of wine.

128. *he that darted mountains*] one of the Titans who warred on Jove.

129. *Atlas*] a Titan, made to shoulder the earth in punishment for his part in the revolt.

Whereat thou trembling hidd'st thee in the air,   130
Clothed with a pitchy cloud for being seen.—
And now, ye cankered curs of Asia,
That will not see the strength of Tamburlaine
Although it shine as brightly as the sun,
Now you shall feel the strength of Tamburlaine,   135
And by the state of his supremacy
Approve the difference 'twixt himself and you.
Orcanes. Thou show'st the difference 'twixt ourselves and
  thee
In this thy barbarous damnèd tyranny.
Jerusalem. Thy victories are grown so violent   140
That shortly heaven, filled with the meteors
Of blood and fire thy tyrannies have made,
Will pour down blood and fire on thy head,
Whose scalding drops will pierce thy seething brains
And with our bloods revenge our bloods on thee.   145
Tamburlaine. Villains, these terrors and these tyrannies
(If tyrannies war's justice ye repute)
I execute, enjoined me from above,
To scourge the pride of such as heaven abhors;
Nor am I made arch-monarch of the world,   150
Crowned and invested by the hand of Jove,
For deeds of bounty or nobility.
But since I exercise a greater name,
The scourge of God and terror of the world,
I must apply myself to fit those terms,   155
In war, in blood, in death, in cruelty,
And plague such peasants as resist in me
The power of heaven's eternal majesty.
Theridamas, Techelles, and Casane,
Ransack the tents and the pavilions   160
Of these proud Turks, and take their concubines,

---

131. *for being seen*] to avoid being seen.
133. *will not see*] blind yourselves to.
137. *Approve*] see demonstrated.
141–5.] Jerusalem predicts that the bloody rain caused by Tamburlaine's cruelty to his victims, including the Turkish kings themselves, will inflict a scalding retribution on him.
147.] if you think honourable military action mere tyranny.
148. *execute*] carry out.
153. *exercise*] employ.

Making them bury this effeminate brat,
For not a common soldier shall defile
His manly fingers with so faint a boy.
Then bring those Turkish harlots to my tent,   165
And I'll dispose them as it likes me best.
Meanwhile, take him in.
Soldiers. We will, my lord.
        [*Exeunt* THERIDAMAS, TECHELLES, *and* USUMCASANE,
                and Soldiers *with the body of* CALYPHAS.]
Jerusalem. O damnèd monster, nay, a fiend of hell,
Whose cruelties are not so harsh as thine,   170
Nor yet imposed with such a bitter hate!
Orcanes. Revenge it, Rhadamanth and Aeacus,
And let your hates, extended in his pains,
Expel the hate wherewith he pains our souls!
Trebizond. May never day give virtue to his eyes,   175
Whose sight, composed of fury and of fire,
Doth send such stern affections to his heart!
Soria. May never spirit, vein, or artier feed
The cursèd substance of that cruel heart,
But, wanting moisture and remorseful blood,   180
Dry up with anger and consume with heat!
Tamburlaine. Well, bark, ye dogs! I'll bridle all your tongues
And bind them close with bits of burnished steel
Down to the channels of your hateful throats,
And with the pains my rigour shall inflict   185
I'll make ye roar, that earth may echo forth
The far-resounding torments ye sustain,
As when an herd of lusty Cimbrian bulls

---

166. *likes*] pleases.
170.] i.e. the cruelties of a fiend of hell are not so harsh as Tamburlaine's.
172. *Rhadamanth and Aeacus*] sons of Zeus and judges of the dead.
173. *extended . . . pains*] made even more fierce by his cruelties.
174. *Expel*] banish, do away with (by the death of Tamburlaine).
175. *virtue*] power.
177. *affections*] feelings. The eyes are thought of as transmitting strong feelings of fury and vengeance to the heart in a physiological process involving the 'humours' or bodily fluids.
178. *artier*] artery.
180. *remorseful*] compassionate.
188. *Cimbrian bulls*] The Cimbri were a Teutonic tribe.

Run mourning round about the females' miss,
And stung with fury of their following   190
Fill all the air with troublous bellowing.
I will, with engines never exercised,
Conquer, sack, and utterly consume
Your cities and your golden palaces,
And with the flames that beat against the clouds   195
Incense the heavens and make the stars to melt,
As if they were the tears of Mahomet
For hot consumption of his country's pride;
And till by vision or by speech I hear
Immortal Jove say 'Cease, my Tamburlaine',   200
I will persist a terror to the world,
Making the meteors that, like armèd men,
Are seen to march upon the towers of heaven,
Run tilting round about the firmament
And break their burning lances in the air   205
For honour of my wondrous victories.—
Come, bring them in to our pavilion.   *Exeunt.*

SCENE 2

OLYMPIA *alone [holding a bowl of ointment].*

Olympia. Distressed Olympia, whose weeping eyes
　　Since thy arrival here beheld no sun,
　　But close within the compass of a tent
　　Hath stained thy cheeks and made thee look like death,

---

189. *the females' miss*] the loss or lack of females.

190. *their following*] chasing after the females.

192. *engines never exercised*] military contrivances never yet invented or used in war.

196. *Incense*] set on fire, consume with fire.

198.] shed for the burning of his country's proud cities and palaces.

200.] echoing Jehovah's instruction 'stay now thy hand' to the angel sent to destroy Jerusalem: 1 Chronicles 21.15, 2 Samuel 24.16.

202–5.] the fiery impression of 'burning spears', formed by the kindling of an exhalation in the highest region of air: portents transformed into signs which Tamburlaine has occasioned in honour of his own victories.

4.2. Location: at Balsera.

4. *Hath*] normal Elizabethan plural, agreeing with 'eyes'.

Devise some means to rid thee of thy life   5
Rather than yield to his detested suit
Whose drift is only to dishonour thee.
And since this earth, dewed with thy brinish tears,
Affords no herbs whose taste may poison thee,
Nor yet this air, beat often with thy sighs,   10
Contagious smells and vapours to infect thee,
Nor thy close cave a sword to murder thee,
Let this invention be the instrument.

Enter THERIDAMAS.

Theridamas. Well met, Olympia. I sought thee in my tent,
But when I saw the place obscure and dark   15
Which with thy beauty thou wast wont to light,
Enraged, I ran about the fields for thee,
Supposing amorous Jove had sent his son,
The winged Hermes, to convey thee hence.
But now I find thee, and that fear is past.   20
Tell me, Olympia, wilt thou grant my suit?
Olympia. My lord and husband's death, with my sweet son's,
With whom I buried all affections
Save grief and sorrow which torment my heart,
Forbids my mind to entertain a thought   25
That tends to love, but meditate on death—
A fitter subject for a pensive soul.
Theridamas. Olympia, pity him in whom thy looks
Have greater operation and more force
Than Cynthia's in the wat'ry wilderness,   30
For with thy view my joys are at the full,
And ebb again as thou depart'st from me.
Olympia. Ah, pity me, my lord, and draw your sword,

---

7. *drift*] purpose.

11. *Contagious smells*] i.e. affords no contagious smells.

12. *close*] secret.

13. *invention*] contrivance (involving the deception with the 'magical' ointment).

18–19.] Theridamas echoes Tamburlaine's conceit at *Two* 2.4.107.

23. *affections*] emotions.

29. *operation*] efficacy.

30.] i.e. than the moon's influence on tides.

31. *thy view*] my seeing you.

Making a passage for my troubled soul,
Which beats against this prison to get out   35
And meet my husband and my loving son.

Theridamas. Nothing but still thy husband and thy son?
Leave this, my love, and listen more to me:
Thou shalt be stately queen of fair Argier,
And, clothed in costly cloth of massy gold,   40
Upon the marble turrets of my court
Sit like to Venus in her chair of state,
Commanding all thy princely eye desires;
And I will cast off arms and sit with thee,
Spending my life in sweet discourse of love.   45

Olympia. No such discourse is pleasant in mine ears
But that where every period ends with death
And every line begins with death again.
I cannot love to be an emperess

Theridamas. Nay, lady, then if nothing will prevail,   50
I'll use some other means to make you yield.
Such is the sudden fury of my love,
I must and will be pleased, and you shall yield.
Come to the tent again.

Olympia. Stay, good my lord! And will you save my honour,   55
I'll give Your Grace a present of such price
As all the world cannot afford the like.

Theridamas. What is it?

Olympia. An ointment which a cunning alchemist
Distillèd from the purest balsamum   60
And simplest extracts of all minerals,
In which the essential form of marble stone,
Tempered by science metaphysical

---

41. *turrets*] rounded ornamental towers.
44. *cast off arms*] lay aside military pursuits.
47. *period*] (1) sentence; (2) any ending, especially a final one.
49.] i.e. (1) I cannot love you even for the sake of becoming an empress; or (2) I do not wish to be an empress.
55. *will you . . . honour*] if you will respect my chastity.
60. *balsamum*] healthful preservative essence.
61. *simplest extracts*] i.e. the alchemical elements.
62. *form*] property.
63. *Tempered*] brought to a proper consistency.
    science metaphysical] supernatural skill—the 'metaphysics of magicians' (*Dr Faustus*, A-text, I.1.51.).

And spells of magic from the mouths of spirits,
With which if you but 'noint your tender skin,   65
Nor pistol, sword, nor lance can pierce your flesh.
Theridamas. Why, madam, think ye to mock me thus
    palpably?
Olympia. To prove it, I will 'noint my naked throat,
    Which when you stab, look on your weapon's point,
    And you shall see't rebated with the blow.   70
Theridamas. Why gave you not your husband some of it,
    If you loved him, and it so precious?
Olympia. My purpose was, my lord, to spend it so,
    But was prevented by his sudden end.
    And for a present easy proof hereof,   75
    That I dissemble not, try it on me.
Theridamas. I will, Olympia, and will keep it for
    The richest present of this eastern world.
                             She 'noints her throat.
Olympia. Now stab, my lord, and mark your weapon's point,
    That will be blunted if the blow be great.   80
Theridamas. Here then, Olympia—   [*He stabs her.*]
    What, have I slain her? Villain, stab thyself!
    Cut off this arm that murderèd my love,
    In whom the learned Rabbis of this age
    Might find as many wondrous miracles   85
    As in the theoria of the world!
    Now hell is fairer than Elysium;
    A greater lamp than that bright eye of heaven
    From whence the stars do borrow all their light

---

66. *Nor*] neither.

70. *rebated*] blunted.

73. *spend it so*] use it thus (to protect my husband's life).

80. *if*] even if.

81 ff.] Ariosto lends plausibility to the episode by having Isabel's suitor 'overlayed / With wine, that in his idle braine did work' (*Orlando Furioso*, Book 29, st. 26). A producer of *Tamburlaine* could achieve much by introducing a spirit of playfulness, in tune with the incredulity expressed at 67, and by having Olympia herself virtually thrust the blade home.

84. *Rabbis*] sages.

86. *theoria*] contemplation, survey (?).

87 ff.] Hell is more beautiful than Elysium, to Theridamas here, because the soul of his dead beloved hovers there now in the eternal darkness.

Wanders about the black circumference,   90
And now the damnèd souls are free from pain,
For every Fury gazeth on her looks.
Infernal Dis is courting of my love,
Inventing masques and stately shows for her,
Opening the doors of his rich treasury   ————95
To entertain this queen of chastity;
Whose body shall be tombed with all the pomp
The treasure of my kingdom may afford.

> *Exit, taking her away.*

SCENE 3

[Enter] TAMBURLAINE, *drawn in his chariot by*
TREBIZOND *and* SORIA *with bits in their mouths, reins in*
his left hand, in his right hand a whip, with which he
scourgeth them. TECHELLES, THERIDAMAS,
USUMCASANE, AMYRAS, CELEBINUS; [ORCANES *of*]
NATOLIA *and* JERUSALEM *led by with five or six common*
Soldiers.

Tamburlaine. Holla, ye pampered jades of Asia!
What, can ye draw but twenty miles a day,
And have so proud a chariot at your heels,
And such a coachman as great Tamburlaine,
But from Asphaltis, where I conquered you,   5
To Byron here where thus I honour you?
The horse that guide the golden eye of heaven

---

93. *Dis*] Hades, ruler of the underworld; as at *One* 2.7.37. Elsewhere, 'infernal Jove' (e.g. *Two* 1.3.143).

96. *entertain*] receive, welcome. The affinity of this speech to Tamburlaine's lament as Zenocrate dies is focused in the close recall of the refrain 'To entertain divine Zenocrate' (*Two* 2.4.17 ff.).

4.3. Location: at Byron (see 6), on the march to Babylon.

0.1. drawn in his chariot] Cf. *One* 4.2.78n.

0.6–7. led by with . . . *Soldiers*] pulled across the stage with indignity by a few ordinary troops.

5. *Asphaltis*] the bituminous lake near Babylon; cf. *Two* 5.1.17n.

6. *Byron*] a town near Babylon and Asphaltis Lake.

I honour you] i.e. I honour you by being your coachman.

7. *horse*] plural form. The horses are here drawing the chariot of the sun.

And blow the morning from their nosterils,
Making their fiery gait above the clouds,
Are not so honoured in their governor   10
As you, ye slaves, in mighty Tamburlaine.
The headstrong jades of Thrace Alcides tamed,
That King Aegeus fed with human flesh
And made so wanton that they knew their strengths,
Were not subdued with valour more divine   15
Than you by this unconquered arm of mine.
To make you fierce, and fit my appetite,
You shall be fed with flesh as raw as blood
And drink in pails the strongest muscatel.
If you can live with it, then live, and draw   20
My chariot swifter than the racking clouds;
If not, then die like beasts, and fit for nought
But perches for the black and fatal ravens.
Thus am I right the scourge of highest Jove,
And see, the figure of my dignity   25
By which I hold my name and majesty.
Amyras. Let me have coach, my lord, that I may ride
    And thus be drawn with these two idle kings.
Tamburlaine. Thy youth forbids such ease, my kingly boy.
    They shall tomorrow draw my chariot   30
    While these their fellow kings may be refreshed.
Orcanes. O thou that sway'st the region under earth,

---

8. *nosterils*] nostrils.
10. *governor*] charioteer.
12–14.] In his seventh labour, Hercules (Alcides) subdued the savage human-flesh-eating horses of Diomedes of Thrace. In one version, the king in question is Aegeus, thus repaid for his villainy in feeding his horses with human flesh.
14. *wanton*] unmanageable.
19. *muscatel*] a strong sweet wine.
21. *racking*] driven before the wind; galloping at full stretch.
23. *fatal*] ominous.
24. *right*] indeed, aright.
25. *figure*] image, emblem; in particular, scourge.
28. *idle*] worthless; unused—i.e. Orcanes and Jerusalem.
32–8.] Dis or Hades abducted Proserpina, daughter of the goddess of harvest, Ceres. During her yearly absence winter reigns in the world. Dis carried her off from *Sicily* (34).

And art a king as absolute as Jove,
Come as thou didst in fruitful Sicily,
Surveying all the glories of the land!   35
,And as thou took'st the fair Proserpina,
Joying the fruit of Ceres' garden plot,
For love, for honour, and to make her queen,
So for just hate, for shame, and to subdue
This proud contemner of thy dreadful power,   40
Come once in fury and survey his pride,
Haling him headlong to the lowest hell!
Theridamas. [*To Tamburlaine*] Your Majesty must get some
        bits for these,
To bridle their contemptuous cursing tongues
That like unruly never-broken jades   45
Break through the hedges of their hateful mouths,
And pass their fixèd bounds exceedingly.
Techelles. Nay, we will break the hedges of their mouths
And pull their kicking colts out of their pastures.
Usumcasane. Your Majesty already hath devised   50
A mean as fit as may be to restrain
These coltish coach-horse tongues from blasphemy.
                                [*Celebinus bridles Orcanes.*]
Celebinus. How like you that, sir king? Why speak you not?
Jerusalem. Ah, cruel brat, sprung from a tyrant's loins,
How like his cursèd father he begins   55
To practise taunts and bitter tyrannies!
Tamburlaine. Ay, Turk, I tell thee, this same boy is he
That must, advanced in higher pomp than this,
Rifle the kingdoms I shall leave unsacked
If Jove, esteeming me too good for earth,   60
Raise me to match the fair Aldebaran

---

40. *contemner*] despiser.
41. *once*] once and for all.
46. *hedges*] teeth.
49.] i.e. and pull their saucy tongues out of their mouths.
51. *mean*] means.
52.1.] Orcanes is evidently here bridled and yet is able to speak at 77–80. Perhaps he is released, then bridled in earnest, with Jerusalem, at *Two* 5.1.147.1.
61.] *Aldebaran* is the bright red 'eye' in the constellation Taurus.

Above the threefold astracism of heaven
Before I conquer all the triple world.
Now fetch me out the Turkish concubines.
I will prefer them for the funeral   65
They have bestowed on my abortive son.

The Concubines *are brought in.*

Where are my common soldiers now that fought
So lion-like upon Asphaltis' plains?
Soldiers. Here, my lord.
Tamburlaine. Hold ye, tall soldiers, take ye queens apiece—   70
I mean such queens as were kings' concubines.
Take them, divide them and their jewels too,
And let them equally serve all your turns.
Soldiers. We thank Your Majesty.
Tamburlaine. Brawl not, I warn you, for your lechery,   75
For every man that so offends shall die.
Orcanes. Injurious tyrant, wilt thou so defame
The hateful fortunes of thy victory,
To exercise upon such guiltless dames
The violence of thy common soldiers' lust?   80
Tamburlaine. Live content, then, ye slaves, and meet not me
With troops of harlots at your slothful heels.
Concubines. Oh, pity us, my lord, and save our honours!
Tamburlaine. [*To Soldiers*] Are ye not gone, ye villains, with
    your spoils?
                    They [Soldiers] *run away with the* Ladies.
Jerusalem. Oh merciless, infernal cruelty!   85

---

62. *threefold astracism*] three prominent stars near Aldebaran; or earth,
planet, and star.
63. *the triple world*] the world as known in Tamburlaine's time, compris-
ing Europe, Asia, and Africa.
65. *prefer*] promote, advance.
66. *abortive*] worthless. The concubines were ordered to bury Calyphas in
Two 4.1.161–2.
70. *tall*] bold, valiant.
queens] punning on 'queans', harlots.
73. *serve all your turns*] be raped by all in turn.
75.] i.e. Do not, I warn you, quarrel over your women.
81–2.] Tamburlaine may be admonishing his own soldiers here, in line
with 72–3; alternatively, he may be mocking the captive kings.

Tamburlaine. Save your honours! 'Twere but time indeed,
  Lost long before you knew what honour meant.
Theridamas. It seems they meant to conquer us, my lord,
  And make us jesting pageants for their trulls.
Tamburlaine. And now themselves shall make our pageant,   90
  And common soldiers jest with all their trulls.
  Let them take pleasure soundly in their spoils
  Till we prepare out march to Babylon,
  Whither we next make expedition.
Techelles. Let us not be idle, then, my lord,   95
  But presently be prest to conquer it.
    [*Tamburlaine mounts the chariot, drawn by Trebizond
                                            and Soria.*]
Tamburlaine. We will, Techelles. Forward then, ye jades!
  Now crouch, ye kings of greatest Asia,
  And tremble when ye hear this scourge will come
  That whips down cities and controlleth crowns,   100
  Adding their wealth and treasure to my store.
  The Euxine Sea, north to Natolia,
  The Terrene, west, the Caspian, north-north-east,
  And on the south Sinus Arabicus,
  Shall all be loaden with the martial spoils   105
  We will convey with us to Persia.
  Then shall my native city Samarcanda
  And crystal waves of fresh Jaertis' stream,
  The pride and beauty of her princely seat,
  Be famous through the furthest continents;   110
  For there my palace royal shall be placed
  Whose shining turrets shall dismay the heavens

86.] In 'Save your honours!' Tamburlaine mockingly repeats the concubines' plea in 83. ''Twere but time indeed' suggests sardonically how unlikely
it is for something like this to happen.
  89. *jesting pageants*] derisory exhibits.
  trulls] strumpets.
  94. *expedition*] haste; warlike march.
  96. *prest*] in readiness.
  100. *controlleth crowns*] holds sway over kings.
  102. *Euxine Sea*] Black Sea.
  103. *Terrene*] Mediterranean.
  104. *Sinus Arabicus*] the Red Sea.
  108. *Jaertis*] the Jaxartes. Cf. *Two* 4.1.105–10.

And cast the fame of Ilion's tower to hell.
Thorough the streets with troops of conquered kings
I'll ride in golden armour like the sun,   115
And in my helm a triple plume shall spring,
Spangled with diamonds dancing in the air,
To note me emperor of the threefold world,
Like to an almond tree ymounted high
Upon the lofty and celestial mount   120
Of ever-green Selinus, quaintly decked
With blooms more white than Herycina's brows,
Whose tender blossoms tremble every one
At every little breath that thorough heaven is blown.
Then in my coach, like Saturn's royal son,   125
Mounted his shining chariot, gilt with fire,
And drawn with princely eagles through the path
Paved with bright crystal and enchased with stars,
When all the gods stand gazing at his pomp,
So will I ride through Samarcanda streets   130
Until my soul, dissevered from this flesh,
Shall mount the milk-white way and meet him there.
To Babylon, my lords, to Babylon!

>   *Exeunt* [*with* TAMBURLAINE *in his chariot,*
>   *drawn by the Kings of* TREBIZOND *and* SORIA].

>   *Finis Actus quarti.*

---

113. *Ilion's*] Troy's.
114. *Thorough*] through. Also in 124.
118. *threefold world*] See 63 above.
121. *Selinus*] Sicilian town, site of a temple of Jupiter.
122. *Herycina's*] Venus's.
125. *Saturn's royal son*] Jupiter.
126. *Mounted*] mounted in.
   gilt] gilded, made golden. Fire was often thought to be golden in
appearance.
   127. *the path*] the Milky Way, highway to the palace of Jove, *Saturn's royal*
son (125). See 'milk-white way' in 132.

Act 5

SCENE I

Enter the GOVERNOR OF BABYLON *upon the walls with*
[MAXIMUS *and*] *others.*

Governor. What saith Maximus?
Maximus. My lord, the breach the enemy hath made
    Gives such assurance of our overthrow
    That little hope is left to save our lives
    Or hold our city from the conqueror's hands.   5
    Then hang out flags, my lord, of humble truce,
    And satisfy the people's general prayers
    That Tamburlaine's intolerable wrath
    May be suppressed by our submission.
Governor. Villain, respects thou more thy slavish life   10
    Than honour of thy country or thy name?
    Is not my life and state as dear to me,
    The city and my native country's weal,
    As any thing of price with thy conceit?
    Have we not hope, for all our battered walls,   15
    To live secure and keep his forces out,
    When this our famous lake of Limnasphaltis
    Makes walls afresh with every thing that falls
    Into the liquid substance of his stream,
    More strong than are the gates of death or hell?   20
    What faintness should dismay our courages
    When we are thus defenced against our foe
    And have no terror but his threat'ning looks?

5.1. Location: at Babylon, on the third (black) day of siege.
0.1. *the walls*] presumably the gallery above the main stage.
14.] as anything you would prize.
15. *for*] despite.
17. *Limnasphaltis*] the burning bituminous lake near Babylon; making a
natural defensive structure out of objects fallen into it (17–19).

Enter another [Citizen *above*], *kneeling to the Governor.*

Citizen. My lord, if ever you did deed of ruth
    And now will work a refuge to our lives,   25
    Offer submission, hang up flags of truce,
    That Tamburlaine may pity our distress
    And use us like a loving conqueror.
    Though this be held his last day's dreadful siege
    Wherein he spareth neither man or child,   30
    Yet are there Christians of Georgia here,
    Whose state he ever pitied and relieved,
    Will get his pardon, if Your Grace would send.
Governor. How is my soul environèd,
    And this eternised city Babylon   35
    Filled with a pack of faint-heart fugitives
    That thus entreat their shame and servitude!

    [*Enter another* Citizen *above, kneeing to the Governor.*]

Second Citizen. My lord, if ever you will win our hearts,
    Yield up the town, save our wives and children!
    For I will cast myself from off these walls   40
    Or die some death of quickest violence
    Before I bide the wrath of Tamburlaine.
Governor. Villains, cowards, traitors to our state!
    Fall to the earth and pierce the pit of hell,
    That legions of tormenting spirits may vex   45
    Your slavish bosoms with continual pains!
    I care not, nor the town will never yield
    As long as any life is in my breast.

    Enter THERIDAMAS *and* TECHELLES, *with other* Soldiers
    [*on the main stage*].

Theridamas. Thou desperate governor of Babylon,
    To save thy life, and us a little labour,   50
    Yield speedily the city to our hands,

---

    24. *ruth*] pity.
    31–3.] a return to the concept of Tamburlaine as the scourge of the
Christian God. Cf. *One* 3.3.44n.
    33. *Will*] who will.
    35. *eternised*] everlastingly famous.

> Or else be sure thou shalt be forced with pains
> More exquisite than ever traitor felt.

Governor. Tyrant, I turn the traitor in thy throat,
> And will defend it in despite of thee.—   55
> Call up the soldiers to defend these walls.

Techelles. Yield, foolish governor. We offer more
> Than ever yet we did to such proud slaves
> As durst resist us till our third day's siege.
> Thou seest us prest to give the last assault,   60
> And that shall bide no more regard of parley.

Governor. Assault, and spare not! We will never yield.

> *Alarm; and they [Tamburlaine's forces] scale the walls.*
> *[Exeunt* Citizens *and* GOVERNOR *above, followed in by*
> THERIDAMAS, TECHELLES, *and their* Soldiers.]

> *Enter* TAMBURLAINE *[all in black, on the main stage, drawn*
> *in his chariot by* TREBIZOND *and* SORIA*], with* USUMCASANE,
> AMYRAS, *and* CELEBINUS, *with* others; *the two spare kings*
> [ORCANES *of* NATOLIA *and* JERUSALEM].

Tamburlaine. The stately buildings of fair Babylon
> Whose lofty pillars, higher than the clouds,
> Were wont to guide the seaman in the deep,   65
> Being carried thither by the cannon's force,
> Now fill the mouth of Limnasphaltis' lake
> And make a bridge unto the battered walls.
> Where Belus, Ninus, and great Alexander
> Have rode in triumph, triumphs Tamburlaine,   70

---

53. *exquisite*] excruciating.
54. *turn the traitor in*] return the charge of 'traitor' down.
55. *it*] the city.
60. *prest*] ready.
61. *bide . . . parley*] wait no longer for negotiations.
62.6 spare kings] i.e. not in harness, awaiting their turn.
69–70.] 'The three successive masters of Babylon here come before Tamburlaine: Belus, the legendary founder, himself the son of Poseidon; Ninus, the hardly less legendary founder of the empire of Nineveh, whose queen, Semiramis, built the famous walls of Babylon; and Alexander of Macedon, who overcame the then effete Babylonian empire in 331 B.C.' (Ellis-Fermor).

Whose chariot wheels have burst th'Assyrians' bones,
Drawn with these kings on heaps of carcasses.
Now in the place where fair Semiramis,
Courted by kings and peers of Asia,
Hath trod the measures, do my soldiers march;   75
And in the streets where brave Assyrian dames
Have rid in pomp like rich Saturnia,
With furious words and frowning visages
My horsemen brandish their unruly blades.

Enter THERIDAMAS *and* TECHELLES, *bringing the*
GOVERNOR *of* BABYLON.

Who have ye there, my lords?   80
Theridamas. The sturdy governor of Babylon,
    That made us all the labour for the town
    And used such slender reckoning of Your Majesty.
Tamburlaine. Go, bind the villain. He shall hang in chains
    Upon the ruins of this conquered town.—   85
    Sirrah, the view of our vermilion tents,
    Which threatened more than if the region
    Next underneath the element of fire
    Were full of comets and of blazing stars
    Whose flaming trains should reach down to the earth,   90
    Could not affright you; no, nor I myself,
    The wrathful messenger of mighty Jove,
    That with his sword hath quailed all earthly kings,
    Could not persuade you to submission,

---

71. *burst*] broken, shattered.
72. *with*] by.
73. *Semiramis*] See *Two* 3.5.36–7 and note, and 69–70n. above.
75. *measures*] stately dances.
76. *brave*] finely-dressed, grand.
77. *Saturnia*] Juno.
81. *sturdy*] refractory.
83. *used . . . of*] so lightly estimated.
86. *Sirrah*] an insulting form of address, said to the Governor.
87–90.] In received Aristotelian theory, a comet was an ignited mass of exhalations at the uppermost limits of the earth's atmosphere.
91. *Could . . . you*] Tamburlaine speaks sarcastically: No, you couldn't be bothered to worry about my terrible menace, could you?
93. *quailed*] overpowered, caused to quail.

But still the ports were shut. Villain, I say,   95
Should I but touch the rusty gates of hell,
The triple-headed Cerberus would howl
And wake black Jove to crouch and kneel to me;
But I have sent volleys of shot to you,
Yet could not enter till the breach was made.   100

Governor. Nor, if my body could have stopped the breach,
Shouldst thou have entered, cruel Tamburlaine.
'Tis not thy bloody tents can make me yield,
Nor yet thyself, the anger of the Highest,
For, though thy cannon shook the city walls,   105
My heart did never quake, or courage faint.

Tamburlaine. Well, now I'll make it quake.—Go, draw him
up.
Hang him in chains upon the city walls,
And let my soldiers shoot the slave to death.

Governor. Vile monster, born of some infernal hag,   110
And sent from hell to tyrannise on earth,
Do all thy worst! Nor death, nor Tamburlaine,
Torture, or pain can daunt my dreadless mind.

Tamburlaine. Up with him, then; his body shall be scarred.

Governor. But Tamburlaine, in Limnasphaltis' lake   115
There lies more gold than Babylon is worth,
Which when the city was besieged I hid.
Save but my life and I will give it thee.

Tamburlaine. Then, for all your valour, you would save
Your life? Whereabout lies it?   120

Governor. Under a hollow bank, right opposite
Against the western gate of Babylon.

Tamburlaine. [*To Soldiers*] Go thither some of you, and take
his gold.   [*Exeunt* Soldiers.]

---

95. *ports*] gates.

97. *Cerberus*] the dog guarding Hades and captured by Hercules; cf. *One*
1.2.160.

98. *black Jove*] Pluto.

104. *the anger . . . Highest*] you who embody God's wrath and are his
scourge.

112. *Nor*] neither.

113. *dreadless*] undaunted.

123. *take*] seize.

The rest, forward with execution!
Away with him hence; let him speak no more.—   125
I think I make your courage something quail.
        [*The* GOVERNOR *is taken away by* Soldiers.]
When this is done, we'll march from Babylon,
And make our greatest haste to Persia.
These jades are broken-winded and half tired;
Unharness them, and let me have fresh horse.   130
        [Soldiers *unharness* TREBIZOND *and* SORIA.]
So, now their best is done to honour me,
Take them and hang them both up presently.
Trebizond. Vile tyrant, barbarous, bloody Tamburlaine!
Tamburlaine. Take them away, Theridamas, see them
    dispatched.
Theridamas. I will, my lord.   135
        [*Exit* THERIDAMAS *with* TREBIZOND *and* SORIA.]
Tamburlaine. Come, Asian viceroys, to your tasks a while,
    And take such fortune as your fellows felt.
Orcanes. First let thy Scythian horse tear both our limbs
    Rather than we should draw thy chariot
    And like base slaves abject our princely minds   140
    To vile and ignominious servitude.
Jerusalem. Rather lend me thy weapon, Tamburlaine,
    That I may sheathe it in this breast of mine.
    A thousand deaths could not torment our hearts
    More than the thought of this doth vex our souls.   145
Amyras. [*To Tamburlaine*] They will talk still, my lord, if you
    do not bridle them.
Tamburlaine. Bridle them, and let me to my coach.
                They bridle [*and harness*] *them.*

      [*The* GOVERNOR *appears hanging in chains.*
        Re-enter THERIDAMAS.]

Amyras. See now, my lord, how brave the captain hangs!

---

    124. *execution*] speed.
    126. *something*] somewhat. (Said sardonically.)
    131. *now*] now that.
    132. *presently*] immediately.
    140. *abject*] degrade, debase.
    147.2. appears] a 'discovery' effect, perhaps arranged behind a curtain.
    148. *brave*] courageous (sarcastically).

Tamburlaine. 'Tis brave indeed, my boy. [*To Theridamas*]
    Well done!
  Shoot first, my lord, and then the rest shall follow.   150
Theridamas. Then have at him to begin withal.
               Theridamas shoots[*, wounding the Governor*].
Governor. Yet save my life, and let this wound appease
  The mortal fury of great Tamburlaine.
Tamburlaine. No, though Asphaltis' lake were liquid gold
  And offered me as ransom for thy life,   155
  Yet shouldst thou die.—Shoot at him all at once.
                     They shoot.
  So, now he hangs like Baghdad's governor,
  Having as many bullets in his flesh
  As there be breaches in her battered wall.
  Go now and bind the burghers hand and foot,   160
  And cast them headlong in the city's lake.
  Tartars and Persians shall inhabit there,
  And, to command the city, I will build
  A citadel, that all Africa,
  Which hath been subject to the Persian king,   165
  Shall pay me tribute for, in Babylon.
Techelles. What shall be done with their wives and children,
    my lord?
Tamburlaine. Techelles, drown them all, man, woman, and
    child;
  Leave not a Babylonian in the town.   170
Techelles. I will about it straight. Come, soldiers.
              Exeunt [TECHELLES *with* Soldiers].
Tamburlaine. Now, Casane, where's the Turkish Alcoran
  And all the heaps of superstitious books
  Found in the temples of that Mahomet
  Whom I have thought a god? They shall be burnt.   175
Usumcasane. [*Presenting books*] Here they are, my lord.
Tamburlaine. Well said. Let there be a fire presently.
  In vain, I see, men worship Mahomet.
  My sword hath sent millions of Turks to hell,
  Slew all his priests, his kinsmen, and his friends,   180

---

149. *brave*] excellent.
157. *like Baghdad's governor*] i.e. as Baghdad's governor should
hang. *Baghdad* here equated with Babylon.

And yet I live untouched by Mahomet.
There is a God full of revenging wrath,
From whom the thunder and the lightning breaks,
Whose scourge I am, and him will I obey.
So, Casane, fling them in the fire.   185
                              [*They burn the books.*]
Now, Mahomet, if thou have any power,
Come down thyself and work a miracle.
Thou art not worthy to be worshippèd
That suffers flames of fire to burn the writ
Wherein the sum of thy religion rests.   190
Why send'st thou not a furious whirlwind down
To blow thy Alcoran up to thy throne
Where men report thou sitt'st by God himself,
Or vengeance on the head of Tamburlaine,
That shakes his sword against thy majesty   195
And spurns the abstracts of thy foolish laws?—
Well, soldiers, Mahomet remains in hell;
He cannot hear the voice of Tamburlaine.
Seek out another godhead to adore,
The God that sits in heaven, if any god,   200
For he is God alone, and none but he.

                [*Re-enter* TECHELLES.]

Techelles. I have fulfilled Your Highness' will, my lord.
    Thousands of men, drowned in Asphaltis' lake,
    Have made the water swell above the banks,
    And fishes, fed by human carcasses,   205
    Amazed, swim up and down upon the waves
    As when they swallow asafoetida,

---

182. *a God . . . wrath*] the power that 'thundered vengeance' at the cost of
Sigisimond, *Two* 2.3.2. As apocalyptic deity, cf. Psalm 18.7–14.

186–7.] It is possible that Marlowe refers provocatively to the challenge to
Christ on the Cross (cf. Matthew 27.40); Kocher, 88.

194. *Or vengeance*] i.e. or why do you not send vengeance (continuing the
construction from 191).

196. *abstracts*] epitome, i.e. the Koran.

200–1.] There are Judaic parallels in Deut. 32.39, and 4.35: 'the Lord he is
God, and there is none else beside him'.

206. *Amazed*] dazed.

207. *asafoetida*] a bitter resin.

Which makes them fleet aloft and gasp for air.
Tamburlaine. Well then, my friendly lords, what now remains
    But that we leave sufficient garrison   210
    And presently depart to Persia,
    To triumph after all our victories?
Theridamas. Ay, good my lord. Let us in haste to Persia,
    And let this captain be removed the walls
    To some high hill about the city here.   215
Tamburlaine. Let it be so. About it, soldiers.—
    But stay. I feel myself distempered suddenly.
Techelles. What is it dares distemper Tamburlaine?
Tamburlaine. Something, Techelles, but I know not what.
    But forth, ye vassals! Whatsoe'er it be,   220
    Sickness or death can never conquer me.

        Exeunt [TAMBURLAINE, *drawn in his chariot by*
                ORCANES *and* JERUSALEM.].

Scene 2

Enter CALLAPINE, AMASIA, [Captain, Soldiers,]
with drums and trumpets.

Callapine. King of Amasia, now our mighty host
    Marcheth in Asia Major, where the streams
    Of Euphrates and Tigris swiftly runs,
    And here may we behold great Babylon,
    Circled about with Limnasphaltis' lake,   5
    Where Tamburlaine with all his army lies—
    Which being faint and weary with the siege,
    We may lie ready to encounter him
    Before his host be full from Babylon,
    And so revenge our latest grievous loss   10
    If God or Mahomet send any aid.

---

208. *fleet aloft*] float on the surface.

214. *removed*] removed from.

217.] The onset of illness can be taken variously, as a punishment for impiety or as coincidental with it. Tamburlaine's defiance of Mahomet was itself in the name of another God-figure.

5.2. Location: in sight of Babylon.

9. *full from Babylon*] i.e. back to full strength after the siege of Babylon.

Amasia. Doubt not, my lord, but we shall conquer him.
   The monster that hath drunk a sea of blood
   And yet gapes still for more to quench his thirst,
   Our Turkish swords shall headlong send to hell;   15
   And that vile carcass drawn by warlike kings
   The fowls shall eat, for never sepulchre
   Shall grace that baseborn tyrant Tamburlaine.
Callapine. When I record my parents' slavish life,
   Their cruel death, mine own captivity,   20
   My viceroys' bondage under Tamburlaine,
   Methinks I could sustain a thousand deaths
   To be revenged of all his villainy.
   Ah, sacred Mahomet, thou that hast seen
   Millions of Turks perish by Tamburlaine,   25
   Kingdoms made waste, brave cities sacked and burnt,
   And but one host is left to honour thee,
   Aid thy obedient servant Callapine
   And make him, after all these overthrows,
   To triumph over cursèd Tamburlaine!   30
Amasia. Fear not, my lord. I see great Mahomet
   Clothèd in purple clouds, and on his head
   A chaplet brighter than Apollo's crown,
   Marching about the air with armèd men
   To join with you against this Tamburlaine.   35
Captain. Renownèd general, mighty Callapine,
   Though God himself and holy Mahomet
   Should come in person to resist your power,
   Yet might your mighty host encounter all
   And pull proud Tamburlaine upon his knees   40
   To sue for mercy at Your Highness' feet.
Callapine. Captain, the force of Tamburlaine is great,
   His fortune greater, and the victories
   Wherewith he hath so sore dismayed the world
   Are greatest to discourage all our drifts.   45
   Yet when the pride of Cynthia is at full
   She wanes again, and so shall his, I hope,

---

   19. *record*] call to mind.
   45. *drifts*] purposes.
   46. *Cynthia*] the moon, as goddess of fortune.

For we have here the chief selected men
Of twenty several kingdoms at the least.
Nor ploughman, priest, nor merchant stays at home;   50
All Turkey is in arms with Callapine.
And never will we sunder camps and arms
Before himself or his be conquerèd.
This is the time that must eternise me
For conquering the tyrant of the world.   55
Come, soldiers, let us lie in wait for him,
And if we find him absent from his camp
Or that it be rejoined again at full,
Assail it and be sure of victory.   *Exeunt.*

SCENE 3

[Enter] THERIDAMAS, TECHELLES, USUMCASANE.

Theridamas. Weep, heavens, and vanish into liquid tears!
Fall, stars that govern his nativity,
And summon all the shining lamps of heaven
To cast their bootless fires to the earth
And shed their feeble influence in the air!   5
Muffle your beauties with eternal clouds,
For hell and darkness pitch their pitchy tents,
And Death with armies of Cimmerian spirits
Gives battle 'gainst the heart of Tamburlaine.
Now, in defiance of that wonted love   10
Your sacred virtues poured upon his throne
And made his state an honour to the heavens,
These cowards invisibly assail his soul
And threaten conquest on our sovereign;

---

54. *eternise*] immortalise.
58. *Or that*] before.
rejoined] reassembled.

5.3. Location: near Babylon.
4. *bootless*] unavailing.
5. *influence*] an etherial fluid by means of which the stars act on the character and destiny of men; see *Two* 3.2.39.
8. *Cimmerian*] The Cimmerii of legend lived in perpetual darkness. Used of clouds at *One* 3.2.77, and of the Styx, *One* 5.1.234.

But if he die, your glories are disgraced,   15
Earth droops and says that hell in heaven is placed.
Techelles. O then, ye powers that sway eternal seats
    And guide this massy substance of the earth,
    If you retain desert of holiness,
    As your supreme estates instruct our thoughts,   20
    Be not inconstant, careless of your fame;
    Bear not the burden of your enemies' joys
    Triumphing in his fall whom you advanced;
    But as his birth, life, health, and majesty
    Were strangely blest and governèd by heaven,   25
    So honour, heaven, till heaven dissolvèd be,
    His birth, his life, his health, and majesty.
Usumcasane. Blush, heaven, to lose the honour of thy name,
    To see thy footstool set upon thy head,
    And let no baseness in thy haughty breast   30
    Sustain a shame of such inexcellence,
    To see the devils mount in angels' thrones
    And angels dive into the pools of hell.
    And though they think their painful date is out
    And that their power is puissant as Jove's,   35
    Which makes them manage arms against thy state,
    Yet make them feel the strength of Tamburlaine,
    Thy instrument and note of majesty,
    Is greater far than they can thus subdue;
    For if he die, thy glory is disgraced,   40
    Earth droops and says that hell in heaven is placed.

---

19. *desert of holiness*] worthiness of religious worship.
20. *estates*] station, rank.
22. *Bear . . . burden*] do not join in the chorus.
25. *governèd*] cared for.
26. *heaven*] O heaven (addressed in apostrophe). (*Honour* here is an imperative verb.)
31.] bear so vile an indignity.
34. *they . . . out*] they (the devils) think their allotted period of suffering is over.
36. *thy*] i.e. heaven's, Jove's.
37. *feel*] feel that.
38. *note*] mark, sign.
40–1.] In choric mode, these lines closely echo 15–16.

[*Enter* TAMBURLAINE *in his chariot, drawn by* ORCANES *of*
NATOLIA *and the King of* JERUSALEM, *and attended*
by AMYRAS, CELEBINUS, *and* Physicians.]

Tamburlaine. What daring god torments my body thus
 And seeks to conquer mighty Tamburlaine?
 Shall sickness prove me now to be a man,
 That have been termed the terror of the world?   45
 Techelles and the rest, come take your swords
 And threaten him whose hand afflicts my soul.
 Come, let us march against the powers of heaven
 And set black streamers in the firmament
 To signify the slaughter of the gods.   50
 Ah, friends, what shall I do? I cannot stand.
 Come, carry me to war against the gods,
 That thus envy the health of Tamburlaine.
Theridamas. Ah, good my lord, leave these impatient words,
 Which add much danger to your malady.   55
Tamburlaine. Why shall I sit and languish in this pain?
 No! Strike the drums, and, in revenge of this,
 Come, let us charge our spears and pierce his breast
 Whose shoulders bear the axis of the world,
 That if I perish, heaven and earth may fade.   60
 Theridamas, haste to the court of Jove.
 Will him to send Apollo hither straight
 To cure me, or I'll fetch him down myself.
Techelles. Sit still, my gracious lord. This grief will cease
 And cannot last, it is so violent.   65
Tamburlaine. Not last, Techelles? No, for I shall die.
 See where my slave, the ugly monster Death,
 Shaking and quiv'ring, pale and wan for fear,
 Stands aiming at me with his murd'ring dart,
 Who flies away at every glance I give,   70

---

44. *a man*] a mere mortal.
53. *envy*] second syllable stressed.
58. *charge*] level.
his] i.e. Atlas's.
62. *Apollo*] as god of healing.
64. *grief*] pain, suffering.
64–5. *will . . . violent*] a proverbial idea.

And when I look away comes stealing on.—
Villain, away, and hie thee to the field!
I and mine army come to load thy bark
With souls of thousand mangled carcasses.—
Look where he goes! But see, he comes again   75
Because I stay. Techelles, let us march,
And weary Death with bearing souls to hell.
Physician. Pleaseth Your Majesty to drink this potion,
   Which will abate the fury of your fit
   And cause some milder spirits govern you.   80
Tamburlaine. Tell me, what think you of my sickness now?
Physician. I viewed your urine, and the hypostasis,
   Thick and obscure, doth make your danger great;
   Your veins are full of accidental heat
   Whereby the moisture of your blood is dried.   85
   The humidum and calor, which some hold
   Is not a parcel of the elements
   But of a substance more divine and pure,
   Is almost clean extinguishèd and spent,
   Which, being the cause of life, imports your death.   90
   Besides, my lord, this day is critical,
   Dangerous to those whose crisis is as yours.
   Your artiers, which alongst the veins convey
   The lively spirits which the heart engenders,
   Are parched and void of spirit, that the soul,   95
   Wanting those organons by which it moves,

---

73. *thy bark*] Cf. the loading of 'Charon's boat', *One* 5.1.464–5.
78. *Pleaseth*] may it please.
80. *govern*] to govern.
82. *hypostasis*] sediment.
84. *accidental*] inessential, abnormal.
84–90.] Tamburlaine's passions have caused an excess of 'accidental heat', which 'parches his arteries and dries up in his blood the radical moisture (*humidum*) which is necessary for the preservation of his natural heat (*calor*). The depletion of his *humidum* and *calor* (whose admixture in the blood gives rise to the *spirits*) prevents his soul's functions, stops his bodily activities, and thereby causes his death' (Parr, 19).
91–2.] The physician has in mind the unfavourable days in Tamburlaine's horoscope.
93. *alongst*] parallel to.
95. *that*] so that.
96. *organons*] highly-refined substances or fluids.

Cannot endure, by argument of art.
Yet if Your Majesty may escape this day,
No doubt but you shall soon recover all.
Tamburlaine. Then will I comfort all my vital parts   100
And live in spite of Death above a day.

Alarm within.

[*Enter a* Messenger.]

Messenger. My lord, young Callapine, that lately fled from
Your Majesty, hath now gathered a fresh army, and,
hearing your absence in the field, offers to set upon us
presently.   105
Tamburlaine. See, my physicians, now, how Jove hath sent
A present medicine to recure my pain.
My looks shall make them fly, and, might I follow,
There should not one of all the villain's power
Live to give offer of another fight.   110
Usumcasane. I joy, my lord, Your Highness is so strong,
That can endure so well your royal presence,
Which only will dismay the enemy.
Tamburlaine. I know it will, Casane.—Draw, you slaves!
In spite of Death I will go show my face.   115

Alarm. TAMBURLAINE *goes in*[, *riding his chariot,*]
and comes out again with all the rest.

Tamburlaine. Thus are the villains, cowards, fled for fear,
Like summer's vapours vanished by the sun.
And could I but a while pursue the field,
That Callapine should be my slave again.
But I perceive my martial strength is spent;   120
In vain I strive and rail against those powers

---

97. *argument of art*] i.e. the logic of medicine.
100. *comfort*] husband.
101. *above*] longer than.
104. *offers*] makes as if.
107. *present*] ready.
recure] cure.
112. *endure*] harden, strengthen.
113. *only*] i.e. Tamburlaine's royal presence is capable in itself of dismaying his opponents.
117. *vanished*] caused to disappear.

That mean t'invest me in a higher throne,
As much too good for this disdainful earth.
Give me a map, then, let me see how much
Is left for me to conquer all the world,   125
That these my boys may finish all my wants.

One brings a map.

Here I began to march towards Persia,
Along Armenia and the Caspian Sea,
And thence unto Bithynia, where I took
The Turk and his great empress prisoners;   130
Then marched I into Egypt and Arabia,
And here, not far from Alexandria,
Whereas the Terrene and the Red Sea meet,
Being distant less than full a hundred leagues,
I meant to cut a channel to them both,   135
That men might quickly sail to India.
From thence to Nubia near Borno lake,
And so along the Ethiopian sea,
Cutting the tropic line of Capricorn
I conquered all as far as Zanzibar.   140
Then by the northern part of Africa
I came at last to Graecia, and from thence
To Asia, where I stay against my will—
Which is from Scythia, where I first began,
Backward and forwards near five thousand leagues.   145
Look here, my boys, see what a world of ground
Lies westward from the midst of Cancer's line
Unto the rising of this earthly globe,
Whereas the sun, declining from our sight,
Begins the day with our Antipodes;   150
And shall I die, and this unconquerèd?

132–6.] Tamburlaine's dream anticipates the Suez Canal.

133. *Whereas*] where.

137. *Borno lake*] Lake Chad, in North Central Africa.

147.] 'In Ortelius the meridian 0° cuts the Tropic of Cancer just off the coast of north-west Africa. Tamburlaine traces the map westward from this point' (Woolf).

150. *our Antipodes*] 'here, the dwellers in the Western Hemisphere, and the southern half of it (that is, South America, the source of Spanish gold and the riches of the fabulous El Dorado)' (Ellis-Fermor).

Lo, here, my sons, are all the golden mines,
Inestimable drugs, and precious stones,
More worth than Asia and the world beside;
And from th'Antarctic Pole eastward behold   155
As much more land, which never was descried,
Wherein are rocks of pearl that shine as bright
As all the lamps that beautify the sky;
And shall I die, and this unconquerèd?
Here, lovely boys: what Death forbids my life,   160
That let your lives command in spite of Death.

Amyras. Alas, my lord, how should our bleeding hearts,
Wounded and broken with Your Highness' grief,
Retain a thought of joy or spark of life?
Your soul gives essence to our wretched subjects,   165
Whose matter is incorporate in your flesh.

Celebinus. Your pains do pierce our souls; no hope survives,
For by your life we entertain our lives.

Tamburlaine. But sons, this subject, not of force enough
To hold the fiery spirit it contains,   170
Must part, imparting his impressions
By equal portions into both your breasts;
My flesh, divided in your precious shapes,
Shall still retain my spirit though I die,
And live in all your seeds immortally.   175
Then now remove me, that I may resign
My place and proper title to my son.
[*To Amyras*] First take my scourge and my imperial
          crown,
And mount my royal chariot of estate,

---

152. *here*] i.e. in the Americas, the West Indies.

155–6. *from th'Antarctic . . . descried*] Australasia, as yet uncharted, but subject to much rumour.

163. *grief*] pain.

165–6.] i.e. Tamburlaine's sons, as individuals, derive their animal spirits and bodies from him.

168. *entertain*] maintain.

169. *this subject*] I myself.

171. *his*] its.

177, 183. *proper*] own.

178. *scourge*] i.e. chariot whip.

179.] The echo of *One* 5.1.526 ('Mount up your royal places of estate') points up the comparison between the two endings.

That I may see thee crowned before I die.   180
Help me, my lords, to make my last remove.
　　　[Tamburlaine is helped down from his chariot.]
Theridamas. A woeful change, my lord, that daunts our
　　　thoughts
More than the ruin of our proper souls.
Tamburlaine. Sit up, my son, let me see how well
Thou wilt become thy father's majesty.   185
　　They crown him [Amyras, but he declines to ascend the chariot].
Amyras. With what a flinty bosom should I joy
The breath of life and burden of my soul,
If not resolved into resolvèd pains
My body's mortifièd lineaments
Should exercise the motions of my heart,   190
Pierced with the joy of any dignity!
O father, if the unrelenting ears
Of Death and hell be shut against my prayers,
And that the spiteful influence of heaven
Deny my soul fruition of her joy,   195
How should I step or stir my hateful feet
Against the inward powers of my heart,
Leading a life that only strives to die,
And plead in vain unpleasing sovereignty?
Tamburlaine. Let not thy love exceed thine honour, son,   200
Nor bar thy mind that magnanimity
That nobly must admit necessity.
Sit up, my boy, and with those silken reins
Bridle the steelèd stomachs of those jades.
Theridamas. *[To Amyras]* My lord, you must obey His Majesty 205
Since fate commands, and proud necessity.
Amyras. *[Ascending the chariot]* Heavens witness me, with
　　　what a broken heart

186–91.] i.e. 'How hardhearted would be my enjoyment of your gift to me
of life and soul if, instead of dissolving into grief and mortification, I should
gladden my heart at the prospect of such earthly dignity!' (Bevington).

196–9.] How should I take such steps, against the promptings of my heart,
embracing a life of honour when I wish only to die, and pleading in vain with
myself to accept an unwelcome sovereignty?

200. *thine honour*] your devotion to honour.

204. *steelèd stomachs*] hardened spirits ('silken' in 203 is sardonic).

And damnèd spirit I ascend this seat,
And send my soul, before my father die,
His anguish and his burning agony!   210
Tamburlaine. Now fetch the hearse of fair Zenocrate.
    Let it be placed by this my fatal chair
    And serve as parcel of my funeral.   [*Exeunt some.*]
Usumcasane. Then feels Your Majesty no sovereign ease,
    Nor may our hearts, all drowned in tears of blood,   215
    Joy any hope of your recovery?
Tamburlaine. Casane, no. The monarch of the earth
    And eyeless monster that torments my soul
    Cannot behold the tears ye shed for me,
    And therefore still augments his cruelty.   220
Techelles. Then let some god oppose his holy power
    Against the wrath and tyranny of Death,
    That his tear-thirsty and unquenchèd hate
    May be upon himself reverberate.
                    They bring in the hearse [*of Zenocrate*].
Tamburlaine. Now, eyes, enjoy your latest benefit,   225
    And when my soul hath virtue of your sight,
    Pierce through the coffin and the sheet of gold
    And glut your longings with a heaven of joy.
    So, reign, my son! Scourge and control those slaves,
    Guiding thy chariot with thy father's hand.   230
    As precious is the charge thou undertak'st
    As that which Clymen's brain-sick son did guide

---

208. *damnèd*] doomed, wretched.

209–10.] and may heaven vouchsafe me to assume my father's bodily suffering in his hour of death.

212. *fatal chair*] i.e. the chair I am doomed to die in.

213. *parcel*] part.

214. *sovereign*] distinctive, remedial; associating here ironically, perhaps, with the proverbial 'sovereign remedy' effected magically by kings.

216. *Joy*] cherish.

217. *The . . . earth*] i.e. Death. Cf. *One* 5.1.111.

225. *latest*] last.

226.] Freed of the limitations of corporeal sight, the spirit may perceive the soul of Zenocrate.

232. *Clymen's brain-sick son*] Phaethon, child of Apollo and Clymene. The phrase recalls *One* 4.2.49.

When wand'ring Phoebe's ivory cheeks were scorched
And all the earth, like Etna, breathing fire.
Be warned by him, then, learn with awful eye   235
To sway a throne as dangerous as his.
For, if thy body thrive not full of thoughts
As pure and fiery as Phyteus' beams,
The nature of these proud rebelling jades
Will take occasion by the slenderest hair   240
And draw thee piecemeal like Hippolytus
Through rocks more steep and sharp than Caspian clifts.
The nature of thy chariot will not bear
A guide of baser temper than myself,
More than heaven's coach the pride of Phaethon.   245
Farewell my boys; my dearest friends, farewell!
My body feels, my soul doth weep to see
Your sweet desires deprived my company;
For Tamburlaine, the scourge of God, must die.
                                                [He dies.]
Amyras. Meet heaven and earth, and here let all things end!   250
For earth hath spent the pride of all her fruit,
And heaven consumed his choicest living fire.
Let earth and heaven his timeless death deplore,
For both their worths will equal him no more.
      Exeunt [in procession, with AMYRAS *drawn in the chariot].*

                    FINIS.

---

233. *Phoebe*] the moon.
235. *awful*] reverential, awe-struck.
238. *Phyteus' beams*] the sun's (Apollo's, i.e. Pythias's) rays.
239. *jades*] the notorious 'pampered jades' of *Two* 4.3.1.
240. *take . . . hair*] Proverbially, time must be seized by the forelock.
241. *Hippolytus*] dragged to death by his own chariot.
242. *clifts*] cliffs.
245. *Phaethon*] See 232n above.
250. *Meet . . . earth*] i.e. may earth and heaven collapse into one indistinguishable mass.
252. *his*] i.e. heaven's.
253. *timeless*] untimely.